EUROPEAN SECURITY AFTER 9/11

European Security After 9/11

Edited by
PETER SHEARMAN
and
MATTHEW SUSSEX

ASHGATE

Published by
Ashgate Publishing Limited
Gower House
Croft Road
Aldershot
Hants GU11 3HR
England

Ashgate Publishing Company
Suite 420
101 Cherry Street
Burlington, VT 05401-4405
USA

Ashgate website: http://www.ashgate.com

British Library Cataloguing in Publication Data
European security after 9/11
    1.Security, International 2.War on Terrorism, 2001
    3.Terrorism 4.Europe - Foreign relations - 1989-
    I.Shearman, Peter II.Sussex, Matthew
    327.4'00905

Library of Congress Control Number: 2003056879

ISBN 0 7546 3594 5

Printed and bound in Great Britain by Antony Rowe Ltd, Chippenham, Wiltshire

Contents

List of Contributors		*vi*
Acknowledgements		*vii*
List of Abbreviations		*viii*

Introduction — 1
Peter Shearman and Matthew Sussex

1   Reconceptualizing Security After 9/11 — 11
Peter Shearman

2   Cultures in Conflict? Re-evaluating the 'Clash of Civilizations' Thesis After 9/11 — 28
Matthew Sussex

3   America and Europe After 9/11 — 51
Peter Shearman and Matthew Sussex

4   French Security After 9/11: Franco-American Discord — 69
Rémy Davison

5   German Security After 9/11 — 90
Franz Oswald

6   9/11 and Russian Perceptions of Europe and NATO — 107
Alexey D. Muraviev

7   New Lines in the Sand: 9/11 and Implications for British Policy in the Middle East — 128
Peter Hinchcliffe

References — *145*
Index — *159*

List of Contributors

Rémy Davison is Lecturer in Political Science at the University of Tasmania, Hobart, Australia. His research and many publications have focused on European politics and foreign policy, international security, and international political economy. He is Vice President of the Contemporary European Studies Association of Australia (CESAA) and co-editor of the *CESAA Review*. He also edits the *Australasian Journal of European Integration*.

Peter Hinchcliffe is Honorary Fellow at the Edinburgh Institute for Advanced Study of Islam and the Middle East, the University of Edinburgh. He has held a variety of diplomatic posts with the British Foreign and Commonwealth Office, including stints as U.K. Ambassador to Jordan (1993-1997) and Kuwait (1987-1990). He is an expert on the politics of the Middle East and has published widely in scholarly journals on the subject. His most recent publication (with Beverley Milton-Edwards) is *Conflicts in the Middle East since 1945*, London, Routledge, 2002.

Alexey D. Muraviev has been Co-Director of the International Relations and Global Security Research Unit at Curtin University of Technology, where he specializes in Russian foreign and security policy. He has widely published in both Russian and English language journals. His book (with Greg Austin) *Red Star East: The Armed Forces of Russia in Asia*, was published by Allen & Unwin in 2000.

Franz Oswald is Associate Professor and Director of the International Relations and Global Security Research Unit at Curtin University. Franz has extensive experience in German politics, and his research interests include the military and foreign policy formulation in Germany, and the transformation of the transatlantic alliance between Europe and the USA. Among his many publications is the co-edited volume (with M. Perkins), *Europe – United or Divided?* Canberra, Southern Highland Publishers, 2000.

Peter Shearman is Associate Professor of International Relations and Security Studies at The University of Melbourne, Australia, and has published widely in these fields.

Matthew Sussex completed his PhD on Russian foreign policy at the University of Melbourne in 2001. His research interests include international security and international relations theory. He is currently teaching and conducting research in these areas at the University of Queensland, Australia. His forthcoming book (also with Ashgate) is *Power, Interests and Identity in Russian Foreign Policy*.

Acknowledgements

We are indebted to a number of people who assisted either in the preparation of the manuscript or in facilitating the workshop on which this volume in based. The organisation of the workshop and the volume were collaborative efforts. We would especially like to thank Dr Zoe Knox at the Contemporary Europe Research Centre (CERC), The University of Melbourne, for her hospitality and tireless efforts to make us welcome during our workshop, and for cheerfully dealing with any problems that arose (some of which were, naturally, at the last minute). Our thanks are also due to the participants from the Australian Department of Foreign Affairs and Trade and postgraduates from The University of Melbourne who attended and provided valuable comments over the course of the workshop.

We would like to thank all participants from the International Relations and Global Security Research Unit at Curtin University of Technology. In addition to the contributors here we appreciate the efforts of Associate Professor Robert Bruce and Ms Victoria Mason for making the trek from Perth to Melbourne and for providing excellent papers and contributing to a friendly and stimulating debate.

Peter Shearman and Matthew Sussex
December, 2003

List of Abbreviations

ABM	Anti Ballistic Missile Treaty
ANZUS	Australia–New Zealand–US Alliance
AWACS	Airborne Warning and Control Systems
BBC	British Broadcasting Corporation
CDU	Christian Democratic Union (Germany)
CERC	Contemporary Europe Research Centre, University of Melbourne
CFSP	Common Foreign and Security Policy
CIS	Commonwealth of Independent States
CNN	Cable News Network
CSCE	Conference for Security and Cooperation in Europe
CST	Common Security Treaty
CSU	Christian Social Union (Germany)
CTBT	Comprehensive Test Ban Treaty
EC	European Community
ECPR	European Consortium for Political Research
ECSC	European Coal and Steel Community
EDC	European Defence Community
ESDP	European Security and Defence Policy
EU	European Union
FATF	Financial Action Taskforce on Money Laundering
FCO	Foreign and Commonwealth Office (UK)
FDP	Free Democratic Party (Germany)
FRG	Federal Republic of Germany
FTA	Free Trade Agreement
G8	Group of Eight
GCC	Gulf Cooperation Council
GUUAM	Georgia–Ukraine–Uzbekistan–Armenia–Moldova
ICC	International Criminal Court
IFOR	Implementation Force in Bosnia and Herzegovina
IGC	Inter-Governmental Conference
IMF	International Monetary Fund
INF	Intermediate Nuclear Forces Treaty
IR	International Relations
IRA	Irish Republican Army
ISAF	International Security Assistance Force
LNG	Liquid Natural Gas
MdB	Member of the Deutsche Bundestag
MEPP	Middle East Peace Process
MP	Member of Parliament

NATO	North Atlantic Treaty Organization
NMD	National Missile Defense
OECD	Organization for Economic Cooperation and Development
OIC	Organization of Islamic Conferences
OPEC	Organization of the Petroleum Exporting Countries
OSCE	Organization for Security and Cooperation in Europe
PDS	Party of Democratic Socialism (Germany)
PFP	Partnerships for Peace
PJC	Permanent Joint Council
PRC	People's Republic of China
PRO	Partei Rechtsstaaliche Offensive
R&D	Research and Development
RRF	Rapid Reaction Force
SDI	Strategic Defense Initiative
SFOR	Stabilization Force in Bosnia and Herzegovina
SPD	Social Democratic Party (Germany)
TEU	Treaty on European Union
TMD	Theatre Missile Defense
UAE	United Arab Emirates
UN	United Nations
UNSC	United Nations Security Council
UNSCR	United Nations Security Council Resolution
USSR	Union of Soviet Socialist Republics (former)
WEU	Western European Union
WMD	Weapons of Mass Destruction
WP	Warsaw Pact
WTC	World Trade Center
WTO	World Trade Organization

Introduction

Peter Shearman and Matthew Sussex

In his survey of the major scholarly journals dealing with international politics and security studies Bruce Jentleson found that in the three years leading up to 9/11, not one of them published an article that had terrorism as its primary focus.[1] A book published in 2001 dealing with the nature of warfare in the Third World did not contain a single reference to terrorism.[2] A major introductory text on international relations claiming to provide a comprehensive coverage of '...history, theory, structures and processes, and international issues' published the same year contained chapters on gender, human rights, nationalism and Marxism, as well as environmental issues, amongst many others – but it too made no mention of terrorism.[3] Similarly a 'major new handbook' providing a '...state of the art review and essential guide to the study of International Relations', also published in 2001, not only had no separate coverage of terrorism, there was not even a reference to it in the index, even though it included chapters on Foreign Policy, War and Peace, and Security.[4] A day before the terrorist attacks in New York and Washington a major international conference concluded in Kent. This was a pan-European convention of political scientists, under the initiative of the Standing Group on International Relations that grew out of the European Consortium for Political Research (ECPR), an organization that brings together political scientists across Europe. The Pan-European International Relations Conference (along with the General Conference of the ECPR that immediately preceded it) encompassed some 1,500 participants on over 300 panels. Not one of those panels dealt separately with terrorism as a phenomenon, or as a security threat.[5] Then came 9/11, and the ensuing flood of literature on international terrorism, with leading specialists in International Relations who had previously never written on the subject, including many of the authors in the two edited volumes referred to above, offering their assessments, mainly in relation to U.S. perceptions and policies. Many of these works are cited in other contributions to this volume and are listed in the bibliography.

Given three basic facts it is understandable that this immediate post 9/11 coverage focused on the U.S. and its policies. First, the terrorist attacks took place in the U.S., hence one would naturally expect Americans to be profoundly affected. Second, the U.S. is the most powerful country in the world, and clearly its reaction to the attacks would have potentially system-wide implications. And third, American institutions and academics dominate in the disciplines of International Relations and Security Studies, so one would expect to see U.S. experts clamoring to give their views. Yet it is still a remarkable fact that so little coverage was accorded to Europe in these early assessments of 9/11. Many of the terrorists plotted their actions in various parts of Europe: in Germany, the U.K., and Spain. Europe also offered critical support to the U.S., at least in the initial stages of the 'war against terror'. Then, not too long after the war's theatre was expanding to possibly incorporate members of a so-called 'axis of evil', a serious rift developed between Europe and America. Even in a volume edited by two influential academics based in the U.K., in an institution often critical of U.S. dominance of the discipline, there was no chapter on Europe in relation to 9/11.[6] In this book our primary focus is the impact that 9/11 and the wars in Afghanistan and Iraq have had on European security. The volume grew out of a joint workshop between the Contemporary Europe Research Centre (CERC) at The University of Melbourne, and the International Relations and Global Security Research Unit based in Curtin University of Technology in Perth. The workshop examined the impact of 9/11 on various aspects of European security, and was hosted in Melbourne by CERC in July 2001. Each contributor is a specialist in the field to which he has contributed, and each has the foreign language skills necessary for researching primary documents in the countries that are the subject of the book. The countries chosen are those central to security matters on the European continent: the UK, France, Germany and Russia. Given the significance of the Middle East as a region of conflict linked to the war on terror, British policy in this area, particularly given its stance on the war on Iraq (diverging from the other countries examined here), is given special attention.

September 11, 2001 challenged many assumptions about the nature of international politics. Not least of these was the widely held notion that Western states of the trans-Atlantic alliance shared a common approach to vital issues of security, despite the lack of any clear threat in the aftermath of the Cold War. Certainly there was initially pan-European support for the U.S. following 9/11. Yet the partnership became increasingly shaky, tested initially by the war to unseat the Taliban in Afghanistan, and then by a fundamental rift over war in Iraq in 2003, which placed the U.S. and Britain on one side, and France, Germany, and a somewhat equivocal Russia on the other. With hindsight it was ironic that U.S. President George W. Bush chose the principles of the NATO alliance as the best reflection of post-September 11 global unity. In his speech to the joint session of Congress on September 20, 2001, Bush referred to a worldwide perception that '…an attack against one is an attack against all'.[7] It was in a similar vein that the long-time Pentagon hawk Paul Wolfowitz, in his December 2002 remarks at the International Institute of Strategic Studies in London, noted that the U.S.-European relationship had '…more staying power than any historic alliance built purely on a narrow coincidence of interests'.[8] In contrast to the split that emerged soon after, there was no talk here of 'old' and 'new' Europe.

In general terms though, the most enduring message of the September 11, 2001 attacks on the World Trade Centre and Pentagon was that they fundamentally changed the world. From conceptual and policy debates amongst academics, to the international media, to statements by diplomats in the UN, the dominant theme was the same: that visions of a stable and peaceful post-Cold War era had been shattered by the rise to prominence of the threat of global terrorism. Of course, terrorism had been identified as a growing problem prior to the end of the Cold War, and the emergence of a new threat to replace Soviet communism had long been anticipated. Many European states had long been confronted with terrorist threats of one sort or another, although in no case had these posed a major threat to the state. Perhaps a telling statistic is that in three decades of the 'Troubles' in Northern Ireland, terrorist attacks resulted in 3,100 killings. These resulted from 34,000 shootings, and 14,000 bombings.[9] Yet on just one day in September 2001, one terrorist mission on one target in New York (the World Trade Centre) killed a similar number of people to those killed over nearly thirty years of terrorism in Northern Ireland. This was terrorism on a new, mass scale. Thus, while terrorism is not a new phenomenon, there was little indication before 9/11 that bin Laden rather than Beijing, terrorism rather than Taiwan, would come to dominate international politics in the way that they have. And while the overall effects of the threat of terrorism are yet to be fully played out, it is clear that 9/11 was a strategic 'shock' that will continue to pose challenges regardless of whether new and more serious threats to international security materialize. This is partly because (for a variety of reasons) the United States views emergent threats through the prism of its ongoing 'war on terror', identifying so-called 'rogue' states as part of an 'axis of evil' that aids terrorists, destabilizes world order, and threatens the primacy of post-Cold War American hegemony.[10]

To be sure, problems associated with 'traditional' security issues such as the rise of China, the proliferation of weapons of mass destruction in India and Pakistan, the destabilization caused by mass movements of refugees, and the question of NATO expansion remain important. Similarly, other security problems incorporating global pandemics, international drug trafficking, and the continued degradation of the environment are gaining in saliency. However, for the time being at least, the agenda of international politics has been set by the United States as the dominant power – some would say the hyperpower – and its attempts to deal with what it perceives as threats to its own national security and to its own global hegemony. Increasingly the latter (global hegemony – what is increasingly being referred to as the new 'American empire') is being seen in the U.S. as essential to ensure the former (national security – now defined in less narrow terms than in previous conceptions). Rightly or wrongly, as a direct result of 9/11 the Bush administration abandoned its initial proclivity for strategic disengagement, and has challenged the world to either bandwagon with it, or balance against it.

In Europe this has been regarded with varying degrees of cynicism, acceptance, or outright opposition, but with very little enthusiasm. Even in the case of the U.K.

under Tony Blair support for the U.S. is qualified, and is motivated more by an attempt to influence events rather than to simply bandwagon with the stronger power. And where other Europeans, notably the French, are more inclined to balance against the United States, this is not reflective of traditional notions of the balance of power in military terms. Indeed, changes in official attitudes to security policy after 9/11 reflect current debates in the academic and conceptual literature. For the U.K., little has changed in the Atlantic partnership. British support for the U.S. has been stauncher than ever, despite the fact that the Blair and Bush governments have approached the problem of international terrorism from two conceptually different poles. Blair has been more concerned with getting the U.S. to act where possible through multilateral institutions and to commit itself to dealing with what he sees as root causes of much of the terrorist problem: conflict in the Middle East between the Arabs and Israelis. Where this involves the use of military conflict the objectives for Blair are to foster democracy, and to assist in nation-building through cooperative policies under the umbrella of multilateral institutions. Blair sees nothing to be gained from antagonizing the United States; rather his view is that Europe should act with the U.S. in order to have some moderating influence on American policy where desirable. But for practical purposes of analysis what matters most is that the conclusion is the same, and the manner in which one arrives at it matters little. However it is worth stressing that Blair's rhetoric, at least, indicates that he regards the neo-idealist notion that democratization promotes peace as central to British national interests. Blair has combined this with a pragmatic sense that challengers to the current global order will unite to maximize their influence, hence his linking of support for the war in Iraq to international terrorism.[11] A different view, but the same conclusion, is reached by Bush and his advisory team of Condoleeza Rice, Donald Rumsfeld, Paul Wolfowitz and Richard Perle, who epitomize a particularly assertive form of realism that stresses the need for great powers to preserve the status quo (and hence U.S. dominance in the international system) through a mixture of unilateralism, coercion, and reward. There is also a theme – one could argue almost a contradictory one – amongst some of the neo-conservatives in the Bush Administration, that regime change and democratization can lead to a more stable international environment, thereby better ensuring American national interests.

France and Germany, the other major power centers of Europe, have adopted positions that are almost diametrically opposed to the U.S./U.K. partnership, at least in terms of the means of achieving stated common objectives. Both French President Jacques Chirac and Germany's Chancellor Gerhardt Schröder initially supported the U.S. and its war against the Taliban in Afghanistan with enthusiasm. Yet when Washington began to push for war on Iraq it came as a surprise to many that the strongest criticism of U.S. policy came from its traditional European allies. The German government opposed the U.S. from the outset, and government officials made at times heated challenges to the strategic direction of the American leadership, with one minister comparing Bush to Hitler.[12] And although Franco-U.S. relations have been strained in the past, it was generally assumed (incorrectly, as it turned out), that Europe would continue to support the U.S. This was either because European-American interests were regarded as symmetrical in relation to Iraq, or because of the nature of political community that had solidified during the Cold War strategic partnership.

Russia's policy of support for the war on terror was also qualified by opposition to any violations of territorial integrity and the principle of state sovereignty. Russia was keen to prevent interference in the internal affairs of the sovereign state, and was simultaneously an enthusiastic supporter of fighting international Islamic terrorist networks. This reflected Russia's perceived national interests. Russia had long been engaged in an internal war against Chechen rebels, and had argued for some time that support for them came from al Qaeda and other terrorist groups based in Afghanistan and the Muslim territories of the former Soviet Union. The Kremlin wished to both prevent outside interference in its own 'war on terror' in Chechnya, whilst at the same time supporting a wider war on Islamic terror against the Taliban. Russia had fought a costly and drawn-out conflict in the 1980s against Muslim rebels in Afghanistan in support of a Kremlin-installed communist government. The U.S. had supplied these rebels with sufficient support, economic and military, including Stinger ground-to-air missiles, to eventually force the Soviet Union to retreat from Afghanistan in 1989. Once this main goal was achieved, the U.S. lost interest in the region, and the subsequent civil conflict resulted in the Taliban gaining power and ultimately becoming host to Osama bin Laden and his group. Thus one could argue that the origins of the terrorist threats to the U.S. and the specific attacks of 9/11 have their origins in U.S. policies in Afghanistan in the 1980s. In fact, Putin was the first foreign leader to call President Bush offering his support for the 'war on terror'. 9/11 provided an opportunity for Russia to counter terrorist groups in Central and West Asia that had been supporting the Chechens in Russia, whilst simultaneously legitimizing the struggle to subdue the Chechens as part of a war against terrorism. This would permit the Kremlin to conduct its policy without outside interference or criticism. For Putin, extending the war to Iraq could not be seen within the framework of this campaign against terror, and hence Russia registered its opposition. In addition to resisting any military undermining of the principle of state sovereignty, the Putin administration's reluctance to endorse a war on Iraq was based upon preserving its influence in the Middle East, and acting as a diplomatic counterweight to the U.S.

Many academics in their post 9/11 assessments saw the U.S. and the West as defenders of peace, liberty and democracy.[13] Others decried the injustices perpetuated via globalization by a wealthy North on an impoverished South, thus giving rise to international terrorism as the desperate act of those marginalized by a Western-inspired politics of resentment.[14] Yet others have referred to the U.S. as the principle terrorist state.[15] But while academics have quickly shifted gear into rationalization and debate, it is worth remembering that the initial writings conveyed above all else a sense of shock and puzzlement. One early collection of essays from prominent analysts in the field even adopted the plaintive title *How Did This Happen?*[16] This was analogous to the situation after the end of the Cold War, when the field of international relations was criticized from within and without for failing to predict the end of bipolarity. Policy specialists complained that theory was vague and incomplete, which made the task of prediction on the basis of a variety of competing 'isms' virtually impossible. Theorists countered by criticizing policy specialists for neglecting the wider structural picture, and concentrating too deeply on the nitty-gritty of everyday events in the Soviet Union, which resulted in a host of assessments from analysts so focused in their work that they could not see the forest for the trees.[17]

Yet although 9/11 demonstrated that the study of international politics suffered again from its inability to foresee major events, either through too close attention to detail, or insufficient attention to theory that related to the real empirical world, it also demonstrates that once a major event occurs, IR has no shortage of explanations and conceptual blueprints for policy action. Immediately after 9/11, Samuel Huntington's 'Clash of Civilizations' thesis was exhumed from under the weight of criticism that had buried it shortly after its publication in 1993 as an article in *Foreign Affairs*. Huntington quickly gained a host of new adherents who joined him in demanding that the academic community repent for doubting that the next world conflict would pit the 'West against the Rest' (and especially the West against Islam).[18] Fred Halliday rushed into publication a collection of old essays, accompanied by what was essentially an editorial footnote stressing the urgency of intercultural dialogue between the West and Islam.[19] Kenneth Waltz was accorded the last word in a series of papers on terrorism and global order, and typically used the opportunity to demonstrate the shortcomings of neorealism's critics. Waltz argued that terrorism changed nothing about international order, and in fact contributed to its continuity by reinforcing the current global power imbalance.[20] Others have argued that on the contrary realism and other 'tired' theories of international politics are no longer applicable in an age of terror, for traditional notions of 'balancing' and 'great powers' and 'shifting alliances' are of no utility whatsoever in countering these new threats.[21]

But what is clear in all of this is that Europe's role is a major component that has been neglected in the earlier academic analyses and debates on the ramifications of 9/11. There have been many discussions of modernity in Islamic societies, and whether or not Islam or capitalism is to blame for terrorism, and much talk of understanding the 'root causes' of terrorism as an unintended by-product of globalization. There has been work on reconceptualizing security from a focus on the state to the human, global, or societal levels. Still others have focused on the nature of 'new wars' that transcend levels of analysis, incorporate new actors, and are based on the politics of identity rather than issues of material power.[22] Amidst all this there has been little attention to the effects, role, and implications of 9/11 for the geopolitical space that incorporates most of the powerful states in the contemporary international system (the current American hegemon excluded). In a sense this is understandable. Major shifts in the landscape of security studies tends to lead first to a re-evaluation of core assumptions, and this process stimulates debate initially on the philosophical level. But for the specialist on Europe, many questions remain. Some pertain to recent issues. For instance, if 9/11 in fact *did* mark a major shift in world politics, then what will be the long-term responses of European states? Is the role of culture in international politics more important as a result of 9/11, and if so, what is Europe's role as a core component of the 'West'? How does 9/11 alter the relationship between Europe and the United States, especially in regard to the nature of alliances and competing interests of major European powers? There are also questions to be answered about more 'traditional' problems, of policy, diplomacy and statecraft that remain important in European security. Can France realistically balance against the U.S., and should it follow such a policy path? Does Tony Blair's view that theories that focus on balancing are outdated and dangerous imply an irresolvable rift between France and the United Kingdom? What does 9/11 imply for German security policy as Berlin continues to foster an image as a 'normal' state after the ending of the Cold War? What is Britain's role in the Middle East now that the U.S. has taken the lead? Can European security planning accommodate Russia, which already perceives a threat from NATO expansion?

We hope this book will help fill the gap by addressing these questions. As a group of researchers, we are puzzled by the fact that Europe has received such little attention in discussions relating to the impact of 9/11 on security studies. Europe remains vitally important to the maintenance of international order, especially since it is currently so divided over the best security path to follow in the aftermath of not only 9/11 but also the Cold War. Some prominent academics like William Wallace have attempted to address this in terms of institutionalization through the EU, and such work has been thought provoking and useful.[23] Others like John Mearsheimer focus on the nature of power in Europe. Mearsheimer blends Waltz's structural realism with Morgenthau's classical realist theory, with its focus on power-maximization, leading to what he labels a theory of 'offensive realism'. Mearsheimer's theory is counter-posed then to Waltz's 'defensive realism' in which security and survival are the primary interests of states.[24] Based on the logic and assumptions of his theory Mearsheimer suggests that Europe will be a rival power centre in an emerging multipolar world order. It is certainly not clear how 'offensive realist theory' can apply to the war on terror and the events that have unfolded from 9/11. There has also been little discussion of European solidarity in relation to the events of 9/11, even though – as is pointed out in many of the chapters here – the cracks in Europe's perceived unity have been visible for some time.

As a result, we believe that this book is particularly timely, given the deepening schisms on security not only between European states, but also between parts of Europe and America. In the first chapter, Peter Shearman examines the changing notion of security in the aftermath of the Cold War and 9/11, and discusses the implications of this for Europe. He argues that rather than representing a new structural phenomenon of international politics, the 'war on terror' represents a response to challenges to global U.S. interests, leading to an assertion of American hegemony, with important consequences for European security. The second chapter takes up the notion of culture in world politics, and Matthew Sussex re-evaluates Samuel Huntington's 'Clash of Civilizations' thesis in relation to Europe's position as part of the West. He finds that Huntington's case remains problematic, particularly given the disunity between civilizations as a result of 9/11 and the war in Iraq. He argues instead that although culture is important as an instrument of power, material forces represent more appropriate factors in guiding and determining states' foreign policies, and that they can even ameliorate the possibility of a war between the 'West and the rest'.

The rest of the book is devoted to case studies of security policies in major European states. Peter Shearman and Matthew Sussex examine in Chapter 3 the changing relationship between the U.S. and Europe, and suggest that the transatlantic partnership, often identified as a zone of peace and stability, may be under threat due to U.S. unilateralist tendencies and changing strategic interests. Remy Davison analyses French security policy after 9/11, focusing on the emphasis placed on multipolarism in Paris, coupled to the perceived need to balance against the U.S. in order to safeguard French interests. In his chapter on German security policy, Franz Oswald looks at the changing nature of German defense policy in relation to the war in Afghanistan. He argues that changes in German security doctrine following 9/11 are not reflective of sudden shifts in Germany's stance, but rather are part of the broader pattern of Germany's emergence as a 'normal' state in the aftermath of the Cold War. Chapter 6, by Alexei Muraviev, examines Russian responses to 9/11 in the context of Moscow's troubled relationship with the member states of the NATO alliance. Muraviev charts the process by which Russia's position shifted from outright hostility to the expansion of a Cold War-era security organization to its borders, to a grudging acceptance that NATO expansion was inevitable. In the aftermath of 9/11, Muraviev identifies the opportunity for broader security cooperation between the U.S. and Russia, provided the issue of NATO enlargement is settled by the provision of a new architecture for pan-European security that includes all former republics of the USSR. In the last chapter of this volume Peter Hinchcliffe addresses the implications of 9/11 for British policy in the Middle East. As a former ambassador to two states in the region, he delivers unique insights on the need for Britain to pursue a policy that does not alienate those Islamic states that are important to British interests. In order to turn this from vision into reality, Hinchcliffe argues that Tony Blair should continue to make the resolution of the Israeli-Palestinian problem a priority for his foreign policy team.

Finally it is pertinent to note that we still live in turbulent and uncertain times. Much will possibly have happened in the international security environment during the period that will have elapsed between the production stage of this volume and its final publication. The war in Iraq, although looming, had not yet been fought when we held the original workshop in July 2002. However, subsequently, we have been able to revise each chapter to account for the Iraq war and its aftermath. This task was simplified by the (as it turned out) remarkably prescient conclusions reached by all of us that there were considerable cracks in the transatlantic alliance which had underpinned European security both during and following the Cold

War. But we are well aware of the occupational hazard presented by writing on contemporary issues, particularly at a time of such rapid change. The shifting and fluid nature of U.S. responses to perceived threats to its interests, and the impact of U.S. policies in various parts of the world, may mean that this volume will lose its immediate contemporary topicality. But the aim of the volume is not to provide a journalistic analysis or record of current events, but to offer a contribution to our understanding of European security and international relations after 9/11. We hope also that this book will make some contribution to ongoing debates about the future of the transatlantic relationship.

Notes

1   Jentleson, B.W., 'The Need for Praxis: Bringing Policy Relevance Back In', *International Security*, vol. 26, no. 4, 2002, pp. 169-183. The journals included: *American Journal of Political Science, American Political Science Review, International Organization, Security Studies*, and *World Politics*. Jentleson points out that U.S. graduate programmes in political science '...convey early on to PhD students that the track they have chosen is more about the discipline than it is about the world', p. 171.

2   Harkavy, R.E. and Neuman, S.G., *Warfare and the Third World*, New York, Palgrave, 2001.

3   Baylis, J. and Smith, S. (eds), *The Globalization of World Politics: An Introduction to International Relations*, Oxford, Oxford University Press, 2nd edition, 2001. The quote here is taken from the cover.

4   Carlsnaes, W., Risse, T., and Simmons, B.A. (eds), *Handbook of International Relations*, London, Sage, 2001. The quote is from the flyleaf.

5   The Programme clearly demonstrates this. One of the editors of this volume presented a paper at the conference: Shearman, P., 'New Wars and Russia's War in Chechnya', 4th Pan-European International Relations Conference, University of Canterbury, Kent, 6-10 September, 2001.

6   Booth, K. and Dunne, T. (eds), *Worlds in Collision: Terror and the Future of Global Order*, Houndsmills, Basingstoke, 2002. This is not to question the quality of the contributions, simply to point out that Europe is largely absent from the book's focus.

7   Bush, G.W., 'Freedom at war with Fear', speech to joint session of Congress, September 20, 2001, at www.whitehouse.gov/news/releases/2002/01/20020129-11.html.

8   Wolfowitz was (and remains at the time of writing) the U.S. Deputy Secretary of Defense. For his December 2, 2002 IISS speech at Arundel House in London, see www.defenselink.mil/speeches/2002/s20021202-depsecdef.html.

9   Figures from Holliday, L., *Children of the Troubles*, New York, Washington Square Press, 1997, p.1.

10   The argument that hegemony is a more useful concept than balance of power to understand the post-Cold War international system has been recently made by Michael Cox. Cox argues that global order rests not on 'shared norms or something vaguely defined as the international community, but the power and policies of one very special kind of state'. This marks a divergence from structural realist accounts focusing on the role of international anarchy to an emphasis on

hierarchy of power as the determinant of international order. See Cox, M., 'September 11 and U.S. Hegemony – or Will the 21st Century be American Too?', *International Studies Perspectives*, vol. 3, no. 1, 2002, pp. 53-70.

[11] See Tony Blair's address to the nation at the onset of the war in Iraq on March 20, 2003: www.primeminister.gov.uk/output/Page3327.asp. Blair noted the world faced a new type of threat '…born either of brutal states like Iraq, armed with weapons of mass destruction; or of extreme terrorist groups… My fear is that these threats come together and deliver catastrophe to our country and world'.

[12] Germany's Justice Minister, Herta Daeubler-Gmelin, was forced to resign in September 2002 after she made this comparison. Her comments prompted Condoleeza Rice to claim that relations with Germany had been 'poisoned'. See www.cnn.com/2002/WORLD/europe/09/23/germany.minister/index.html

[13] See, for example, Elshtain, J.B., *Just War Against Terror: The Burden of American Power in a Violent World*, New York, Basic Books, 2003.

[14] See, for instance, Wallerstein, I., 'America and the World: The Twin Towers as Metaphor', www.ssrc.org/set11/essays/wallerstein.

[15] Zinn, H., *Terrorism and War*, Crows Nest, New South Wales, Allen & Unwin, 2002; and Chomsky, N., *Power and Terror*, New York, Seven Stories Press, 2003.

[16] Hoge Jr., J.F. and Rose, G. (eds), *How Did This Happen? Terrorism and the New War*, New York, Council on Foreign Relations, 2001.

[17] On the failure of IR theory and the problems of 'Sovietology' in not being able to account for the end of the Cold War see Shearman, P., 'Nationalism, the State, and the Collapse of Communism', in Vandersluis, S.O. (ed.), *The State and Identity Construction in International Relations*, Houndsmills, Basingstoke, Macmillan, 2000, pp. 76-108.

[18] On this point see Kaplan, R., 'Looking the World in the Eye', *Atlantic Monthly*, vol. 288, no. 5, 2001, pp. 68-82.

[19] Halliday, F., *Two Days That Shook the World: September 11, 2001: Causes and Consequences*, London, Al Saqi Books, 2002.

[20] Waltz, K.N., 'The Continuity of International Politics', in Booth and Dunne (eds), *Worlds in Collision*, 2002, pp. 348-354.

[21] This was one of the key arguments that Tony Blair made in his speech to the joint sitting of the U.S. Congress in July 2003.

[22] Kaldor, M., *New and Old Wars: Organized Violence in a Global Era*, Cambridge, Polity, 1999. See also Kaldor's 'Beyond Militarism, Arms Races, and Arms Control', available at www.ssrc.org/sept11/essays/kaldor_text_only.htm.

[23] Wallace, W., 'Living With The Hegemon: European Dilemmas', available at www.ssrc.org/sep11/essays/wallace.

[24] Mearsheimer's J., *The Tragedy of Great Power Politics*, New York, McGraw-Hill, 2001. This builds on earlier realist works such as Waltz, K.N., *Theory of International Politics*, Reading, MA, Addison-Wesley, 1979; and Morgenthau, H.J., *Politics Among Nations: The Struggle for Power and Peace* (Brief Edition), New York, McGraw Hill, 1993.

Chapter 1

Reconceptualizing Security After 9/11

Peter Shearman

Introduction

The conservative *Economist* weekly is not noted for its hyperbole, hence its bold headline in September 2001 was clearly a message its readers were expected to take seriously, stating without a qualifying question mark: *The Day The World Changed.*[1] Following the attacks on the World Trade Centre and the Pentagon there quickly emerged a general consensus, at least in the Western media and among Western leaders and many academics, that indeed the world *had* changed. Although newspaper articles offered analogies with Pearl Harbour, reflecting an attempt to understand the events in terms of traditional defence and security patterns, most then went on to argue that this was a *radically different kind* of conflict. Leading academic specialists, intellectuals and political activists rushed into print offering their assessments, many of which called specifically for a radical reassessment of how we should conceive security.[2] The aim of this chapter is to provide some background to how thinking on security, war and defence is changing as a result of the attacks on America. It does this by examining traditional notions of security and war, before going on to assess the impact of September 11 on the nature of war, defence strategies, and global politics more generally.

What do we mean by 'security'?

First we should note that security is a slippery concept, one of those in the social sciences that are 'essentially contested' (one of those about which there is no overall agreement in academic circles as to its exact meaning).[3] There has been disagreement about who or what should be the most important referent objects of security. Should it be the individual, giving rise to conceptions of human security? Or should the focus be upon social groups, whether based upon religion, culture, or ethnicity, facilitating conceptions of societal security? Or is the global community the appropriate object, leading to conceptions of cosmopolitan or world security?[4] There has been disagreement among analysts about what should be on the security agenda, and about what should be viewed as the most salient threats to security (military, either conventional or weapons of mass destruction; environmental problems; economic issues; resource scarcities; demographic trends; transnational crime; or terrorism). This debate and uncertainty became particularly intense with the ending of the bipolar conflict between the superpowers. To what extent has

9/11 resolved this problem? Does the 'war on terror', what President George Bush has referred to as the first war of the twenty-first century, mark a shift in thinking on security where transnational terrorism is the most salient threat, and will this then help to define strategic thinking during the emerging new era in global politics, and hence determine defence planning and deployments?[5] If 9/11 did mark a radical change in thinking about war and peace, and the defence and security policies of the major powers, especially in the U.S., then this would mark a major shift in the conduct of world politics, which would be certain to have consequences for Europe.

To be secure, simply, is to be out of harm's way. If something threatens harm then, depending upon what it is, individuals or communities can develop strategies and policies to deter, counter, or in the final analysis fight off threats. At the domestic level, *within* the state community, security from harm is provided traditionally by law enforcement agencies and other institutions. Courts of law, police, jails, and health authorities help ensure security against threats, whether from armed robbers, corruption, or pandemics. People might have a generally positive view of human nature and trust in their fellow citizens, but nevertheless most of us feel the need to insure our personal property against crime, even though we might have a general trust in our neighbours not to do us any harm. Security at the domestic level, then, is provided through a mixture of legal mechanisms and insurance policies. No such mechanisms exist when it comes to *external* threats to the state. The international system of states is defined by anarchy: the absence of an overriding political authority with the power to impose legal authority or offer insurance against international misbehaviour. States traditionally have had to rely upon their own resources to deter and counter threats, and the tragedy of the system dictates that they inevitably seek to enhance their own power by building up their own military capabilities and forging alliances with other states. This creates a 'security dilemma' whereby the provision of one state's security through military build up will be viewed as potentially threatening by others, making them feel *less* secure. This is how Realist theory, which was dominant during the Cold War, perceives international politics and security. Security in this conventional view focuses upon states, with power defined in terms of material (and principally military) capabilities as the key variable, with national security determined by the anarchical nature of the international system.[6]

States and warfare

In the modern era, since the Treaty of Westphalia in 1648, international security has been associated with states, and war came to be established as primarily a state activity. Scholars have focused on the Great Powers, for it is these most powerful states that were seen to determine the overall balance of power and the stability of the system. When there is a crisis in the state system and order breaks down, war as an instrument (what Hedley Bull termed an 'institution') is used as a last resort to ensure a new stable order emerges.[7] War has been a phenomenon in human relations since the beginning of recorded history, but during the modern system of nation states for the past 500 years it has been associated with states, most often the most powerful among them. Great Power War has also been for the most part concentrated during the last 200 years on the European continent. European states fought amongst themselves for much of the modern era. One should remember also that the Cold War was centred in Europe, symbolized by the wall dividing Germany, with East-Central Europe and the USSR pitted against Western Europe and the United States. War as a socially sanctioned phenomenon developed rules and norms, mainly devized by Europeans, to ensure combatants' behavior remained within certain limits, and to safeguard non-combatants. War was distinguished from crime, and soldiers from police. States were accorded the legitimate use of military power. Only soldiers representing the state were permitted to engage in combat, in the name of the state.

War has also been seen as having a specific purpose. Wars traditionally have defining battles, followed by surrender and/or the negotiation of peace treaties. Conventional encounters on the battlefield in the modern era have most often been decisive for the ending of wars. Those conducting war need an exit strategy. There needs to be an end goal which is achievable and from which it is then possible to arrange an exit for deployed troops and a return if not to the status quo ante, then at least a return to a non-violent, more stable and secure environment.

War on terror as a new type of war

The war against terror, although its most spectacular manifestation has been in using traditional national military forces and hardware, first in Afghanistan and later in Iraq, is not a war against a state or coalition of states in alliance. We can use the continuous present tense in discussing the war against terror, because it has no obvious exit strategy and no logical end point. It is an ongoing war against a largely invisible enemy, an enemy that does not recognize the norms and customs associated with the modern conceptions of war, traditionally associated with states. The bombing of Afghanistan was designed to remove terrorist networks from a state that had essentially failed, with a regime that even before the war began was recognized by only three other states. The Taliban was also the only regime to give official recognition to the rebels fighting against Russian control in Chechnya. It is not a war amongst the Great Powers, but one that has pitted the world's sole remaining superpower – or what some refer to as a 'hyperpower' – against the world's poorest countries that have provided havens to terrorists or thought to be in league with them. The stated purpose of the war on Iraq was to prevent a rogue regime from providing weapons of mass destruction to terrorists who threatened to harm the United States. In a radical departure from previous state practice the world's most powerful state unilaterally preempted war against another state in order to remove a regime that was thought to pose a possible future threat – one of providing WMD to terrorist groups. Yet the real target of the longer war is not a state at all, but essentially a transnational terrorist organization.

The war is a direct response to what would have previously been termed a criminal act, not an act of war.[8] The opponent in the war did not really articulate clearly the purpose of the attacks in September 2001 (although statements by Osama bin Laden pointed to America's support for Israel, its opposition to Iraq, and the presence of U.S. troops in Saudi Arabia as the key concerns). The 9/11 attacks were not traditional in the sense that they were not clearly linked to a demand for territory, nor to a change in government or regime, nor to impose an ideology. Although not having a great track record of success, where terrorism has succeeded in the past it has been linked to direct political objectives. Terrorism has usually had a distinct political purpose relating to territory and nationalism. For example, the Irish Republican Army (IRA), the Basques, the Tamil Tigers, and various groups of Palestinians have as their central motivating cause claims over territory. Left wing terrorist groups in Europe in the 1970s (such as the Red Brigades and the Baader-Meinhoff gang) operated in the name of a radical ideology whose purpose was to destabilize incumbent governments. Terrorists have also most often been careful to target military or security personnel or political leaders, or at least given warnings of bombs before they are detonated. Many innocent civilians not associated with the security forces have, it is true, been killed. But flying aircraft into the most densely populated building in the world, with workers going about their daily business, marked a radical departure from previous terrorist practice.[9]

Traditionally, security challenges have a focal point that produces crises that threaten to spill over into war. Here, to take a salient example, Kashmir provides a focal point of conflict between Pakistan and India. Diplomatic and/or military energies and attention are focused upon this issue. Similarly in recent 'conventional' wars there have been clear focal points around which the conflict has centered, and out of which crises grew into wars (Britain and Argentina over the Falklands/Malvinas; the U.S. under Bush Senior and Iraq over Kuwait). Transnational terrorism is distinguished from traditional security threats by not having a focal point of conflict out of which crises result in war over clearly defined issues. Conventional combatants in war also seek to identify, define, and destroy an enemy's principle capacities essential for operations. In the Falklands war it was a case of removing hostile invading forces from the Islands. In the Gulf war over Kuwait it was the Iraqi command and control system.

Yet in the case of transnational terrorism this is not possible. Transnational terrorists operate in small cells with no clear central command station, with each individual cell often not even knowing the identity of others in the organization. There are simply many centres in many places all operating under strict secrecy. The U.S. saw Afghanistan as the centre of gravity, but it is generally acknowledged that fulfilling the objective of destroying the Taliban and the terrorist camps in that country would not effectively destroy al Qaeda's ability to operate. Terrorists move on, some lie low, waiting an opportunity to strike again. It could be from anywhere, aimed against anything, at any time. The Bali bombings in October 2002 demonstrated this fact, with large numbers of innocent, mainly young, holidaymakers blown to pieces in a nightclub. Terrorist atrocities in Casablanca and Riyadh, in both cases in almost simultaneous explosions in multiple locations (including housing complexes, and social clubs) showed, some eighteen months after 9/11, that the war on terror was far from over. The battlefield is indeterminate. The U.S. has threatened to expand the war to other states that might sponsor terrorism, but terrorists hide away deep within societies, making many countries unwilling and/or unknowing hosts to such groups. As September 11 demonstrated terrorists are not from the middle ages, but from the middle classes, not necessarily from the poorest segments of the community, but also from the very wealthiest, not ignorant of the ways of the world, but highly educated, technically competent, and able to blend into American society itself.[10] Part of the U.S. justification for waging war on Iraq in March 2003 was the links that Washington claimed the Saddam regime had with al Qaeda, and other terrorist groups in the Middle East, and the danger of Iraq providing them with WMD. No such connections have since been proven, or any solid proof yet discovered of Iraq being in possession of WMD. And many would see the important ultimate consequence of the U.S. led war on Iraq to be more recruits for the terrorists' cause. This could be another case of 'blowback' in the making, as aggressive American foreign policies provide the seeds for later negative consequences for U.S. long-term interests.

Terrorists also do not operate in accordance with the norms and customs of conventional warfare, or even pretend to recognize laws of war. On the contrary, they are defined in large part by their non-conventional methods. Clearly there is no prospect of the warring parties sitting around a table and negotiating a settlement. Not only are their demands, in so far as they can be ascertained, unlikely to be considered the legitimate basis for diplomacy, the terrorists themselves do not play by the same state-based rules of international politics. It is not possible to contain or to deter an invisible enemy that is willing to commit suicide in the name of an unspecified cause. To complicate things further, even where a cause *is* the motivating factor for joining a terrorist group, over time 'terrorism can become a career as much as a passion'.[11] The United States, in conducting a war against global terrorism, has set itself objectives that are unlikely ever to be fulfilled (at least through the traditional means of military power). There is no simple exit strategy. It is unlikely, unless the root causes of terrorism against the United States can be identified and dealt with effectively, that Americans will be confident in their security in the foreseeable future.

This is therefore an asymmetrical war on a number of levels. The United States as the most powerful state in the system had a defence budget, even before September 11 of over $300 billion per year. This represented ten times the British defence budget and twice that of the other NATO states put together.[12] The U.S. has the greatest power projection capacity of any state since ancient Rome – it has more aircraft carriers again than all other NATO states combined. Despite the military hardware and power projection capabilities of the United States armed forces, a small group of terrorists conducted an operation that would have cost possibly only a couple of million dollars to execute. The operation had as great an impact on

American perceptions of its vulnerability than did the more conventional attack at Pearl Harbour. Clearly then, on almost any indicator or definition of security and warfare, the attacks on the U.S. and the subsequent war on terror mark a major divergence from the practice of war and security policies that dominated during the Cold War period. Before going on to assess in detail the actual consequences of this for security policies it is instructive to return briefly to the confusion of the early post-Cold War years in this area.

Confusion about security after the Cold War

During the interregnum following the end of the Cold War up until the attacks on the United States, U.S. foreign and security policies appeared to lack cohesion, clarity or long-term strategic thinking. As the Cold War was winding down there was a brief triumphal moment when it was considered that the world was heading towards a new order based upon an expanded community of democratic states.[13] There soon followed a less optimistic prediction that the world was heading for a clash of civilizations, as cultural identities were said to be replacing ideology as the major determinant of international divisions and conflict.[14] Meanwhile, U.S. foreign policy zigzagged with no apparent overriding strategy. Interventions were carried out for 'humanitarian purposes' where U.S. (and other Western, most often British) troops were employed in a new style of combat in which soldiers were deliberately and carefully kept out of harm's way. It seemed that although U.S. troops were prepared to kill, they were not prepared to die, as evidenced in the operations in the former Yugoslavia. At the same time a debate ensued about the relative merits of containing or engaging China, the assumption on both sides being that China was in any case destined to be a Great Power.[15] The enlargement of NATO, variously justified either in terms of expanding the zone of democracy, or in more traditional realist terms, presented problems for Russia's leadership as many in Moscow perceived this as a deliberate move to bolster U.S. hegemony. Although America's European allies in the Atlantic Alliance supported NATO enlargement and participated in the interventions in Bosnia and Kosovo, there was concern about Washington's unchecked power and the tendency of the U.S. to act unilaterally. Immediately prior to the September attacks U.S. relations with the Russians, the Europeans, and the Chinese were, for different reasons and with different intensities, becoming complicated. Leaders in Paris, Beijing, and Moscow all spoke critically about American 'hegemony', and the need for a proper multipolar balance to counter U.S. power. Under the new Presidency of George W. Bush the U.S. withdrew or threatened to pull out of a number of international treaties and agreements (including the Kyoto Protocol and the ABM Treaty), while simultaneously pursuing a National Missile Defence programme. The U.S. appeared to be moving toward a clash not only with China, the next Great Power in Asia, but also with Russia, its former ideological adversary stretching across Eurasia, whilst raising tensions with its old Cold War partners in Western Europe.

The Bush defence team was packed with hard-nosed advocates of the unilateral utilization of military power in defence of U.S. national interests. Donald

Rumsfeld, the Defence Secretary, had previously served in that position (the youngest ever to hold the portfolio, under President Ford). Rumsfeld's deputy, Paul Wolfowitz, was Under Secretary for Defence when Dick Cheney was in charge of the Pentagon under Bush Senior. Cheney became Bush Junior's Vice President. Richard Perle, until early in 2003 chair of the Defence Policy Board, was one of the hard-liners in the Reagan Administration. These defence officials shared a general view that U.S. power should not be constrained by legal agreements, arms control treaties, or any detente-type relationships.[16] Condoleeza Rice, the National Security Adviser, worked for Bush Senior as an expert on the Soviet Union and in particular Soviet military and defence policies. President Bush himself had very little experience or knowledge in the areas of foreign affairs and defence, and has relied heavily on his ministers and advisers. The general expectation was for an increasing tendency towards American unilateralism, undertaken through influence of this group of so-called 'neo-conservatives'.

The shock of September 11

Then came September 11, and everything suddenly changed. Perhaps the most significant impact the attacks of 9/11 had was psychological, as they dented America's perceptions of its own invulnerability. More people were killed in New York than at Pearl Harbour, and more than in any battle in Vietnam. And those killed were civilians in their offices, not soldiers in combat. The terrorist acts of just nineteen men had the effect of making over 280 million American citizens feel vulnerable.

It is absolutely remarkable that the U.S. and Russia forged such strong and close ties in such a rapid period of time, culminating in a new arms treaty and Russia's new relationship with NATO. It would have been inconceivable before 9/11, that Russia would not only agree, but also help to facilitate the deployment of U.S. troops in the former Central Asian republics of the USSR, and accept the deployment of U.S. troops in the former Soviet republic of Georgia. This was possibly the most radical and rapid change in strategic relationships that had occurred since 1945. The U.S. also quickly dropped the sanctions against Pakistan and India that had earlier been imposed following the nuclear tests by those two states. China also came on board. The Australian Prime Minister invoked Article 4 of the ANZUS Treaty, and George Robertson, Secretary General of NATO invoked, for the first time ever, Article 5 of the NATO Treaty, thereby committing both organizations in support of the U.S.[17]

The question to ask is: do these changes mark simply a shift in international alliances on the basis of shared interests, with those interests being shaped principally by traditional national concerns, or do they represent a more radical departure from previous patterns of international politics? Is the war on terror really a new type of war? And does this reflect a new trend that will shape and determine not only the security policies of the major states in the system, but also the very nature of global politics? In the past, strategic shocks (such as oil shocks and economic shocks) have resulted in rapid changes in the way we think about security. Wars have broken empires, shifted territorial boundaries, removed regimes, stimulated domestic revolutions, and altered the global balance of power. Previous major wars have also had an impact on the way both practitioners and academics have thought about international relations and security. Indeed, the separate development of International Relations as an academic discipline is closely associated with the experience arising from the World War of 1914-1918.[18] The liberal idealist theories that dominated at this time grew out of a general consensus that collective security through international institutions was necessary for the prevention of war. With the onset of another major global conflict in 1939 realist theories came to dominate, where security was to be ensured through a balance of power and alliance systems based upon the principle of collective defence.

The point here is that major events, direct experience and sudden shocks impact both on the way we theorize the world in which we live, and on the development of policy making. Are we once more at a point in time when both academic analysts and foreign and security policy practitioners are developing new ideas and policies in the security realm, as a direct result of a new strategic shock (the attacks of September 11)? Are we entering a new era in world politics? The Great Powers have always determined the overall pattern of international relations. During the Cold War, global politics and international security clearly centred around the two superpowers, the U.S. and the USSR. During the 1990s global politics became confused as the U.S., as the sole superpower, sought to develop a new role for itself in an increasingly complex world. The direction the U.S. has taken as a consequence of September 11 has impacted globally, hence it is vitally important that we understand thinking on security in Washington. What has been learned from the shock of 9/11?

Rapid learning?

In 1946 Albert Einstein stated that with the advent of the nuclear age everything, 'save our modes of thinking' had changed, and as a result the world would drift toward 'unparalleled catastrophe'.[19] A nuclear holocaust has not yet eventuated, but the genie has not been put back into the bottle, and danger still confronts us from nuclear tensions in South Asia, and with the threat of nuclear terrorism. However, the events of September 11 appear to be leading to rapid learning, which could have a radical impact on the way in which security is applied. The initial reaction to the attacks of September 11 could be interpreted as a restoration of state power, and a demonstration of the effectiveness of traditional military instruments in pursuit of the national interest. States were quickly coerced or persuaded to join with the United States in the war against terror. Alliances were made, clearly (in some cases at least, for example, in the case of Pakistan) on the basis of threats and promises emanating from the world's sole superpower. Yet the war on terror marked a learning curve for the Bush defence team. Donald Rumsfeld called it a 'war like no other', stating that it is easier to talk about what it is not than about what it is: 'This war will not be waged by a grand alliance. Instead it will involve floating coalitions...The uniforms of this conflict will be bankers' pinstripes just as assuredly as desert camouflage'.[20] More recently Rumsfeld has articulated a much more thoughtful assessment of security threats. He has stated that to meet the challenge of future threats '...we must put aside comfortable ways of thinking and planning – take risks and try new things – so we can deter and defeat adversaries that have not yet emerged to challenge us'.[21] Rumsfeld argued that it was necessary to move away from the old 'threat-based strategy' that had dominated defence planning for the previous half a century, and develop and adopt a 'capabilities-based approach'. What the Defence Secretary has in mind here is rather than focusing upon who, or which *states*, might threaten the U.S., to redirect attention to an assessment of *what* might threaten, and how to deter and defend against these threats. It is necessary, he continued, *to identify U.S. vulnerability*, and build the armed forces around this, rather than organizing the armed forces to fight this or that country. He concludes by stating that 'we must change not only the capabilities at our disposal, but also how we think about war'.[22] Clearly, September 11 has had a major impact on how key officials in the Bush Administration now think about security, threats, war, and the structure of the military and defence policy.

However, it should be noted that Rumsfeld, although talking about the need for a radical reassessment of how we define security threats and think about war, is not advocating a new world order, or broader cooperation through global institutions. This is not in any way reflective of shifting the referent object of security to a lower or a higher level. Rumsfeld is not prescribing a cosmopolitan approach to global security. Rather what we have is a clear reassertion of U.S. national, *state* interests as the primary object of security. In his address to the joint sitting of Congress after the attacks, in which he essentially declared war on Afghanistan, Bush stated that other states are either with the U.S. in the war or against.[23] Rumsfeld put it this way: 'In this war the mission will define the coalition – not the other way around.'[24]

As Michael Mandelbaum has aptly put it, 'Wars shape diplomacy. Victory becomes the supreme goal of foreign policy and diplomatic alignments are adjusted to achieve it. This can make for strange bedfellows'.[25] Yet the U.S. administration's behaviour in the conduct of the war was to ensure that it was not in any way hampered by alliances, either traditional or recently found ones. For example, although NATO's Article 5 was invoked, the U.S. proceeded to mount its own independent military operation in Afghanistan. Ultimately NATO as an institution did not play a role at all. Other NATO members such as Britain and France participated as individual actors under the general leadership of the U.S., and not as part of a military alliance. ANZUS was invoked, but the Australian contingent operated not under the institutional banner of that alliance, but independently, although essentially following the U.S. lead. In June 2002 President Bush announced the most radical institutional reform in the security realm since the early Cold War years with the establishment of a new Department for

Homeland Security. In addition, it has been clearly acknowledged that it is not possible to deter or contain transnational terrorism in the way that it was against the USSR during the Cold War by using nuclear deterrence or traditional military strategies. In the wake of September 11 the Bush Administration has been developing pre-emptive strategies in which military strikes, and overt or covert operations, will be conducted against terrorist groups or those that harbour or support them before they are able to inflict damage on the U.S. This, again, is a radical departure from previous strategies and policies. This new principle of pre-emption was put into effect against Iraq in 2003.

But 'Why Us'? Identifying root causes

One question that Americans immediately asked themselves after the attacks of September 11 was 'why us'? Bush asked the same question in his address to Congress. This is a significant question. In any conflict it is first necessary to identify the root causes before being able to construct an appropriate long-term strategy to deal with it. Even if the war against terrorist networks is successful, unless the underlying root problem is resolved, then the war may not be won. Soon after September 11 many commentators suggested that the root cause is to be found in the gross inequalities between Americans and the impoverished peoples of the Third World. Whilst it is a truism to note that power inevitably brings envy and even hatred and feelings for revenge, it does not necessarily result in a commitment to carefully plan one's own suicide in order to cause mass destruction of civilian populations. Although Americans are clearly not the direct or deliberate cause of all the injustices and miseries of the world, because the U.S. is the global superpower, as Immanuel Wallerstein has put it, they perhaps are the 'prime beneficiaries'.[26] Yet this is not sufficient for an explanation of September 11 and the war on terror. It was not poverty that precipitated war, although those who started it took advantage of the poor in mobilizing support against the U.S. In seeking to identify the roots of any conflict it is common to look at three factors of causation: deep causes, intermediate causes, and precipitating causes.

In seeking to identify the deep causes of the current war on terror one could refer to the structural parameters of power in global politics and U.S. foreign policies and interventions. Also, perhaps the U.S., as the current centre of global power, is paying the price of centuries of resentment against the West, and Western imperialism. When assessing more intermediate causes it is worth remembering that perceptions are often more important than reality, and different groups often will have radically different interpretations of important events. Many Muslims consider that they have been the disproportionate victims of U.S. power, both military and economic, in the first Gulf War and subsequent sanctions against Iraq, and in America's support for Israel in the Middle East. The Afghan war against the Soviets was also important in the creation of a transnational terror network, as it attracted Muslims from around the world, especially from Arab states, in a common struggle against 'infidels'. Funded by the United States as part of its bipolar confrontation with the USSR, these groups, once the Soviets withdrew from Afghanistan in 1989, returned to their home countries or infiltrated elsewhere with objectives of spreading terror aimed against incumbent governments or against U.S. interests. The precipitating cause of the current war, of course, was the specific attacks of September 11.

If one accepts that these are the deep, intermediate, and precipitating causes of the war, then victory against the Taliban, as a regime sponsoring terrorism, and removing Osama bin Laden and al Qaeda from Afghanistan does not equate with overall victory in the war. Nor will the removal of Saddam Hussein and the installation of a pro-U.S. regime in the virtually secular state of Iraq contribute significantly to the defeat of global terrorism. Indeed, ultimately, it could result in a strengthening of radical Islamism and anti-Americanism, and act as a recruitment campaign for terrorist networks. It logically follows that it would be necessary as part of a strategy to deter future attacks to seek a solution to the deep and intermediate causes. Bush and Blair and (most) other Western leaders have been careful not to further inflame the Muslim world by making clear at every opportunity that the war is not against Islam. This of course indicates that they realize the danger for this to eventuate, and the significance of this factor as a deep cause for the resentment aimed at the West. Another important issue is the question of U.S. troops in Saudi Arabia, and the intractable conflict over Palestine and U.S. support for Israel. Given current trends and thinking in Washington, it is most unlikely that the U.S. will radically change its policies in these areas. U.S. troops in the Gulf are considered important for strategic reasons, not least the safeguarding of oil interests. Even if American military bases are closed in Saudi Arabia, the presence of U.S. troops in Iraq and other neighbouring states will provide continuing motivation for resentment among Muslims. Support for Israel, although there are occasional criticisms of Israeli policies, is not likely to alter fundamentally. Most specialists on the Middle East do not see the Bush-inspired 'Road Map' as offering any real prospects of resolving the Palestinian problem and the wider Arab-Israeli dispute. American foreign and security policies are likely to continue to be based upon traditional notions of the national interest, defined in terms of power. American citizens might simply have to get used to transnational (as well as home grown) terrorism. There will of course be radical changes in the way the United States structures sections of its armed forces and in the relationships between its branches. There will be changes in the collection of intelligence and the alliances between agencies, especially the FBI and the CIA, and whom the U.S. considers its friends and potential enemies. And there is a new Cabinet-level Department looking after Homeland Security. The wars in Afghanistan and Iraq have demonstrated clearly the awesome powers of America's post-modern military, and just how far the actual conduct of war has changed in the information age. U.S. forces in Iraq utilized effectively a system of network-centric warfare, in which computers facilitated a seamless battlefield, in which various components, from unmanned aerial vehicles, central command, and soldiers on the ground had the same information and data stream. Iraq confirmed what was already widely appreciated: the absolutely overwhelming superiority of U.S. military power. It should be noted also that the development of this revolution in warfare was conducted largely under the two terms of Bill Clinton's presidency. Not only the military technology, but also much of the new political thinking on warfare was already developed and salient before the neo-conservatives gained influence in the White House under George W. Bush. 9/11 did not change the world; but it did provide the opportunity and justification for the neo-conservatives to implement a policy of reasserting American global power through pre-emption against regimes considered hostile and threatening.   The seemingly successful outcomes of the wars against Afghanistan and Iraq have also demonstrated to the U.S. that America has the ability to act alone where necessary, with less need for the bases of allies for forward projection. Allies become less important given the effectiveness of precision weapons systems, space-based weapons, long-distance bombers, and other advancements in military technology. Allies are not only made less important, they are even considered by some in Washington as a nuisance. However, there is little indication that much energy is going into identifying and dealing with the root causes of the transnational terrorism against the United States.

America and Europe

As is demonstrated in the other chapters in this volume, all this could have a serious impact on European security concerns and policies, and also on U.S. relations with its traditional European allies. During the Cold War the United States and Western Europe often had disagreements, but these never materialized into a serious confrontation of interests due to the common overriding determining mutual priority of containing and deterring the USSR. Today things are far more complex, the world is far more turbulent, and alliance patterns and national interests do not always neatly intersect due to a single structural feature of international politics. The attacks on America in September 2001 could ultimately have very serious consequences for global politics generally, and Europe will not be immune. To briefly refer to two issues the possible tensions between the U.S. and European states becomes readily apparent.   The first relates to America's support for Israel in the current conflict in the West Bank. This support is not matched by most European governments, which have more sympathy for the Palestinians. A poll taken after the Israeli incursion into the West Bank in March 2002 revealed that whereas Americans sympathized with the Israelis by a three-to-one margin, Europeans supported Palestinians by a margin of two-to-one.[27] The second issue is Iraq. The U.S. assault against Baghdad in order to remove Saddam Hussein from power led to serious tensions in relations with Europe. The tendency for the U.S. to act independently of its European allies to a much greater extent than hitherto is causing anxiety in European capitals. Although it has yet to occur, the asymmetry in perceived interests between Washington and Europe could result, as William Wallace has suggested, in the EU seeking to counterbalance U.S. power by further integrating its foreign and security policies, international diplomacy, and even military force structures.[28] The war on Iraq, although causing some rifts within Europe itself, has nevertheless clearly shown how extending the war on terror caused serious tensions in transatlantic relations, a potential harbinger for the future.

The nature of warfare and security threats is changing in radical ways. Since the demise of the Cold War perceptions of threats and who represent the main adversaries has altered fundamentally. This has resulted in radical thinking among leading states, but with important differences of view between them, reflecting the complexities of defining the national interest in the contemporary era. Despite forces of globalization and the growth of transnational terrorism, politics still takes place within the territorial boundaries of the nation state. It is instructive to note how 9/11 has resulted in a strengthening of the already existing tendency of Western states to restrict and take a harder stance against illegal immigration. Rather than developing a more humane approach to problems associated with these issues, the response has been in the opposite direction. The state is reasserting its powers in defending what it perceives to be new kinds of threats to its territorial integrity. Defence and security strategies might be changing to deal with new types of threats, but there is very little evidence that the state is being replaced as the main object of security or the main actor in global politics. Nor is there evidence that the traditional instruments of 'hard' power and diplomacy are being replaced with other, 'soft' forms of power.[29] However, there are important differences in perceptions about the nature of the main dynamics in global politics between the United States and some of its European allies.

It is interesting here to note that the person who has done more to articulate a radical approach to security, which runs counter to that of U.S. conceptions under Bush, is British Prime Minister Tony Blair. Blair has been Bush's closest supporter in the war on terror, yet his basic orientation in its pursuit differs greatly from that of the U.S. Blair set out his ideas in his so-called 'Doctrine of the International Community' in April 1999. Central to this doctrine is the assumption that the 'national interest is to a significant extent governed by international collaboration'.[30] Blair was positing a conception of international security that is no longer state based, but one guided by a 'subtle blend of mutual self interest and moral purpose in defending the values we cherish...The spread of our values makes us safer'.[31] Blair concluded by noting that Britain for the first time in three decades has a government that is both pro-Europe and pro-American, having done away with what he called the 'false proposition' that the U.K. had to choose between the two. However, as the war on terror continues to reflect a unilateral tendency to use American military power in the pursuit of U.S. national interests (rather than that of the international community), Britain could in the long run be pulled closer still to Europe while becoming more critical of the United States. The war on terror has demonstrated the hegemonic status of the U.S. in global politics, both in the military and economic realms. The outcome of September 11 could ultimately leave Europe having to make a choice of whether or not to continue to work within an international architecture of U.S. hegemony, or to develop its own institutions to counter what is presently an unfettered U.S. power. William Wallace puts it this way: the Europeans will either have to bandwagon with the United States, or balance against it.[32]

Conclusions

In conclusion it could be suggested that the war on terror can be seen as reinforcement for the theories that have been developed about new wars, in which old ways of managing international conflict is not only inappropriate, but ultimately dangerous, for they do not deal with the root causes. To deal with transnational terrorism, which thrives and is financed by international crime and seeks support through mobilizing hatred and ethnic and/or religious intolerance designed to legitimate its leadership, requires a more radical, cosmopolitan approach. This would involve a mixture of humanitarian intervention, and other legal enforcement mechanisms through emerging institutions of global governance, which limit the sovereignty of territorially-based states. Mary Kaldor is one of the most influential proponents of a cosmopolitan approach to security. Kaldor argues that 'new wars' depart radically from earlier wars on the basis of the actors involved, the objectives sought, the methods used, and in how they are financed.[33] The war against terror would appear to fit her typology of a new war. However, in concluding a recent article that prescribes international and especially humanitarian law as the way forward to deal with the war on terror, she concedes, in light of U.S. reactions to September 11, that her approach 'sounds impossibly utopian'. At the same time it is clear that it is not possible to bomb an idea out of existence, or to deal with the underlying factors that allow for the mobilization of this idea among a wider audience through military means.

Ultimately the war on terror is riddled with contradictions and moral dilemmas. It lacks coherence or clarity in its objectives, and the U.S. has itself been divided over the goals and methods of warfare. Indeed often it has seemed as though it has competing objectives, as the Bush Administration swings between support and criticism of Israel, military threats against Iraq, followed by diplomacy, ending in war. Whilst Bush has stated his war in the first instance was against al Qaeda, he asserts that '...it does not end there. It will not end until every terrorist group of global reach has been found, stopped and defeated'.[34] However it is clear that this is not a war against 'global terrorism', but only against terrorism that harms or threatens the American state and its interests. It is these overriding state interests that are determining U.S. reactions to September 11, and for this reason one could already see difficulties in holding the coalition together as the U.S. broadened its war aims to include the 'liberation' of Iraq. Regarding the controversy over intelligence reports relating to WMD Rumsfeld admitted that the information on this might not have changed – but since 9/11 the U.S. perceives the world through a new prism. 9/11 has clearly had a major impact on U.S. foreign and security policies. The subsequent emphasis by Washington on temporary coalitions to 'fit the mission' could have serious ramifications for European security, and for U.S. relations with its current allies in Europe. Other chapters in this volume take up these themes in detail.

Notes

1   *Economist*, 15 September, 2001.

2   Just to list some of them: Talbott, S. and Chanda, N. (eds), *The Age of Terror: America and The World After September 11*, New York, Basic Books 2001; Harris, S. et al, *The Day The World Changed? Terrorism and World Order*, Keynotes, RSPAS, The Australian National University, Canberra, October 2001; Baxter, J. and Downing, M., *The Day That Shook The World: Understanding September 11*, London, BBC Worldwide, 2001; Hoge Jr., J.F. and Rose, G. (eds), *How Did This Happen? Terrorism and the New War*, New York, Council on Foreign Relations, 2001; Snow, D.M., *September 11, 2001; The New Face of War?*, New York, Longman, 2001; Chomsky, N., *September 11*, Crows Nest, New South Wales, Allen & Unwin, 2001; Silvers, R.B. and Epstein, B. (eds), *Striking Terror: America's New War*, New York, New York Review Books, 2002; and Booth, K. and Dunne, T. (eds), *Worlds in Collision: Terror and the Future of Global Order*, Houndmills, Palgrave, 2002. Text book publishers also sought to cash in by offering quick supplements designed for undergraduate teaching in International Relations: eg, *Prentice Hall Authors Speak Out: September 11 and Beyond*, Prentice Hall, Upper Saddle River, NJ, 2002; and Tuman, M. (ed), *September 11, 2001: Readings for Writers*, New York, Longman, 2002. Other works have since been published, and there are many more works in the pipeline, and journals and websites are also full of articles, debates, analysis, and commentary on questions concerning defence, security, and war after September 11.

3   For a brief description of security as a concept in International Relations see Griffiths, M. and O'Collaghan, T., *International Relations: The Key Concepts*, London, Routledge, 2002, pp. 291-293. See also Baylis, J., 'International and Global Security in The Post-Cold War Era', in Baylis, J. and Smith, S. (eds), *The Globalization of World Politics: An Introduction to International Relations*, Oxford, Oxford University Press, 2nd edition, 2001, pp. 253-276.

4   For an early post Cold War discussion of individual security see Buzan, B., *People States and Fear: An Agenda for International Security Studies in the Post-Cold War Era*, Hemel Hempstead, Harvester Wheatsheaf 1991, pp. 35-56; On human security see Suhrke, A., 'Human Security and the Interests of States', *Security Dialogue*, vol. 30, no. 3, 1999, pp. 265-276. On societal security see Waever, O., Buzan, B., Kestrup, M. and Lemaitre, P., *Identity, Migration and the New Security Agenda in Europe*, London, Pinter, 1993, esp. pp. 17-40; for ideas relating to cosmopolitan security see Held, D., *Democracy and the Global Order: From the Modern State to Cosmopolitan Governance*, Cambridge, Cambridge University Press, 1995, and Kaldor, M., *New and Old Wars: Organized Violence in a Global Era*, Cambridge, Polity, 1999, esp. pp. 112-137. For a detailed assessment of various conceptions of security cooperation see Muller, H., 'Security Cooperation', in Carlsnaes, W., Risse, T. and Simmons, B.A. (eds), *Handbook of International Relations*, London, Sage, 2002, pp. 350-368.

5   It should of course be noted that Palestinians, Chechens, Sri Lankans, and many other groups would take issue with the idea that the 'war on terror' is the first war of the twenty-first century!

6   Morgenthau, H.J., *Politics Among Nations: The Struggle for Power and Peace*, 2nd edn, New York, Alfred A. Knopf, 1948; Waltz, K.N., *Theory of International*

Politics, Reading, MA, Addison-Wesley, 1979; and Mearsheimer, J., *The Tragedy of Great Power Politics*, New York, W.W. Norton, 2001.

[7]   Bull, H., *The Anarchical Society: A Study of Order in World Politics*, London, Macmillan, 1977.

[8]   Indeed there are many critics of U.S. policy who argue that the perpetrators of the attacks were criminals and should be treated as such, requiring the use of legal instruments, not military ones, to bring them to justice. For different perspectives on this issue see Chomsky, N., *September 11*, Crows Nest, NSW, Allen & Unwin, 2001; Price, R., 'Is It Right To Respond With Military Attacks?, in Harris, S. et al, *The Day the World Changed? Terrorism and International Order*, Canberra, ANU, 2001, pp. 25-31; and Roberts, A., 'Counter-terrorism, Armed Force and the Laws of War', *Survival*, vol. 44, no. 1, 2002, pp. 7-32.

[9]   It could be noted, however, that this was not the first September in which four planes were hijacked simultaneously from different airports. Members of the Popular Front for the Liberation of Palestine attempted a similar feat on September 6, 1970 ('Black September'). One should also note that there is no single agreed definition of terrorism or on who should be labelled as a terrorist. Indeed, one person's 'terrorist' is another person's 'freedom fighter'. Others speak of 'state terrorism'. For a discussion of terrorism as a concept see Townsend, C., *Terrorism: A Very Short Introduction*, Oxford, Oxford University Press, 2002. Also see Laqueur, W., *The New Terrorism: Fanaticism and the Arms of Mass Destruction*, Oxford, Oxford University Press, 1999.

[10] On bin Laden and his organization see Reeve, S., *The New Jackals*, London, Andre Deutsch, 1999; Bergen, P.L., *Holy War: Inside the Secret World of Osama bin Laden Inc*, London, Weidenfeld & Nicolson, 2001; Bodansky, Y., *Bin Laden: The Man Who Declared War on America*, Roseville, Calif, Prima Publishing, 2001; Gunaratna, R., *Inside Al Qaeda: Global Network of Terror*, Carlton, Victoria, Australia, Scribe Publications, 2002; and Fouda, Y. and Fielding, N., *Masterminds of Terror*, Camberwell, Victoria, Australia, Penguin, 2003.

[11] See Stern, J., 'The Protean Enemy', *Foreign Affairs*, vol. 82, no. 4, 2003, pp. 27-40, p. 28.

[12] See Cohen, E., 'A Tale of Two Secretaries', *Foreign Affairs*, vol. 81, no. 3, 2002, pp. 33-46, p. 37.

[13] Fukuyama, F., *The End of History and the Last Man*, New York, Free Press, 1992.

[14] Huntington, S., *The Clash of Civilizations and the Remaking of World Order*, New York, Touchstone, 1996.

[15] For example see Gill, B., 'China: Can Engagement Work?', *Foreign Affairs*, vol. 78, no. 4, July/August 1999, pp. 65-76.

[16] See Fallows, J., 'The Unilateralist: A Conversation With Paul Wolfowitz', *The Atlantic Monthly*, March 2002, available on the World Wide Web at www.theatlantic.com/issues.2002/03/fallows.

[17] Thereby setting precedents by invoking the treaties to combat *terrorism*.

[18] The first department of International Relations was established at the University of Wales at Aberystwyth after and as a direct result of the war.

[19] Cited in Garrity, P. and Maaranen, S. (eds), *Nuclear Weapons in a Changing World: Perceptions from Europe, Asia and North America*, New York, Plenum Press, 1992, p. 16.

[20] Rumsfeld, D., 'A War Like No Other', reprinted in the *Guardian Weekly*, 4-10 October, 2001, p. 11.

[21] Rumsfeld, D., 'Transforming the Military', *Foreign Affairs*, vol. 81, no. 3, May/June, 2002, pp. 20-32, p. 23.

22 Rusmfeld, 'Transforming the Military', p. 29.
23 See Bush's speech to the joint sitting of Congress, 21 September, 2001, available at www.whitehouse.gov.
24 Rumsfeld, 'Transforming the Military', p. 29.
25 Mandelbaum, M., in Hoge and Rose (eds), *How Did This Happen?*, pp. 255-268, p. 257.
26 Wallerstein, I., 'America and the World: The Twin Towers as Metaphor', www.ssrc.org/sept11/essays/wallerstein.
27 *Economist*, 20 April, 2002, p. 33. Another Gallup Poll, this time in six Islamic states found that only 18% of Muslims believed that the attacks on America on September 11 were carried out by fellow Muslims. See *Time*, 11 March, 2002, p. 13.
28 See also Hutton, W., *The World We're In*, New York, Little Brown, 2002, in which he argues that the UK should see Europe as the logical choice for its interests and as a counterweight to the United States.
29 For a discussion about the nature of hard and soft power see Nye, J., *The Paradox of American Power*, New York, Longman, 2002.
30 Tony Blair's speech at the Economic Club in Chicago – 'Doctrine of the International Community', 23 April, 1999, www.primemister.gov.uk.
31 Blair, 'Doctrine of the International Community'.
32 Wallace, W., 'Living with the Hegemon: European Dilemmas', available at www.ssrc.org/sept11/essays/wallace, 2002.
33 See Kaldor, M., 'Beyond Militarism, Arms Races, and Arms Control', available at www.ssrc.org/sept11/essays/kaldor_text_only.htm. See also Kaldor, M., 'American Power: from "compellance" to "cosmopolitanism?"', *International Affairs*, vol. 79, no. 1, 2003, pp. 1-22.
34 See Bush's speech on 21.9.01, at www.whitehouse.gov.

Chapter 2

Cultures in Conflict? Re-evaluating the 'Clash of Civilizations' Thesis After 9/11

Matthew Sussex

Introduction

Shortly after the September 11 attacks on the World Trade Centre and the Pentagon, Robert Kaplan published a thought-provoking article in the *Atlantic Monthly*, which documented the many obstacles encountered by Samuel Huntington throughout his career. Certainly no stranger to controversy, Huntington was initially denied tenure at Harvard University because the establishment felt that his 1957 book on civil-military relations, *The Soldier and the State*, was too stinging in its attacks on liberal values and represented an apologia for militarism.[1] Later, in *The Third Wave*, published in 1991 and building on his more acclaimed work *Political Order in Changing Societies*, Huntington predicted a scramble for democratization *before* the collapse of the USSR to howls of derision from a variety of influential commentators.[2] Most recently his 'Clash of Civilizations' thesis, which claimed to have identified the emergence of a new world order that would pit the 'West against the rest' and particularly against Islam,[3] was roundly dismissed for a variety of sins. These included conflating identity with civilization; ignoring the disunity within civilizations (if in fact they existed at all); downplaying the role of states in controlling civilizations rather than vice versa; and creating a hypothesis which could result in a self-fulfilling prophecy.[4] But the point, as Kaplan shrewdly observed, was that Huntington had consistently proven his critics wrong in the past.[5] Why not again?

Yet here is the crux of the problem. On the face of it, Huntington's thesis appears to bear a ring of truth, not least because it has clearly struck a nerve with policymakers in Europe and the U.S., who have gone to great lengths to stress that the 'war on terror' does not target Muslims.[6] But as 9/11 reminded us, culture is a powerful force that can foster adversarial relationships and conflict. For International Relations theorists, in addition to the fact that a precise means of operationalizing cultural forces and their effects has not yet been satisfactorily demonstrated (and probably never will), traditional theories of IR have been unable to consistently predict international outcomes at a systemic level.[7] Neorealism's failure to foresee the end of the Cold War has left the discipline in a state of flux, and without a clearly superior theory to replace it amongst the myriad critical, neoliberal, constructivist and postpositivist approaches, understanding the shape of the evolving post-9/11 security landscape is difficult. Amidst this uncertainty, two prominent scholars have described International Relations theory as a 'failed intellectual project',[8] or as Fred Halliday recently put it, there is a pressing need to strike a balance between 'complacency disguised as realism and irresponsibility posing as conscience'.[9]

It is therefore pertinent to re-evaluate Huntington's theory in the wake of September 11, particularly since Osama bin Laden clearly wishes to foment a cultural war between the West and Islam.[10] According to Huntington, we are moving from an international system in which states are involved primarily in the pursuit of material interest to a system in which states define their identity and interests along civilizational lines. This is similar to Benjamin Barber's claim that the world's population is increasingly falling into either the camp of tribalism or globalism, resulting in a war of 'Jihad vs McWorld'.[11] Yet unlike Barber's emphasis on economic globalization breeding fundamentalism, Huntington focuses specifically on religion and tradition. He argues that it is the responsibility of a Western civilization faced by the prospect of diminishing power, a retreating culture, and a backlash against globalization, to adopt a siege mentality by strengthening its institutions, whilst simultaneously playing divide-and-rule with other less powerful civilizations.[12] For Huntington, then, although states remain the most important actors in world politics, the future of conflict is to be found between different civilizations embodying incompatible cultural and political goals. This incorporates conflict between groups at the micro-level, clashes involving states and groups (including terrorists), and ultimately a power struggle between groups of states as the conflict moves onto the structural level of analysis.[13]

Leaving aside problematic issues such as the definition of civilization,[14] a focus on the predictive and prescriptive elements of Huntington's theory allows us to examine whether 9/11 and the subsequent wars in Afghanistan and Iraq do in fact represent the onset of a clash of cultures. In fairness to Huntington it would be precipitate to expect widespread changes at the structural level, since these take time to evolve. Thus it is unlikely that we should find an international system, only two years or so after 9/11, characterized by wars and balance-of-power shifts between states from competing civilizations.[15] Rather, if Huntington's theory is to be supported at this early stage, the most likely changes would be those in which states come to interpret the nature of the threat as cultural, and then respond to it on the basis of their civilizational identities. This necessitates transformations in policy at the very least, and a consequent refocusing of alliances amongst threatened states in Europe and the U.S. Finally, while there must be a will for civilizations to clash, there must also be relatively comparable means – in other words, both sides must possess comparable power – in order for the conflict to be sustained.[16] Yet the failure of Islamic states to join with Iraq against the U.S. and its allies during the campaign to unseat Saddam in early 2003 makes this problematic. Even if Islamic identity had been strong enough to overcome more rational state interests, uniting Muslims against the West, a combination of power asymmetries and more pressing national interests made such a move potential suicide.

Here I find that ultimately Huntington's thesis remains unsatisfactory, and that analysis of the evolving post-September 11 security environment lends greater weight to classical realist explanations than it does a true clash of civilizations. This is due to three factors: first, the clear imbalance of power between the West and Islam; second, the growing disunity within Western civilization, especially over the war in Iraq, that reflects important policy differences between Europe and the U.S.; and third, the fact that the West's responses both in Afghanistan and in coalition-building over Iraq have reflected rational interests of great powers (and associated bandwagoning from less powerful states) rather than normative cultural considerations. Nevertheless, I also argue that Huntington is correct in identifying culture as a motivating force for conflict on the intra-state level of analysis, and that a clash of cultures remains possible if Europe, the U.S., and the Middle East unwisely interpret their interests in cultural/civilizational terms. Thus although culture is an important mechanism of power for the disenfranchised, a prolonged 'war on terror' is ultimately unsustainable because states remain inherently predisposed to identify serious threats as stemming from like units. Indeed, it is the often-maligned system of states itself that minimizes the likelihood of a global clash of cultures emerging. This is for the simple reason that tribalist conflict does not translate well to an international system that remains dominated by states pursuing material interests rather than elusive civilizational identities. I begin by briefly examining the relationship between culture and power, before moving on to consider whether 9/11 has resulted in policy shifts in Europe and the U.S. conducive to a civilizational clash, taking into account issues of identity, interests, and alliances.

Culture and Power

Amidst the debate surrounding the role of culture and religion in conflict, an overlooked lesson of the post-9/11 security environment is that its dominant theme is not culture, but power and interests. Culture, while important, serves primarily as a rationale for action that motivates followers and is thus itself an instrument of power (albeit what Joseph Nye calls 'soft power').[17] As Fred Halliday has observed, 'religious fundamentalists in all societies have one goal: it is not to convert other people to their beliefs, but to seize power – political, social and gendered – within their own societies'.[18] This is remarkably similar to the views articulated by Morgenthau in *Politics Among Nations*, in which he identified culture as an important element in the attainment of power. Morgenthau saw culture as a significant vehicle for expansionist state policies. As he put it, cultural imperialism was 'the most subtle and, if it were ever to succeed by itself alone, the most successful of imperialistic policies'. Thus, Morgenthau stated, the imposition of culture and ideology on a vanquished nation would cement its position 'on more stable grounds than any military conqueror or economic master'.[19]

In this context, Huntington sees the 'Islamic Resurgence' as an attempt to counter the threat of Western cultural encroachment. He notes that the resurgence is a broad global movement that represents 'an effort to find the "solution" not in Western ideologies but in Islam'. It incorporates 'acceptance of modernity, rejection of Western culture and recommitment to Islam as the guide to life', and is prevalent in both popular and serious writing in the Islamic world, which identifies the West as the source of plots to undermine Islamic culture.[20] There is some truth to this claim – to verify it, we need only look as far as our television screens a few hours after the 9/11 attacks, when major news organizations such as the BBC and CNN were independently broadcasting images of Palestinians rejoicing in the streets. Similar scenes could be found in Egypt and Pakistan, and fundamentalist Muslim imams from Europe to the Israeli Occupied Territories made it clear that they approved of the attacks, despite the fact that many had ongoing theological differences with al Qaeda.

Indeed, cultural and religious clashes have been prominent throughout the post-Cold War era, particularly in the former communist states of Eastern Europe. These included successive wars in the Balkans that pitted Orthodox Serbs first against Catholic Croats and Slovenians, and then against Muslim Bosnians and Albanian Kosovars. Although in these conflicts Europe and the U.S. supported the Muslims, culminating in the NATO bombardment of Belgrade in 1999 (thus negating the possibility of a civilizational clash), the fact remained that old ethno-cultural rivalries with the potential to destabilize regional security were reawakened by the disintegration of strong centralized order. Likewise different civilizations have been involved in the war in Chechnya, in which acts of terror by both Russia and the Chechens have been brought to light. The conflict also resulted in the first – and so far the only – documented case of nuclear terrorism, when Chechen rebels hid a canister of radioactive Cesium at a Moscow marketplace in 1995.[21]

In all these cases, groups engaged in conflict either around so-called 'failed states' like Yugoslavia, in struggles for ethnic self-determination, or in international terrorist organizations such as al Qaeda have been quick to identify emotionally compelling cultural reasons for others to join the crusade, and equally compelling reasons why the 'other' culture is alien and repugnant.[22] Here, Huntington had a point when he stressed the importance of 'fault lines', which foster 'communal conflicts between states or groups from different civilizations'.[23] Yet there are two important problems with this in terms of the evolution of an overarching clash of cultures as the determining characteristic of post-Cold War global politics. First, and most obvious, the notion of fault lines is not new. Only the most cursory knowledge of history reveals that cultures and religions sharing close territorial proximity with intermingled histories inevitably clash at a local level (for instance, Jews and Muslims in the Middle East and Orthodox Serbs and Muslims in Yugoslavia, not to mention Catholics and Protestants in Northern Ireland). But in the post-9/11 context, this does not adequately explain why, if culture is such an important element of international politics, it was specifically the actions of well-educated yet suicidal fanatics in the United States rather than stone-throwing youths in Palestine that would engender a systemic clash of civilizations.

The second problem is that it is primarily the disenfranchised and powerless rather than the elites in societies (Islamic or otherwise) who have identified external cultural threats, and have simultaneously drawn upon their own cultural forces as popular symbols to counter outside interference. Although leaders in states such as Malaysia and Saudi Arabia both fear and resent U.S. cultural imperialism, sometimes going as far as to fund extremist groups, the goal of such policies tends to be directed towards mobilization of support at home as a rationale for more pragmatic ends. As a result, culture is drawn into games and conflicts on the domestic level of intra-state politics more readily than it is into the international environment. This is primarily because it is not in the interests of Islamic or Arab countries to engage in military confrontation with the U.S., especially since there is no Islamic superpower to support such a crusade.[24] Perhaps more significantly though, it also demonstrates that the chances of cultural conflicts becoming a defining characteristic of the post-Cold War international system are vastly reduced. Culture as power can only go so far in promoting conflict, since at the state level cultural claims inevitably run up against the national interest. And while policies to pursue the national interest can be couched in cultural or ideational terms to justify them, state interests themselves remain primarily determined by material forces.

This is neatly demonstrated by the April 2002 meeting of the Organization of Islamic Conferences (OIC) in Kuala Lumpur, which debated a number of issues high on the agenda for Islamic states, including terrorism and the Palestinian issue. During the meeting the OIC declared its opposition to intervention in any Islamic state in the U.S.-led campaign against terrorism. It also sought to extend the definition of terrorism to include 'state terrorism' (a clear reference to Israel), and distinguished between acts of terror and 'legitimate resistance' by people in occupied lands (the Palestinians).[25] While this certainly illustrated the importance of culture and religion, since every Muslim state is compelled by domestic forces to at least *articulate* a pro-Palestinian policy, the major decisions from the meeting continued to reflect the prevalence of material interests. The OIC was particularly outspoken in praising U.S. efforts to combat terror, notably in statements by Saudi delegates, and it also rejected an Iraqi suggestion that Middle Eastern states should use oil as a weapon, on the grounds that this would violate OPEC rules.[26]

The real issue of significance arising from the OIC meeting was that faced with the opportunity to express anti-Western sentiments and push for greater civilizational unity, the major Islamic countries did not do so. Such a move would have violated their more pressing economic interests, even if they possessed the power – which they do not – to match the U.S. Nor for that matter have the Islamic states identified by George Bush as linked to an 'axis of evil' been able to band together in an attempt to unify Muslims. Important members of the U.S.-led coalition against terror, such as Pakistan, Egypt and Saudi Arabia have also refrained from articulating culturally antagonistic policies, despite severe domestic pressure to do so.[27] Culture alone is therefore not enough to unify nations, especially if cultural pressures clash with states' more important material interests and relative power.[28] Given the inability of the Islamic world to defend their civilization with firm alliances, questions arise about whether Europe and the U.S. have come to define their interests in civilizational terms, and the extent to which identity and culture can influence policy. It is to these issues that this analysis now turns.

A changed world? State behavior in the West

A defining feature of the 'war against terror' is that it challenges the traditional institutions and functions of the state in responding to both external and transnational threats. As a result, conceptions of national security may well move beyond orthodox interpretations which see threats arising from clearly identifiable and state-based aggressors, to a broader focus which incorporates not only non-state actors and organized terrorist groups, but also individuals like Richard Reid.[29] As Mary Kaldor and Martin Van Creveld (amongst others) argue, globalization is redefining security by deepening existing economic, political and cultural schisms, exacerbating the gap between rich and poor, and prompting the disenfranchised to challenge intrastate and global elites.[30] Further complicating this issue were the attempts by the former Clinton administration to pursue what Dmitri Simes calls 'global social work' by moving away from Cold War Realpolitik, and towards a naïve 'Moralpolitik' characterized by a faith in human rights and supposedly 'universal' values.[31] This naturally prompted resentment at what was perceived by some as Western cultural imperialism, just as the continued presence of U.S. troops in Saudi Arabia has been identified by bin Laden as an insult to Islam.[32] In this sense Huntington was clearly correct in asserting that the Western belief in the universality of its culture was misguided and dangerous, just as it has been shown in the past that normative foreign and security policies, however well-intentioned, can destabilize international order.[33]

But this alone does not demonstrate that civilization has emerged as the dominant force which guides and shapes conflict between states on the macro-level, arising 'from the interaction of Western arrogance, Islamic intolerance, and Sinic assertiveness'.[34] Although the actions of the terrorists on 9/11 may have been partially motivated by cultural disagreements, this assumes that identity manifests itself as a guiding force behind both individual preferences on one level, and states' interests and security policies on another.[35] So far, however, it is not at all clear that either is the case. For identity to play a role in determining interests, it logically follows that such a normative approach should be overt and intentional. In contrast, the very nature of identity is that its role is subtle, and can be mobilized and guided by both states and individuals in order to realize pragmatic interests.[36] Here one can cite numerous examples, from the collapse of the Soviet Union (in which pressing economic requirements forced more accommodating pro-Western policies, prompting Gorbachev to articulate a new set of 'ideas' to justify them), to the current situation involving bin Laden, who has energetically supported clashes between two separate civilizations (Orthodox and Western). It is not at all coincidental that this has also helped him become perceived in the eyes of many as an Islamic hero, and thus play a powerful role in international politics. This is despite the fact that bin Laden's own motivations have changed radically over time. Indeed, his support for the Palestinian cause is only a recent phenomenon. Bin Laden was first a warrior fighting Soviet troops in Afghanistan, but his views have come to encompass opposition to the presence of U.S. troops in Saudi Arabia and a rejection of Saddam Hussein's regime as secular and socialist, which by 2003 became an *endorsement* by al Qaeda of the need to defend Iraq from U.S. invasion.

Moreover, the response of the United States to the threat of terrorism has been unequivocally to strengthen itself and to simultaneously use traditional mechanisms of power, especially military force and diplomatic bargaining. During the war in Afghanistan Washington constructed an (albeit shaky) international coalition, utilizing numerous economic and political carrots rather than cultural rallying calls, that incorporated states from Orthodox, Sinic, Hindu, Japanese *and* Islamic civilizations. This is a strange tactic to employ if in fact a global cultural clash is imminent. Following Huntington's prescriptions, the U.S. could have acted to unify Western civilization by building an alliance comprised of Western and 'torn' non-Western states, in addition to strengthening global institutions, which largely represent Western preferences.[37] However, whether or not this is appropriate given the nature of the primarily non-state nature of the threat is largely irrelevant. This is because the U.S. has pursued a basically realist policy, with Bush's National Security Adviser having previously stated unequivocally that she regards the idea of an international community as 'illusory'.[38] The U.S. has moved to ensure that the effort to protect its interests targets not only Islamic fundamentalism, but also 'rogue states' such as North Korea. In so doing the U.S. has muddied the water by deflecting attention away from the Middle East and incorporating a broader 'axis' of states (and not non-state actors) that threaten U.S. hegemony.

The military campaign to topple the Taliban also helped to highlight the intrinsically realist nature of the Bush administration's policy. Having identified Afghanistan as al Qaeda's primary base, U.S. and coalition forces participated in a war of intervention that reflected classical balance-of-power mechanisms. By removing a hostile regime and installing a government that was friendly to the U.S., Washington gave itself the ability to play divide-and-rule in Afghanistan, while simultaneously receiving applause from a variety of corners (including countries with large Islamic populations) for ridding the world of a pariah state. When the U.S. broadened the 'war on terror' to incorporate regime change in Iraq it did so on flimsy evidence relating to WMDs that prompted protests across the world, most notably amongst the domestic populations of America's customary allies in Europe. France, Germany and Russia attempted to utilize the UN as a power balancing tool to veto action adversely affecting their economic interests (especially since these states were primary beneficiaries of the 'oil for food' program to Iraq). But in the end, the main product of the war in Iraq was not an intra-civilizational clash, but in fact an intra-civilization spat between the U.S. and major continental European powers that had much more to do with conflicting interests than culture.

Consequently, the world and the West may have been shaken by September 11, but as Fred Halliday, Steve Smith, and Stanley Hoffman have all noted, the world has not yet fundamentally changed.[39] As the wars in Afghanistan and Iraq demonstrated, the global balance of power remains firmly centered upon the U.S., states remain the major constituent units of world politics (indeed as Huntington argued they would), and if anything they have become stronger due to the heightened need to safeguard national security.[40] The acceleration of its National Missile Defense (NMD) programme also shows that the U.S. is extending the unilateralist policy path that marked its earlier refusal to ratify the Comprehensive Test Ban Treaty (CTBT) and the Kyoto environmental protocol. In fact, the Bush administration has made it quite clear that Washington would pursue all means to safeguard its interests against terrorism, and that other states had the option of balancing against the U.S. or bandwagoning with it.[41] Faced with the unattractive option of confronting a hegemon on the warpath, many non-Western states, including Russia, Pakistan, and even China played along, perceiving a greater payoff in supporting the U.S. than challenging it at the height of its power.[42] Indeed, the greatest split resulting from the 'war on terror' has ironically occurred within Western civilization itself: the rift in the transatlantic alliance over war in Iraq, which saw France and Germany line up with a more muted Russia against the U.S. and Britain.

It therefore cannot be claimed with much confidence that civilizations have begun to control state behavior in the West. On the contrary, the U.S. has seized the opportunity to pursue previously unfulfilled security objectives that it had previously failed to achieve in a post-Cold War climate initially characterized by popular enthusiasm for 'peace dividends'. This clashes directly with the preferences and interests of its supposed civilizational allies in Europe, particularly in relation to NMD, a policy towards which many West European states, including France and Germany, have expressed reservations if not outright hostility.[43] Whilst NMD may well be utilized to guard against rogue states, it also poses a problem for the deterrent capabilities of Russia and China (and possibly West European states too), thereby actually potentially acting to undermine international security. Washington's abandonment of the 1972 ABM treaty and its refocusing on NMD is also not a strategy that is compatible with Huntington's recommendation that the West should seek closer ties with Slavic civilization.[44]

However, this raises several questions about the emerging 'new world order' and the extent to which it will be characterized by conflict, cultural or otherwise. The first, and most obvious, is how long the U.S. can sustain its war on terror. This is important not only in relation to international reactions after the war widened to encompass Iraq, but also in terms of the short attention span of the domestic population.[45] By late 2002, before the war in Iraq, Bush's popularity had slipped in U.S. opinion polls to 55 percent. This was still healthy to be sure, but nowhere near the 90 percent he enjoyed in October 2001.[46] Here Huntington was again correct when he argued that the U.S. would inevitably face a new security threat that would require it to once again commit 'major resources to the defense of national interests'.[47] But indignant rage (or as Owen Harries put it, a 'visceral, and implacable demand for revenge') is rarely self-sustaining.[48] With victory in a war on terror difficult to accomplish – much the same as a war against drugs – the campaign lost momentum at home. It also prompted jockeying for position, at least at the rhetorical level, amongst European states. As France and Germany began to edge away from bandwagoning towards a vocal rejection of U.S. policies towards Iraq, causing deep schisms in the NATO alliance, non-Western East European states like Poland tried to fill the void by declaring their wholehearted support for U.S. war plans. By the time U.S. forces captured Baghdad it was not clear whether indeed we could still refer to the 'West', with all the assumptions of unity the term had carried with it prior to 9/11.

Disunity within civilizations

This naturally leads to a second question, which concerns to what extent the U.S. response would undergo 'mission-creep', encompassing ever-wider security issues, and thus inadvertently engendering a clash of civilizations by proxy. The public relations offensive against Iraq and the rest of Bush's 'axis of evil' in March 2002 was an early indication of this phenomenon. In addition, the 9/11 attacks on the U.S. were incorporated into the narrower and historically more enduring Arab-Israeli dispute. It is therefore not surprising that Western states, and in particular the Bush administration, have demonstrated what Hoffman calls a 'schizophrenic' response on this issue, reflecting the influence of countervailing forces at the nexus of domestic and international politics.[49] On the one hand, the West has clearly been mindful of the dangers associated with justifying policy in clear-cut civilizational terms, and European leaders like Tony Blair and Jacques Chirac, together with Bush, have repeatedly stated that the war does not represent a fight against Islam. Yet on the other hand, despite cautions from Europe, the U.S. has been influenced by domestic pressure to support Israel in what it claims to be its own 'war on terror' against the Palestinians.[50]

Here a significant problem associated with mission-creep is that it has further highlighted discord in the alliance between the U.S. and Western Europe, thus betraying the disunity of any nascent Western 'civilization'. Within the Bush administration, Condoleeza Rice, Defense Secretary Donald Rumsfeld and Deputy Defense Secretary Paul Wolfowitz all supported making Iraq the next target of the U.S. campaign, perceiving the toppling of Saddam to be unfinished business.[51] While Washington was unburdened over the Iraqi issue by the need faced by less powerful states to build legitimacy for military action, U.S. pronouncements caused tremors amongst European states already wary of NMD. Prominent European leaders urgently cautioned against precipitate responses, and stressed the importance of dialogue and UN approval.[52] In fact, these cracks were transparent well before the war at a joint summit between Bush and Blair in April 2002. Bush told reporters 'I have made up my mind that Saddam needs to go', but Blair, facing a petition at home against a military campaign in Iraq from 140 British MPs (122 of them from his own Labor Party), emphasized the need for a new round of weapons inspections and 'smart sanctions', diplomatically adding that he would support the plan 'if it were justified and necessary'.[53] As other chapters in this volume demonstrate, the U.K. was the most compliant ally of the U.S. over war in Iraq, whilst its Cold War partners France and Germany flatly rejected any suggestion that they should take part.

Given that the U.S. could not convince its European allies to participate in an extended war against terror on a cultural fault line (Iraq), that also involved key Western interests such as access to oil, Washington will also struggle to maintain a broader global anti-terror coalition comprised of both Western and non-Western states.[54] This was also impeded by the West's ambiguous stance on the Israeli-Palestinian dispute leading up to the publication of the 'Road Map' for peace in mid-2003. The debate was characterized on the one hand by Europe's criticism of Ariel Sharon, and Washington's defense of Israel's right to protect its sovereignty (coupled to Bush's cautious support for the concept of a Palestinian state) on the other.[55]

This does not necessarily mean, however, that a clash of civilizations is avoidable simply because of clashing interests amongst Western states. Indeed, Western ambiguities and tensions play into the hands of radicals in the Islamic world who wish to engender a global clash on cultural lines by depicting the West as a pro-Israeli – or at best indifferent – civilization prepared to fiddle while the Occupied Territories burn. Of potential significance here is the use of unwittingly inflammatory rhetoric by the U.S. and European leaders. Bush for instance has repeatedly invoked the linguistic style of bad Hollywood westerns, like those featuring his idol Ronald Reagan, in which the gunfighter sets forth to 'dry up the swamps' which breed fundamentalists (in Saudi Arabia and Egypt, two key Western allies), and consign them to 'history's unmarked grave of discarded lies'.[56] Immediately after 9/11 Bush called for others to join 'civilization's fight', which comes dangerously close to the rhetorical tone, if not the actual content of Huntington's thesis.[57] Another source of tactless remarks has been Tony Blair, who has adopted a hectoring tone when referring to the 'inevitability' of globalization, which many non-Westerners correctly perceive to be a tool utilized by great powers to advance their economic interests. Other European leaders have also been unhelpful, particularly Italian Prime Minister Silvio Berlusconi, who intemperately remarked after meeting with Russian President Vladimir Putin that Europe 'needed to rediscover its Christian roots'.[58]

Although they may be primarily intended for domestic consumption, comments by Western leaders nonetheless strike jangling chords with moderate Muslims who might otherwise support a fight against the destabilizing effects of international terrorism.[59] As a result, it also places moderate Muslim leaders such as Pakistan's Pervez Musharraf in a difficult position, forcing them to perform a delicate balancing act between external demands from the U.S. for cooperation, and growing irritation from within at Western policies. In a less turbulent international setting this would not represent a problem, as diplomats are well trained in recognizing rhetoric for what it is. Yet 9/11 has also shown that the targets of rhetoric are ordinary people in addition to states. The danger, as Huntington would argue, is that if the West's rhetoric comes to be interpreted as anti-Islamic, there is little that could be done to prevent further attacks on Western interests by disaffected Muslims, and even the unification of Islamic states into an anti-Western bloc. As a consequence, careless statements could make the clash of civilizations a self-fulfilling prophecy. This fear was epitomized by Judith Miller, who prophetically remarked in *Foreign Affairs* during 1993 that 'the United States must acknowledge now that Islamic fervor nurtured overseas is bound to come home'.[60] In an earlier issue of *Foreign Affairs*, Robin Wright argued 'an implicit or declared policy of stopping Islamic movements…could also realize the West's greatest fears: unity of the diverse and disparate Islamic groups into an anti-Western force and the use of extremist and terrorist tactics'.[61]

It is nonetheless pertinent to note that such a union has clearly not yet occurred, despite bombings by militant groups like Abu Sayaff in the Philippines and Jamar Islamia in Bali.[62] Additionally it is hardly surprising that Western rhetoric would further alienate radical Muslims. In fact, it logically follows that this is unavoidable, since radical Muslims (just like radical Russian nationalists or radical anti-globalists) will inevitably identify insidious plots in whatever Western leaders say. More to the point, the organization of Islamic *states* into a coherent bloc is, if anything, less likely for the simple reason that Islamic civilization is more fundamentally fragmented than Western civilization even after the war in Iraq. This is in part due to old explanations, such as the lack of territorial proximity between Asian and Middle Eastern Islamic states, as well as fundamental cultural and theological differences between different Islamic groups. As Jeanne Kirkpatrick noted in 1993, 'the most important and explosive differences involving Muslims are found within the Muslim world'.[63] However, the disunity in Islamic civilization is also linked to pragmatic issues relating to national interests and power. First, the foreign and security policies of Islamic states have predominantly been determined by economic rather than cultural interests. As noted above this has been especially the case (with the exception of Iraq) amongst the OPEC states. But it is also true of Asian countries such as Malaysia and Indonesia, who continue to rely on Western patronage in their attempts to recover from the crippling financial crisis of the late 1990s.

This further suggests that the likelihood of cultural clashes on a global scale are minimized by structural factors such as the nature of the international system, with its Western-dominated institutions, and the juxtaposition of policies to serve national interests. But, as Huntington would argue, while the U.S. has been pursuing essentially unilateralist strategies in the aftermath of 9/11, it is also important to consider the motivations of key participants in the global coalition against terror. In particular, the inclusion of 'torn' countries such as Russia would seem (to Huntington at least) to suggest the evolution of an alliance combining Western civilization with others in close cultural proximity. Put simply, if the current 'war on terror' does not target Islam, then why was Russia, a country currently engaged in an internal conflict against Muslim Chechens, such an earnest ally of the West during the war in Afghanistan? Furthermore, why did the U.S. go to such great lengths to split off Pakistan from the Islamic world?

Interests, culture, and 'coalitions against terror'

Although the basic composition of the international system remains largely the same, the post-9/11 landscape is clearly far different in makeup to the environment that characterized security in the immediate post-Cold War years. By March 2002, over 150 states had formally committed to playing at least some part in the global coalition against terrorism. Amongst these were the 132 Signatories and 32 Parties to the 1999 International Convention for the Suppression of the Financing of Terrorism, incorporating signatures from Cuba, Libya, North Korea, and Syria – all of whom were identified by Bush as linked to an 'axis of evil'.[64] Some seventeen states (including Japan, for the first time since 1945) sent forces to Afghanistan, and states identified as real or potential adversaries, such as Iran and China, made public statements condemning terrorism. As part of the military campaign in Afghanistan and broader attempts to combat terror, U.S. military personnel were deployed into areas as diverse as Uzbekistan, the Philippines, Pakistan, and Georgia.[65]

Of all the many changes in security relationships after 9/11 – many of which have been for the better – Russia enjoyed the most radical of reversals in fortune. Prior to 9/11 Russia was gradually moving towards a strategic partnership with China in order to counterbalance American power, through the expansion of bilateral ties as well as the formulation of the multilateral 'Shanghai Five' group. After 9/11, however, Russia was touted by the White House as one of America's closest allies. In fact, it is probably fair to say that America's security ties with Russia have gone from a frosty 'cold peace' to a much warmer arrangement which eclipses the Franco-U.S. security relationship, damaged heavily by disagreements over war in Iraq. Russia now enjoys a new special relationship with NATO, and despite Washington's abandonment of the 1972 ABM treaty and refocusing on NMD, Russia joined the U.S. in a major bilateral nuclear arms reduction deal in May 2002. In the same month, during a meeting with Putin in Moscow, Bush flagged his support for Russian entry into the WTO, and asked Congress to repeal the Jackson-Vanik amendment to the U.S. Trade Act, a relic of the Cold War that had been a major sticking point in relations between the two countries.[66] By acting as a participant in the coalition against terror (if not against Saddam) Russia also sought to link its own struggle against Chechen Muslims to the anti-terrorism effort.

All this seems to very neatly confirm Huntington's claims that the West will encourage torn countries (such as Russia) from nearby civilizations to join the fight against Islam.[67] However, to make this assumption would be overly simplistic and ultimately erroneous, since the new Russian-U.S. relationship overwhelmingly reflects material interests rather than cultural affinity. In fact, since the end of the Cold War Russia has consistently identified the U.S. as the avenue through which its pressing economic interests could best be pursued. Russia initially attempted to be 'friends with everyone' (especially the U.S.), which has been described as an 'accommodating realist' stance. Later, Russia adopted a more 'assertive realist' posture late in Andrei Kozyrev's tenure as Foreign Minister.[68] This was based on a pragmatic attempt to diversify Russian foreign policy in order to meet its interests, and not simply to rely on the West, which Russia perceived to be encroaching on its regional sphere of influence via NATO expansion, highlighted by NATO's involvement in Kosovo during 1999. While catch-phrases such as 'multipolarism' (a term increasingly used also by France) and 'strategic triangles' with China and India came into vogue in the latter years of the Yeltsin Presidency, it was still recognized in Russia's 2000 Foreign Policy Concept that Moscow needed to pursue 'consistency, predictability, and mutually advantageous pragmatism' by focusing on the West, especially in terms of economics.[69] Huntington himself has conceded this point, having noted in an interview with *The New York Times* in January 2002 that Russia was engaging in a partnership with the U.S. in the aftermath of 9/11 'for pragmatic and ad hoc reasons'.[70]

The rewards of bandwagoning with the U.S. have also tempted other states, including those with significant Muslim majorities. A prime example here was the overnight establishment of a U.S.-Pakistan relationship, when prior to 9/11 President Musharraf was *persona non grata* in Washington for his leading role in the derailment of Pakistani democracy. For providing little more than overflight rights, logistical assistance, and accepting small U.S. support contingents, economic sanctions were lifted virtually immediately, dialogue on military aid commenced, and moves were made towards a trade agreement.[71] The relationship developed so well that Pakistan and India, two nuclear-armed neighbors from different civilizations locked in a bitter territorial dispute over Kashmir, now ironically find themselves on the same side in the global anti-terror campaign.

China has also improved its relations with the U.S. by supporting the war on terror, partly because it has an interest in preventing Muslim Uigher rebels in Xinxiang province from pressing ahead with their independence campaign, but also because of the lack of gain to be had from obstructionist tactics that may make the U.S. push a policy of 'constrainment' more rigorously.[72] As U.S. State Department negotiators were sent scuttling from Riyadh to Jakarta, outlining the economic benefits of partnership and the risks associated with defiance, the vast majority of states facing internal cultural pressure to articulate foreign policies influenced by radicalism – including Saudi Arabia, Somalia, and Yemen amongst others – have thus far chosen the national interest ahead of civilizational identity.

However, it proved impossible to maintain the coalition for Afghanistan to the onslaught on Iraq in 2003, due to the myriad competing interests of regional and extra-regional states. Indeed, prior to the campaign to unseat Saddam a view articulated by more hawkish members of the U.S. foreign policy community, such as Richard Perle, came to be accepted as the norm in Washington. According to Perle, broad alliances are not in Washington's interests at all.[73] Having developed such a wide coalition for war in Afghanistan, the U.S. could not utilize cultural or civilizational rhetoric as a motivating force to promote unity in the alliance, because such tactics would not be appreciated by over half of its partners.[74] This was the primary logic behind U.S. preferences for short-term and smaller coalitions during the conflict in Iraq, and for future wars linked to the campaign against terrorism, in which the coalition fits the mission, and not the other way around.

In addition to being difficult to keep together, the challenges in sustaining the conflict against terror itself may mean that it is inevitably temporary, or alternatively used as a rationale for America's desire to fulfill its interests, as the war in Iraq has arguably demonstrated. This is reinforced by the fact that despite Washington's progress in mending fences with some of its competitors, old threats have also not disappeared entirely. This is especially true of China, which, following its recent accession to the WTO, will gain increasing leverage and power in international politics provided its economy is not derailed by internal politics. With the Bush administration making it clear that no concessions to China on the issue of Taiwan would be forthcoming as a *quid pro quo* for Beijing's continued support for America's new anti-terrorist struggle, serious quarrels between the two remain a distinct possibility as China's relative power continues to increase.[75]

While the U.S. struggles to juggle an increasingly complex system of multifaceted 'coalitions of the willing' to combat terrorism whilst simultaneously being mindful of possible tensions from more orthodox threats, other problems will also help to set the agenda for conflict in the post-9/11 world. In particular, the number of so-called 'failed states' will increase as globalization continues its momentum. But although culture will play its part in this process, just as it did on 9/11 itself, the dominant themes will more than likely revolve around material factors of power and collisions between mutually incompatible state interests. As demonstrated above, although the nature of the threat of terrorism seems initially to support Huntington's thesis, it is clear that it fails when subjected to critical inquiry. It also reinforces pragmatic explanations for the war on terror and systemic obstacles to cultural clashes writ large.

Conclusions: averting a clash of cultures

This chapter has argued that state interests relating to hard material factors of power help ameliorate the possibility of states adopting foreign policies that foster inter-civilizational wars. Consequently clashes over culture are likely to be of low intensity and will be found in communal terms primarily within Islamic states and along cultural 'fault lines'. This is not the all-encompassing structural phenomenon that Huntington predicted, but it is nonetheless an important feature of post-9/11 international politics. Indeed, cultural clashes are likely to continue to cause disharmony in key areas of conflict in the Middle East, as they have done for centuries, as well as closer to home amongst diaspora Islamic communities in Eastern Europe and displaced Muslim refugees in EU member states.

This nonetheless confirms what many have suspected for some time – that Huntington's clash is aimed at the wrong level of analysis. Rather than pitting civilizations against each other in a new bipolar era based on conflicting culture, the clash is largely being carried out on the intra-state level, reflecting struggles between secularists, fundamentalists, and moderates, all of whom share a desire to attain domestic power as their ultimate aim and interest. Yet while we are fortunate to have a system of states in which interests minimize cultural conflicts, it does not rule out the possibility of a clash gaining a hold on world politics by proxy for the simple reason that 'it depends how people react to it'.[76] Nor, for that matter, does it reduce the likelihood of new terror attacks on Europe and the United States. This is because the West is both the perceived source of encroachment on Muslim cultures, and more generally as the root cause of disenfranchisement in the Global South. How, then, can a clash of civilizations be averted?

The most ambitious plans for preventing cultural conflict come from the idealist tradition in international relations, where the old guard (like Fred Halliday) and the new (constructivists like Chris Reus-Smit) have found common ground in the perceived need to reduce tension and build trust through institutions and values, thus addressing some of the negative consequences of globalization.[77] Sadly this is most unlikely to happen, since it would require a reversal of Western policies on globalization not only in the Middle East, but also Latin America, the African subcontinent, and Asia. It is also not in the interests of Europe or the U.S., because as Hedley Bull famously noted, the most fundamental interest of a great power is to maintain the status quo and therefore its privileged position.[78] Moreover, such a reversal would amount to an admission of guilt by the West, resulting in serious damage to its prestige. Nor is giving democracy a chance in Islamic states particularly feasible, because it could subject transitional states to anarchy and the rise of domestic nationalism.[79]

Unfortunately the most realistic answer is that cultures cannot be prevented from conflicting at the local level. However, serious attempts can be made by European states and the U.S. to prevent the clash of civilizations from becoming a self-fulfilling prophecy. Europe and the U.S. must continue to consciously avoid linking terror to Islam, and focus on pragmatic policies to achieve their national interests. As shown by the war in Iraq, these interests do not always intersect, and may in fact be diverging.[80] In this respect, the clearest need for policy change is on the Palestinian issue. Despite domestic pressures the U.S. has yielded somewhat by giving cautious backing to the concept of Palestinian independence. But more concessions are necessary to produce a measured policy based on offshore balancing rather than a commitment to the defense of an already nuclear-capable

Israel. This is based not on the need to support the underdog or abstract and supposedly 'universal' (though inherently subjective) humanitarian values, but a logical extension of U.S. post-Cold War interests. Showing flexibility on Israel would not merely placate Islamic states under pressure from domestic groups, but would also open up a potential opportunity for the West to play divide and rule in the region. However, the release of the long-awaited 'Road Map for peace' in 2003, a policy blueprint developed in Washington and supported by the 'Quartet' of the EU, the Russian Federation, the U.S. and the UN, does not bode well for this goal. Only a few weeks after its publication, European and Middle Eastern elites were already claiming that the document privileges Israel over Europe by putting the overwhelming onus for ensuring stability on a new Palestinian state.

Europe and the U.S. also need to pay greater attention to the changing nature of power and threats at all levels. Here we should avoid making a knee-jerk reaction by regarding 9/11 as a major transformation of security. A far more important event was the end of the Cold War and the gradual move from unipolarity to hegemony and eventually a more complex and potentially tense multipolar international system. States may be ill equipped to fight, let alone defeat international terrorism, and the future patterns of global security will in all likelihood be punctuated by repeated terrorist attacks, but this does not mean they will be the defining characteristic of world politics. Rather, cultural clashes are likely to be just a part of many different attempts to challenge the American 'hyperpower', perhaps even from within 'Western' civilization itself. The reality is that having achieved its unchallenged status, the U.S. must be prepared for a struggle from an increasingly diverse array of sources if it is to maintain it.

Notes

[1] Kaplan, R.D., 'Looking the World in the Eye', *Atlantic Monthly*, vol. 288, no. 5, 2001, pp. 68-82. See also Huntington, S., *The Soldier and the State: The Theory and Politics of Civil-Military Relations*, New York, Belknap, 4th edition, 1981.

[2] Huntington, S., *The Third Wave: Democratization in the Late 20th Century*, Norman, University of Oklahoma Press, 1991. See also Huntington's *Political Order in Changing Societies*, New Haven, Yale University Press, 1968.

[3] It has been well documented that Huntington borrowed this term from the essayist Bernard Lewis. Indeed, Huntington's initial article on this topic was accused of being highly derivative of Lewis' work. Lewis' later writings have tended to support Huntington, focusing on what he sees as a 'clear declaration of war' by Islam on the U.S. See Lewis, B., 'The Roots of Muslim Rage', *Atlantic Monthly*, vol. 266, no. 5, 1990, p. 60; and his 'License to Kill: Osama bin Laden's Declaration of Jihad', *Foreign Affairs*, vol. 77, no. 4, 1998, pp. 14-19.

[4] See Huntington, S., *The Clash of Civilizations and the Remaking of World Order*, New York, Simon and Schuster, 1996; and also his earlier article 'The Clash of Civilizations?', *Foreign Affairs*, vol. 72, no. 3, 1993, pp. 23-49. The subsequent edition of *Foreign Affairs* saw a number of responses. Robert Bartly, amongst others, argued that the greatest potential for conflict was within rather than

between civilizations. This point was reinforced by Jeanne Kirkpatrick, who pointed out that the primary targets for fundamentalist Muslims were their own governments. Fouad Ajami saw Huntington's work as a dangerous rallying call to the right wing in the West (this has been reiterated by others like Edward Said), and Albert Weekes noted that Huntington's work reignited the debate between 'microcosmic' and 'macrocosmic' forces in international relations, but rejected the idea of a 'civilization' controlling world politics. Only Kishore Mahbubani was relatively complimentary towards Huntington, suggesting that the West had become blind to internal institutional weaknesses. See Bartly, R., 'The Case for Optimism', pp. 15-18; Kirkpatrick, J., 'The Modernizing Imperative', pp. 22-25; Ajami, F., 'The Summoning', pp. 26-35; Weeks, A., 'Do Civilizations Hold?', pp. 53-54; and Mahbubani, K., 'The Dangers of Decadence', pp. 14-18, all in *Foreign Affairs*, vol. 72, no. 4, 1993. Later critics have focused on the issue of 'Globalization as Westernization'. See for instance Ikenberry, J. et al., 'The West: Precious not Unique', *Foreign Affairs*, vol. 76, no. 2, March/April, 1997, pp. 162-165.

[5] Although Kaplan's own pessimistic views on the evolution of a dangerous and conflict-ridden international system to replace the apparent 'unipolar moment' of post-Cold War U.S. hegemony are not dissimilar to Huntington's own predictions, he does not share Huntington's conviction in civilizations as the guiding structural forces behind this looming anarchy. His grim, post-Westphalian realist vision is of a world inhabited partly by Hegel's and Fukuyama's privileged Last Man, and primarily by Hobbes's First Man, 'condemned to a life that is nasty, brutish, and short'. See Kaplan, R.D., 'The Coming Anarchy', *Atlantic Monthly*, vol. 273, no. 2, 1994, pp. 44-76.

[6] In a speech to the Workers' Trade Union on September 25, 2001, following talks with Egyptian President Hosni Mubarak and Russia's Vladimir Putin, Gerhard Schröeder stated that he would not 'allow either our selves or the world to slip into inter-civilizational war'. Bush's State of the Union address on January 29, 2002 referred to Islam as a religion of peace and tolerance, and Tony Blair noted on October 7 in a speech to the House of Commons that 'as I've said many times before, this is not a war with Islam. Islam is a peaceful and tolerant religion and the acts of these people are wholly contrary to the teachings of the Koran'. For Schröder's comments, see http://eng.bundesregierung.de/frameset/index.jsp; Blair's speech (on October 8, 2001, shortly after airstrikes on Afghanistan began) is at http://www.pm.gov.uk/output/page3573.asp; and Bush's speech can be found at www.whitehouse.gov/news/releases/2002/01/20020129-11.html.

[7] See Gaddis, J.L., 'International Relations Theory and the End of the Cold War', *International Security*, vol. 17, no. 1, 1992-1993, pp. 5-58; and (amongst many others) Lebow, R.N., 'The Long Peace, the End of the Cold War, and the Failure of Realism', in Lebow, R.N. and Risse-Kappen, T. (eds), *International Relations Theory and the End of the Cold War*, New York, Columbia University Press, 1995, pp. 23-56.

[8] Buzan, B. and Little, R., 'Why International Relations has Failed as an Intellectual Project and What to do About it', *Millennium*, vol. 30, no. 1, 2001, pp. 19-39.

[9] Halliday, F., 'Beyond bin Laden', *Observer*, 23 September, 2001.

[10] See www.bbc.co.uk/hi/english/world/south_asia/newsid_1943000/1943785.stm for bin Laden's statement (on a videotape found in April 2002) that 'One hour in the line of battle, to uphold the name of God against the Jews, the Christians and their cronies…is better than worshipping God for 60 years, or even a century'.

[11] Barber, B., *Jihad vs McWorld – Terrorism's Challenge to Democracy*, New York, Ballantyne Books, 1995.

[12] Huntington, S., 'The Clash of Civilizations?', *Foreign Affairs*, vol. 72, no. 3, 1993, pp. 23-49.

[13] Ibid.

[14] This has been covered in great detail in the literature following publication of Huntington's first paper on the topic.   See for instance Weeks, A., 'Do Civilizations Hold', 1993, p. 24.

[15] Huntington, *The Clash of Civilizations*, 1996, p. 101.

[16] Notwithstanding the changing nature of power in a globalizing world and the potential for asymmetrical warfare that this creates, it is in this last requirement that Huntington's theory is clearly deficient. However, this does not in itself invalidate his thesis.   On the contrary, as has often been noted since 9/11, the current conflict requires the West to win over the hearts and minds of ordinary Muslims in addition to attaining military victories against an elusive and territorially unbounded foe.   See for instance Indyk, M., 'Back to the Bazaar', *Foreign Affairs*, vol. 81, no. 1, 2002, pp. 75-88.

[17] On this point see, for example, Nye, J., *The Paradox of American Power*, New York, Longman, 2002.

[18] Halliday, F., 'Beyond bin Laden', *Observer*, 23 September, 2001.   In the same article he makes the neat point 'Freud once argued that the aim of psychoanalysis was to reduce extreme hysteria to everyday common misery. The function of reasoned argument and an engaged skepticism in international affairs is to do just that'.

[19] Morgenthau, H.J., *Politics Among Nations: The Struggle for Power and Peace* (Brief Edition), New York, McGraw Hill, 1993, p. 72. Morgenthau's work is also used in Mazaar, M., 'Saved From Ourselves?' *Washington Quarterly*, vol. 25, no. 2, 2002, pp. 221-232.

[20] Huntington, *The Clash of Civilizations*, 1996, pp. 110, 215.

[21] Keller, B., 'Nuclear Nightmares', *New York Times Magazine*, 26 May, 2002, pp 1-7.

[22] See bin Laden's comments on America in his videotape released in October 2001, at www.news.bbc.co.uk/hi/english/world/south_asia/newsid_1943000/1943104.

[23] Huntington, *The Clash of Civilizations*, 1996, p. 252.

[24] Goldstone, J., 'Responses to Tilly's 'Predictions'', *SSRC Papers*, www.ssrc.org.

[25] Synovicz, R., 'Islamic Conference Fails To Define 'Terrorism', Condemns Israel', *RFE-RL Newsline*, 3 April, 2002, available on the World Wide Web at www.rferl.org/nca/features/2002/04/03042002083906.asp.

[26] Indeed, divisions within the Muslim world were further highlighted at a March 2003 OIC meeting in Qatar, at which the Iraqi labeled his Kuwaiti counterpart a 'monkey', an 'agent of Zionism', and a 'traitor' to Islam. See Shadid, A., 'Iraqi Hurls Abuse at Kuwaiti Delegate', *Washington Post*, 6 March, 2003, p. A5.

[27] Halliday, F., 'Aftershocks that will eventually shake us all', *Observer*, 25 November, 2001.

[28] Indeed, soft cultural power needs to be backed up by hard military power, including the ability to seize and hold territory. This does not mean that vast damage cannot be done with minimal means – the events of 9/11 and after demonstrated that airliners and scare campaigns linked to 'dirty bombs' can wreak havoc on a state's economy and people's sense of security.   But while this suggests that nature of power is changing, it is not yet enough to indicate that individuals articulating any radical cultural belief can fight a sustained campaign against the

'other' on a global scale. Whether or not the international system is unipolar (or 'uni-multipolar', as Huntington would have it), asymmetrical warfare waged by groups against nations has resulted in U.S. pressure, inducements, and coercion on terrorist 'sanctuaries' that has proven difficult for governments in Pakistan, Afghanistan, Yemen, (amongst others) to resist.

[29] Reid is the would-be 'shoeicide' bomber who was apprehended in midair during early 2002 when he (almost comically) attempted to ignite a fuse in his shoes that were laden with plastic explosives. At the time of writing his links to organized terrorist networks remained unclear, although reports from the U.S. suggest he had ties to Khalid Sheikh Mohommad, al Qaeda's 'chief of operations'.

[30] See Kaldor, M., *New Wars: Organized Violence in a Global Era*, Princeton, Princeton University Press, 1999; and Van Creveld, M., *The Rise and Decline of the State*, Cambridge, Cambridge University Press, 1999.

[31] Simes, D., 'What War Means', *National Interest*, vol. 65, no. 4, 2001, pp. 34-42.

[32] As Huntington himself put it, when participating in the Bradley Lecture series at the American Enterprise Institute for Public Policy Research, the U.S. has come to be perceived as 'intrusive, interventionist, exploitative, unilateralist, hegemonic, hypocritical, applying double standards, engaging in "financial imperialism" and "intellectual colonialism", and with a foreign policy driven overwhelmingly by domestic politics'. See Huntington, S., 'Global Perspectives on War and Peace (or Transiting A Uni-Multipolar World)', available on the World Wide Web at: www.aei.org/bradley/b1051198.htm.

[33] On Western values, see Huntington, *The Clash of Civilizations and the Remaking of World Order*, 1996, p. 310. Huntington made a similar point in 'The West: Unique, Not Universal', *Foreign Affairs*, vol. 75, no. 6, 1996, pp. 28-46.

[34] Huntington, *The Clash of Civilizations and the Remaking of World Order*, 1996, p. 215.

[35] The empirical record on this claim, made primarily by the relatively new social constructivist school in international relations (and also amongst some in the so-called 'English School') is not strong, despite showing early promise. On this point, see for instance Brooks, S. and Wohlforth, W., 'Power, Globalization, and the End of the Cold War: Reevaluating a Landmark Case for Ideas', *International Security*, vol. 25, no. 3, 2000-2001, pp. 5-53; Sussex, M., *Power, Interests and Identity in Russian Foreign Policy*, PhD dissertation, The University of Melbourne, 2001; and Sofka, J., 'American neutral rights reappraised: identity or interest in the foreign policy of the early Republic?', *Review of International Studies*, vol. 26, no. 4, 2000, pp. 599-622. On early attempts to show the links between identity and interests, see Katzenstein, P. (ed.), *The Culture of National Security: Norms and Identity in World Politics*, New York, Columbia University Press, 1996; Checkel, J., 'The Constructivist Turn in International Relations Theory' (Review Article), *World Politics*, vol. 50, no. 1, 1998, pp. 324-48; and Lapid, Y. and Kratochwil, F. (eds), *The Return of Culture and Identity in IR Theory*, Boulder, Colorado, Lynne Reimer, 1996.

[36] See Mearsheimer, J., 'A Realist Reply', *International Security*, vol. 20, no. 1, 1995, pp. 82-93.

[37] Huntington, 'Clash of Civilizations', 1993, p. 38.

[38] Rice, C., 'Promoting the National Interest', *Foreign Affairs*, vol. 79, no. 1, 2000, pp. 45-62. The quote appears on p. 62.

[39] Halliday, F., 'New World, But the Same Old Disorder', *Observer*, 10 March, 2002; Hoffman, S., 'On the War', *New York Review of Books*, 10 November,

2001, pp. 4-5; and Smith, S., 'The End of the Unipolar Moment: September 11 and the Future of World Order', *SSRC Papers*, www.ssrc.org.

[40] A useful illustration of this point can be seen in the sudden marginalization of the UN from the public spotlight. Prior to the terrorist attacks Kofi Annan had adopted a prominent global role on humanitarian intervention issues, which had come to dominate the international agenda after NATO's war in Kosovo and the UN's role in East Timor. Yet after September 11 he and the UN were relegated to virtual obscurity, as the world watched to see when George Bush would respond, and what type of coalition he (not the UN) would build to combat terrorism.

[41] Bush has repeatedly uttered variations on the solemn phrase 'either you're with us pause or you're against us': see for example his landmark (and frequently quoted) 20 September 2001 address to the joint session of Congress at http://www.whitehouse.gov/news/releases/2001/09/20010920-8.html.

[42] On the debate over the possible decline of American power, see Kissinger, H., 'America and the Apex: Empire or Leader?', *National Interest*, vol. 64, no. 1, 2001, pp. 1-17.

[43] See, for instance, *RFE-RL Newsline*, www.rferl.org, 16 July, 2001 for comments by European leaders on the inadvisability of NMD. See also 'Missiles Over the Moors', *Economist*, 20 January, 2001; and 'A Shield in Space', *Economist*, 3 June, 2000.

[44] This is despite the fact that a revamped U.S.-Russian security partnership, which endured disagreement over Iraq, has been the most surprising strategic reorientation engendered by September 11. On torn countries and the West see Huntington, 'Clash of Civilizations', 1993, p. 41.

[45] Daalder, I. and Lindsay, J.M., 'Nasty, Brutish, and Long: America's War on Terrorism', *Current History*, December, 2001, pp. 403-406.

[46] Poll data (from Gallup) is at www.gallup.com/poll/releases/pr020614.asp.

[47] Huntington, S., 'The Erosion of American National Interests', *Foreign Affairs*, vol. 76, no. 5, 1997, pp. 26-49 (p. 28).

[48] Harries, O., 'An End to Nonsense', *National Interest*, vol. 65, no. 4, 2001, pp. 117-120.

[49] Hoffman, 'On the War', 2001, p. 4.

[50] Israel, of course, considers Hamas and Hezbollah to be equivalent to al Qaeda. See Falk, R., 'Appraising the War Against Afghanistan', *SSRC Papers*, www.ssrc.org.

[51] Dibb, P., 'The Future of International Coalitions: How Useful? How Manageable?', *Washington Quarterly*, vol. 25, no. 2, 2002, pp. 131-144.

[52] The concerns of European nations were voiced from a number of quarters, but especially German foreign minister Joschka Fischer's criticism of Bush's 'axis of evil' speech in February 2002. Fischer also announced that there was no majority in the Bundestag that would support a military campaign against Iraq – a position reiterated by deputy foreign minister Ludger Vollmer. Hubert Vedrine, the French foreign minister, called Bush's approach 'simplistic', and the U.S. was also criticized by Javier Solana, the EU's foreign policy 'tsar' for acting as a global unilateralist. Likewise Russian foreign minister Igor Ivanov urged caution, stating in late March that Moscow would only support an offensive against Iraq if it was backed by the UN Security Council – which, of course, it was not, partly due to pressure from Russia. See *RFE/RL Newsline*, 27 February, 18 March, 19 March, and 27 March, 2002.

[53] For the comments by both leaders, see Recknagel, C., 'Iraq: Bush and Blair Opt for Diplomatic Offensive for Now', *RFE/RL Newsline*, 8 April, 2002.

54   Indyk, 'Back to the Bazaar', 2002, pp. 75-88.
55   Indyk, 'Back to the Bazaar', 2002, pp. 75-88.
56   See Bush's speech to the joint session of Congress on September 20, 200: George W. Bush, 'Freedom at War with Fear', 20 September, 2001. Available online at www.whitehouse.gov/news/releases/2001/09/20010920-8.html.
57   www.whitehouse.gov/news/releases/2001/09/20010920-8.html.
58   Berlusconi's comments are reprinted in Glinski-Vassiliev, D., 'Suffocation by Embrace: The Putin-Bush Alliance and the Cultural Threat to Western Democracy', *Program on New Approaches to Russian Security (PONARS)*, Harvard University, memo no. 226, 25 January, 2002.
59   Takeyh, R., 'Two Cheers From the Islamic World', *Foreign Policy*, vol. 21, no. 3, 2001, pp. 70-71.
60   Miller, J., 'The Challenge of Radical Islam', *Foreign Affairs*, vol. 72, no. 2, 1993, pp. 43-56, p. 56.
61   Wright, R., 'Islam, Democracy, and the West', *Foreign Affairs*, vol. 71, no. 3, 1992, pp. 131-145, p. 145.
62   See Hefner, R.W., 'Muslim Politics in Indonesia After September 11', paper prepared for the House Committee on International Relations. Available at: www.house.gov/international_relations/hefn1212.htm; and 'U.S. Security Policy in Asia and the Pacific: The View From Pacific Command', House Committee on International Relations, 27 February, 2002, available on the World Wide Web at www.house.gov/international_relations/77895.pdf.
63   Kirkpatrick, J., 'The Modernizing Imperative', *Foreign Affairs*, vol. 72, no. 4, 1993, p. 23. This also brings to mind some of the other earlier and broader criticisms of Huntington's thesis – that (for instance) it equates Malaysia with Jordan, and Indonesia with Sudan.
64   The Convention came into force on 10 April, 2002. Details on the Convention can be found at http://untreaty.un.org/ENGLISH/Status/Chapter_xviii/treaty11.asp.
65   Indeed, prior to 9/11 any suggestion that American troops would shortly be stationed near Tblisi, let alone Tashkent, would undoubtedly have been laughed off by officials in Washington (and met with disbelieving horror in Moscow).
66   The 1974 Jackson-Vanik amendment to the U.S. Trade Act was designed to restrict trade between American and Soviet companies during the Cold War. The amendment was interpreted after the Cold War as effectively claiming that Russia had an unfair emigration policy that necessitated punitive limits on U.S. investment. Intense Russian lobbying succeeded in lifting some but not all of these restrictions in 1996. See the *Proceedings of the U.S.-Russia Binational Commission (GCC-6)*, Washington, D.C, 29-30 January, 1996.
67   Huntington, 'Clash of Civilizations', 1993, p. 41.
68   See, for instance, Shearman, P. and Sussex, M., 'Foreign Policy-making and Institutions', in Robinson, N. (ed.), *Institutions and Political Change in Russia*, London, Macmillan, 2000, pp. 151-172.
69   The Foreign Policy Concept, one of the three major documents underpinning Russia's foreign and security policy (in addition to the Military Concept and Strategic Concept) , was unveiled by Foreign Minister Igor Ivanov in March 2000. See *Izvestiya*, 29 March, 2000, pp. 1-3.
70   *New York Times*, 15 January, 2002, p. 16.
71   For details, see cnn.com/world/SPECIALS/terorr.html.
72   I borrow this term from Gerald Segal, 'East Asia and the 'constrainment' of China', *International Security*, vol. 20, no. 2, 1996, pp. 107-35.

73 Perle has argued that 'as a practical matter, a broad coalition is not terribly important ... if the price of coalition-building is to shackle our operation so that in the end we cannot be effective. Alliances, like coalitions, are made to accomplish a mission, and if we start with the alliance and then look for the mission, we will end up with something that reflects the whole range of interests and outlooks of the coalition partners'. Long known as a Washington hawk (despite never having served in the military), Perle was at the time of writing acting in an advisory role for Donald Rumsfeld as Chairman of the Defense Policy Board. His remarks were made at a symposium at the Nixon Centre in Washington DC on the implications of September 11, featuring participants such as James Schlesinger, Charles Krauthammer, Anthony Cordesman, Dmitri Simes, Joseph Nye, and Fred Ikle. Their discussion was published as 'After September 11: A conversation', *National Interest*, vol. 65, no. 4, 2001, pp. 66-116.

74 This is recognized by the Bush administration, which has noted on several occasions that the war on terror will be comprised of a number of different coalitions to be formed when the need arises. The notion of 'floating coalitions' challenges traditional approaches to understanding bilateral and multilateral security arrangements between states. On this issue see Albinski, H. and Tow, W., 'ANZUS – Alive and Well After 50 Years', *Australian Journal of Politics and History*, vol. 48, no.2, 2002, pp. 153-172.

75 Indeed, Bush was been the first President to state unambiguously that the U.S. would defend Taiwan from military invasion as part of its obligations under the Taiwan Relations Act of 1979. See for instance his remarks at Tsinghua University, Beijing, on 22 February, 2002, available at www.state.gov.

76 Huntington, S., 'Cultures in the 21st Century: Conflicts and Convergences', Keynote address at Colorado College's 125th Anniversary Symposium, February 4, 1999. See www.coloradocollege.edu/anniversary/Transcripts/HuntingtonTXT.

77 In his latest book Halliday calls for a heightened role for global norms and law, whilst Reus-Smit argues that 'ways must be found to combat chronic poverty and economic inequality in the regions of the world economy outside of the advanced industrial core, ways that avoid the creation of dependency traps and the enrichment of local elites...development of open and responsive political institutions should be fostered to encourage the pursuit of intra-institutional politics'. See Halliday, F., *Two Days That Shook the World: September 11, 2001: Causes and Consequences*, London, Al Saqi Books, 2002. For Reus-Smit's paper (in a short collection of essays by leading Australian analyst addressing the consequences of 9/11) see Reus-Smit, C., 'The Return of History', in Reus-Smit, C., Saikal, A., Maley, W., Price, R. and Harris, S., *The Day the World Changed? Terrorism and World Order*, Canberra, Department of International Politics (RSPAS), Australian National University, 2001, pp. 1-8. See also the introductory chapter to Booth, K. and Dunne, T. (eds), *Worlds in Collision: Terror and the Future of Global Order*, Houndsmills, Palgrave, 2002.

78 Bull, H., *The Anarchical Society*, 2nd edition, London, Macmillan, 1995.

79 On the problems of democratic transition see Mansfield, E. and Snyder, J., 'Democratization and the Danger of War', *International Security*, vol. 20, no. 1, 1995, pp. 5-38. Snyder has expanded on his initial thesis. See Snyder, J., *From Voting to Violence: Democratization and Nationalist Conflict*, New York, W.W. Norton, 2000.

80 As John Mearsheimer dryly commented in his latest book, 'it pays to be selfish in a self-help world'. For Mearsheimer's new work (labeled by Glenn Snyder a new

form of 'offensive realism') see Mearsheimer's *The Tragedy of Great Power Politics*, New York, McGraw-Hill, 2001, p. 33.

Chapter 3

America and Europe After 9/11

Peter Shearman and Matthew Sussex

Introduction

The apparently deep rift between U.S. strategic policies and those of European
states after 9/11 (and particularly over the 2003 war in Iraq), came as a surprise to
many analysts. In part this was because by the mid-1990s the much-anticipated
contraction of the transatlantic partnership, following the removal of the Cold War
threat that had sustained it, seemed unlikely. Indeed, NATO was expanding to
encompass former communist states in Central and Eastern Europe. Before 9/11
major debates on European security centered not on the viability of the 'Western'
alliance, but on its formidable strength. Specifically, analysts debated whether
NATO was a stabilizing influence, or represented a threat to Russia, prompting it to
seek new ties with China, and merely shift the boundaries of bipolarism rather than
realize George Bush Snr's much-heralded 'new world order'. The failure of the
transatlantic partnership to collapse on cue after the disintegration of the USSR lent
weight to arguments pointing to the power of pluralism in establishing 'zones of
peace' based on trust, reciprocity, and Kantian norms associated with the belief that
democracies do not wage war against one another.[1]

But September 11 forced a change in this perception when the unilateral approach
of the U.S. in its war against terror, with its emphasis on short-term coalitions rather
than enduring alliances, prompted European states to voice their frustration at being
marginalized by Washington's stance. A variety of commentators provided
explanations, which ranged from banal offerings (Robert Kagan's suggestion that
Americans are from Mars and Europeans from Venus being a prime example), to
more sensible assessments from scholars such as Michael Mandelbaum,
emphasizing the importance of geopolitics and history.[2]

What many of these assessments lack, however, is analysis of U.S-European
relations that focuses on more than just 9/11 and the 'war on terror' as fundamental
changes in international politics. Consequently this chapter examines the history
and rationales for U.S.-European security cooperation, the role of 9/11 in altering
threat perceptions on both sides of the Atlantic, and some possible future paths for
the transatlantic partnership. In so doing we focus on the nature and process of
alliance politics, and argue that the relationship must be considered in terms of

power and the role of interests, rather than ideas and norms, as key determinants of state behavior.

Before assessing the contemporary transatlantic partnership in detail, it is useful to briefly place U.S.-European relations in historical context. As has often been noted, America's relationship with Europe during the second half of the twentieth century was largely determined by the bipolar superpower confrontation with the former USSR. Europe was the central strategic theatre of the Cold War, and transatlantic relations during this period were determined by the geopolitical and ideological challenges posed by the Soviet threat. Historically, the emergence of a potential dominant power in the international system has attracted countervailing power to restrain it. This unrelenting cycle, in John Mearsheimer's view, is the *Tragedy of Great Power Politics.*[3] The bipolar conflict between the USA and the USSR was a reflection of the power configuration that emerged with the defeat of Germany and Japan in 1945. Although the United States was economically and militarily dominant during this period, it faced a formidable protagonist in the form of a second 'superpower'. Following the devastation caused by the war against Nazi Germany, and faced with the emergent threat of communist Russia, the United States, through political, military, and economic programmes helped to rebuild and then defend the countries of Western Europe. Washington acted as an offshore balancer, with the Soviet threat providing a powerful incentive committing the U.S. to protecting its allies in Europe.

However, it is worth recalling that U.S. involvement in European affairs has been by no means a definitive historical characteristic of its foreign policy – far from it, in fact. The lure of isolationism, the need to shun 'entangling alliances' and the desire to avoid engaging in costly wars on the European continent have been at least as significant in the diplomatic history of the United States. During the second half of the nineteenth century the U.S. had no intention, or any incentive in the absence of a potential regional hegemon, to send troops to Europe. American military forces were dispatched to fight the *Entente* powers in 1917 to prevent Germany from gaining victory in World War 1, and thereby gaining hegemony in Europe. From the early 1920s through to the summer of 1940 U.S. troops were once more absent from Europe. It was only when Germany, after the rapid defeat of France in 1940, again threatened to overwhelm the continent that the U.S. reconsidered its previous isolationist stance, and began to provide the British with war materials. It took the Japanese attack on Pearl Harbor and the German declaration of war on the U.S. to force Roosevelt to fully commit American troops to Europe. In joining the war the U.S. was allied with communist Russia in the war against Hitler's fascist Germany, pragmatically supporting one totalitarian regime over another in order to maintain a balance of power that served American national interests.

Cold War cooperation: Strategic and ideological logics of the 'West'

The end of the Second World War saw the emergence of a bipolar international system, with only two major powers that could realistically pose a threat to the other. There was no European state with the capability to contain the Soviet Union. Hence, due to the simple fact that it was the only power with sufficient military means to prevent Soviet hegemony over the whole of Europe, the U.S. retained large numbers of military forces on the continent for the duration of the Cold War conflict. America's former ally against a common enemy had now become its major adversary, due to alterations in global (and especially European) balances of power.

The history of American military commitments to Europe over the past two centuries have been determined in each case by U.S. national interests, and the desire to maintain a balance of power to prevent the emergence of a European or global hegemon. The United States organized its containment strategy against the Soviet Union through a network of multilateral institutions and alliances. NATO, the primary Western military-security organization of the Cold War, was established to counter Soviet power in Europe. The United States supported the integration process in Europe through the establishment of institutions linking the economies of France and Germany, beginning with the European Coal and Steel Community (ECSC). This process was further encouraged by successive U.S. governments. American policies in Europe during the Cold War, whether in the deployment of troops, or in fostering institutional integration among the Europeans themselves, were designed to deter Soviet power.

American preponderance of power during the Cold War, then, did not equate with omnipotence or outright hegemony. As Joseph Nye would put it, America had to cooperate with its allies in order to get what it wanted though multilateral institutions that gave not only voices but also votes to other members.[4] When there *were* disagreements between Washington and Europeans it was incumbent upon the U.S. to persuade others of its viewpoint, rather than coercing them into accepting American unilateralism. The main area of disagreement by the 1970s was over 'burden sharing', in meeting the necessary expenditure on defense to deter Soviet aggression. Influential members of the U.S. Congress were critical of Europeans for not committing a fair share, for essentially taking a 'free ride' on defense spending and hiding under the security umbrella of an American nuclear guarantee, whilst the U.S. picked up the bulk of the bill.

It is instructive to recall that to reinvigorate Atlantic relations, and to encourage European members of NATO to make greater commitments to the alliance, the Nixon administration in 1973 announced the 'Year of Europe'. Nixon's national security adviser, Henry Kissinger, set the scene for the year of Europe, marking out the U.S. vision of a 'new Atlantic Charter' in a major speech. Kissinger stated that the U.S. had 'global interests and responsibilities', going on to point out that America's allies in Europe had 'regional interests'. According to Kissinger, these interests were 'not necessarily in conflict, but in the new era neither are they automatically identical'.[5]

Such a statement could easily be made to describe the state of the Atlantic alliance after 9/11, but it is important to recall that there have long been conflicts of interest between both sides of the Atlantic. The difference is that there was no overriding common threat to hold the alliance together in 2003 when the U.S. went to war on Iraq, as there had been 30 years ago, in 1973. The 'Year of Europe' was also a period of détente, marked by an easing of international tensions and arms control negotiations between the U.S. and the USSR. However arms *control* was simply a new way of managing the arms *race* – and was a limiting process rather than one aimed at dismantling weapons systems through *disarmament*.[6] Therefore, the principle strategic logic of the Cold War remained in place. This kept disagreements between the two sides of the Atlantic alliance in perspective, and moderated American frustration over Europe's apparent unwillingness to contribute proportionally to the defense burden. But with the demise of the Soviet military threat in the region, the key strategic logic of an American commitment to keep large numbers of troops in Europe began to dissipate.

The Cold War also helped to reinforce a psychological sense of belonging to a wider 'Western' world, in counter-distinction to the 'Eastern' bloc of communist countries. In this global competition there was a psychological need to maintain unity and cohesion in the Western bloc against the Soviet 'other'. Hence, the close relationship between the United States and Europe had more than a strategic dimension. Indeed, it also had a psychological, or (perhaps more accurately), an ideological dimension. The point to note is that this was a significant element relating to the politics of identity – in which identity bonded members of a unified 'West' – that had the effect of ameliorating tensions within the Atlantic alliance.

Changes in strategic setting

Following the terrorist attacks on the US in September 2001, Europeans were the first and most committed in offering support to the Bush administration to bring to account those responsible. Indeed, NATO for the first time in its history invoked Article 5 of its treaty, committing its members to support the US in its 'war against terror'. NATO's original mission, to counter the Soviet threat to European security, had disappeared with the demise of communism in the late 1980s, and the subsequent collapse of the USSR itself in 1991. In the interim it had survived and expanded its mission to include so-called 'collective security' engagements 'out of area' in Bosnia and Kosovo. It appeared that although the strategic setting had changed, the psychological glue remained to keep the 'West' united and coherent in its response to these new types of threat.

Furthermore, with the demise of communism and the collapse of the Soviet/Russian empire, the 'West' had expanded through NATO enlargement to incorporate East Central European states that had previously been subjected to Moscow's control during the Cold War, in both institutional and ideological terms. This was also thought to have expanded the zone of the 'democratic peace'. The idea that democracies do not go to war against each other is a powerful one, although there is heated debate and controversy on this question.[7] Nevertheless, even if wars between democratic states are unlikely, this is not to say that the national interests of democratic states will always coincide, or that when they do differ that they cannot lead to important crises in international politics. Extending the 'war on terror' from the Taliban in Afghanistan, to Saddam Hussein in Iraq, had just such an outcome.

It is noteworthy that in responding to 9/11 Washington effectively ignored NATO's declaration of support and its invocation of Article 5. Whilst the U.S. welcomed the symbolic declaration of support from NATO, it was considered that to conduct operations through the alliance would have impeded an effective response. In the end the U.S. managed the war on terror, in the first instance against the Taliban in Afghanistan, and then in Iraq, without being subject to the restrictive parameters of operating in a multilateral context. 9/11, therefore, could ultimately come to be seen as a turning point, not only for the role and functions and future of NATO, but also for the wider context and structure of transatlantic relations. After all, NATO is the principle mechanism that binds the U.S. and Europe together on matters of security and strategic policy. Any fundamental alterations to NATO would alter mutual perceptions in Washington and Europe about the utility and focus of the alliance, and would have subsequent wider ramifications for the relationship.

The original strategic doctrine of NATO offered Europe a guarantee of US military commitment in the event of an attack from a third party. In the 1990s, in the uncertain world of the immediate post-communist period, NATO's doctrine was altered to include humanitarian intervention when security threats appeared on the periphery of the alliance, especially in the former Yugoslavia. However, the Americans were constantly frustrated at European leaders' reluctance to confront rising conflicts being stirred up by nationalists such as Slobodan Milosevic, and were irritated at Europe's procrastination in dealing with security issues within their own region. The conflicts in the former Yugoslavia exposed the relative weakness of European attempts to formulate a coherent Common Foreign and Security Policy (CFSP), or even to act in concert in response to instability on Europe's Eastern frontiers. As a result Europe had to rely upon the leadership of the United States, in both Bosnia and Kosovo, in addressing the problem of Serbia under Milosevic.

Although the U.S. took the lead in Yugoslavia, it was not the original intention of Bill Clinton to play a guiding role in European security. Clinton came to office in 1993 intent on concentrating on the economy, leaving foreign affairs to what was termed a 'flaccid, almost purposefully obscure foreign policy team [providing] further evidence of Clinton's relative lack of interest in this area'.[8] In the end the realities of the international power configuration did not provide Clinton with the luxury of ignoring foreign affairs. As the leading power in the international system the United States, to use a phrase coined by Joseph Nye, was 'bound to lead'.[9] Richard Holbrooke, who became an important and more assertive figure in U.S. diplomacy in Europe during Clinton's second term estimated that '...by the Spring of 1995 it had become commonplace to say that Washington's relations with our European allies were worse than at any time since the 1956 Suez crisis. But this comparison was misleading; because Suez came at the height of the Cold War, the strain then was containable'.[10]

Ultimately U.S.-led NATO interventions in Bosnia and Kosovo appeared to save Europe from itself. Without Clinton's use of American power, Europe would have been subjected to ongoing conflict on its periphery, and faced with increasing numbers of refugees. This would have made the process of EU enlargement much more difficult, putting the future of NATO in doubt, and thereby compromising any further expansion of the alliance. European states themselves would likely have been in conflict with each other over the appropriate response to the Yugoslav problem. Yet in the conduct of the bombing campaigns against the Serbs, American commanders were subjected to what they considered unnecessary and unhelpful interference from Europeans who, it was thought, were overly preoccupied with legal issues. The American commander of NATO forces in the war in Kosovo, General Wesley K. Clark, has referred to some of the specific difficulties within the alliance. Clark has argued that '… we paid the price in operational effectiveness by having to constrain the nature of the operation to fit within the political and legal concerns of NATO member nations'.[11] Clark was summarily removed from his post as the U.S. Commander in Europe immediately after the war in Kosovo.

NATO sidelined

After 9/11 it became clear that the Bush administration was unsure about the merits of NATO, and Europeans were irritated at being sidetracked as the U.S. acted unilaterally, rather than through the multilateral framework of the Cold War period. As Josef Joffe has put it, NATO after 9/11 is becoming for the United States not a military pact with mutual obligations, so much as a pool from which to draw *ad hoc* coalition partners to serve unilateral American national security interests.[12] NATO was not even provided with a *voice*, as the key institution supposedly representing the security interests of the Americans and the Europeans, on the question of war against Iraq. The U.S. had no intention of giving the Germans a veto on this question, let alone in being restricted in what it could or could not do by Luxembourg or Iceland.

The lesson of Kosovo for the U.S. was that on key issues of security, where the U.S. perceives that its interests do not coincide with those of European states, NATO can simply be ignored, even as it expands to incorporate yet more former members of the Soviet and communist bloc.[13] U.S. Defense Secretary Donald Rumsfeld's comment that the mission defines the coalition (and not the other way around) is a clear statement of American attitudes toward NATO. In the coalition in the war against the Taliban, Russia and Central Asian states were more important partners than traditional American allies in Europe. In the subsequent war on Iraq NATO played no role at all, with opposition to the war coming from important allies in the alliance – most critically from Germany. To complicate matters the Turkish parliament, facing imminent elections at the time, chose the populist option of refusing to allow U.S. troops the use of its territory to invade Iraq from the North. France, which under de Gaulle had placed itself outside NATO's command and control structures, yet could be counted on as a key Western ally during the

Cold War era, provided vehement criticisms of U.S. policy along with Germany and Russia.

The marginalization of the transatlantic partnership in U.S. strategic thinking is particularly evident when one considers that, in an influential article on America's security relationship with Europe, hardly a mention is given to NATO. Yet the absence of any detailed treatment of NATO in Robert Kagan's essay, where he argues that Europeans are from Venus and Americans are from Mars, is telling.[14] There can be little doubt about how American neo-conservatives, many influential in the Bush administration, perceive the alliance: as more of a nuisance than a mechanism to secure common interests. Jeffrey Godmin, Director of the Aspen institute in Berlin, argues that US and European views of security are now so radically different that NATO 'holds little promise of figuring prominently in US global strategic thinking'.[15]

The importance of power relativities and interests

The key to understanding the changes in perceptions and policy priorities between Europe and the U.S. does not relate directly to 9/11, although the events on that day have exacerbated them. Rather, the key is in power relativities. During the Cold War U.S. power was moderated, or at least in part subordinated to a wider community as a result of U.S. security partnerships in Europe, and to a lesser extent in Asia, under the San Francisco system of bilateral alliances. Within this framework U.S. power was legitimated, and America enjoyed considerable trust from its allies. Since the collapse of the USSR American power has been unchallenged. In the wake of 9/11 the gap in military capabilities between the U.S. and Europe has escalated further: the mere *increase* in U.S. defense expenditure for 2003 is larger than any European state's entire annual defense outlay. Clearly the United States now has such unbridled power that it no longer perceives the need to conduct its foreign and security policies within the constricting framework of multilateral institutions. U.S. National Security Adviser Condoleeza Rice made it clear that given American power and interests, multilateralism would only be pursued when it served those interests, and where it did not hamper the use of power. With Bush yet to take up residence in the White House Rice let the world know in 2000 that American foreign policy would 'proceed from the firm ground of the national interest and not from the interest of an illusory international community'.[16] It is common knowledge that senior members of the Bush foreign and security policy apparatus regard NATO in a similar manner as they do the UN: little more than a 'talking shop' that hinders rather than helps the pursuit of U.S. goals.

Although a key ingredient in Kagan's assessment of the divergence between Europe and the United States is *power*, differences over *principles* are central to his argument. This is where he is fundamentally wrong. The differences are to do with *interests*, and pragmatic assertions of national goals. The articulation of principles through the tendency to justify policy in rhetorical terms, masks the true pursuit of the national interest. After all, a key feature of American justifications for regime change in Iraq has been the moral issue of defending the rights of the Iraqi people against the evils of a violent dictatorship. Yet few analysts seriously entertain this as the real objective of American policy. Similarly, French and Russian legal arguments against the war, and their concerns that the Security Council was being ignored, represent natural attempts to use such a stance in pursuit of their own national interests. What Stephen Krasner calls the 'organized hypocrisy' of sovereignty[17] is demonstrated by the fact that Russian President Vladimir Putin would clearly not require UN sanction for his war against Chechen rebels.

If U.S. support for war against Iraq was at least in part due to concerns with oil, then opposition to war, especially from French and Russian elites, was also to do with oil. Prior to the war these two countries stood to lose their status as the primary beneficiaries under the old UN-mandated 'oil for food' program to Iraq. Indeed, French and Russian objections were borne out by the subsequent U.S. decision to divide the spoils of war amongst American and British companies in the reconstruction of post-Saddam Iraq. Tony Blair's support for war in Iraq may have been based upon a genuine belief in the benefits of regime change in the name of humanitarian ideals, but generally differences between (and within) America and Europe reflected not moral preferences, but competing strategic visions at a time of global uncertainty. One can make far too much of the differences whilst ignoring the similarities, and the fact that these differences are articulated within the domestic political contexts of each state, in Europe as well as in the U.S.

In the context of international security since 9/11 the most important issue for much of the rest of the world, especially for Arabs and Muslims, is that the global domination of American power merely represents the manifestation of Western imperialism in its present guise. It would be very difficult to make the argument that either American or European policies towards Iraq over the years have been motivated by concerns for the Iraqi people rather than receipts from arms sales and access to oil reserves. In this context it is not only impossible to identify when a supposed normative shift in foreign policy thinking occurred in Europe, but also hypocritical to claim that Europeans have somehow evolved to an ideationally higher plane by adopting cosmopolitan conceptions of their interests guided by pluralistic and peaceful underlying norms. This is for the simple reason that the empirical record shows such claims to be inconsistent at best, and more likely patently false.

If Europeans are concerned primarily about the human rights of the Iraqi people, then a reasonable question to pose is why this concern was only expressed during talk of war against Iraq and not earlier, for the Saddam regime had been inflicting gross human rights abuses for decades. During the Iran-Iraq war in the 1980s Western states provided Saddam's regime with military intelligence and arms, even though it was known that Iraq was employing chemical weapons on the battlefield. Towards the end of that war the regime used chemical weapons against its own Kurdish population in northern Iraq.[18] In the 1990s, keen European participants in the near-global coalition to oust Iraqi forces from Kuwait did not press for an extended UN mandate to remove Saddam from power by pressing allied forces on to Baghdad. In fact, the lone voice advocating such a move was from the *American* theatre commander of coalition forces, General Norman Schwartzkopf. It is also telling that prior to the war against Iraq in 2003, the Europeans, including the Russians, were calling for a lifting of the economic sanctions against Saddam's regime, yet immediately after the war they were, at least initially, in chorus in opposing the lifting of these same sanctions on U.S.-controlled Iraq. This, then is where faith in identity and ideas as underlying determinants of behavior are overextended. Rational interests defined in terms of material power, and not principles, remain central to understanding problems of international security. The differences between Europe and the United States over war in Iraq were no exception.

Threat perceptions

9/11 has altered the balance of interests between the U.S. and Europe, due in part to changing perceptions of threat, and especially those threats posed by so-called 'rogue' states developing weapons of mass destruction. While the United States, with no alternative power centre to balance against it, is intent on unilateral action, where necessary employing pre-emptive strikes and regime change, many European states prefer more traditional deterrence and containment strategies to resolve threats. The problem here is the absence of balance in the international system. 9/11 could ultimately encourage the larger powers in Europe to tip the balance and create an alternative to the unchecked power of the U.S. In this way 9/11 was the catalyst unleashing forces that were already manifest with the radical alterations to global power following the demise of the USSR in 1991.

NATO and the UN can similarly be seen as instruments (if not relics) linked to the Cold War system. The UN Security Council reflects the power configuration of 1945, and not the world of the twenty-first century, whilst NATO was designed to contain and deter the Soviet threat rather than to defeat terrorists and rogue states. International institutions developed in an earlier era to manage a different world require radical restructuring to reflect new realities. A dominant theme emerging from 9/11, albeit slowly, is that the attacks on the United States in 2001 have ultimately forced allies on both sides of the Atlantic to seriously rethink the nature, purpose, and practical utility of those institutions that were so central to the Western world during the second half of the twentieth century. Contemplation of NATO's demise, predictions that the UN may share the fate of the League of Nations, and transatlantic tensions have their origins not in the U.S. stance on the war against Iraq, nor even in the events of 9/11. They are centrally related to the shifting balance of global power that resulted from the end of the bipolar international system that had determined strategic thinking during the second half of the twentieth century.

Towards European unity

Despite the differences over Iraq within Europe, especially between the Blair government and the French and German governments, there has been a remarkable acceleration in cooperation among the EU states. This has taken place not only in the area of Justice and Home Affairs to counter terrorism, but also in long overdue moves towards the eventual development of a European CFSP. This might seem counterintuitive given recent differences between European states, but underneath diverging views on how to deal with Iraq (not, it should be noted, over *whether* it was necessary to prevent Saddam from developing WMDs), 9/11 has resulted in greater awareness across Europe that widening and deepening of the EU in the security realm is important for future prosperity and security.[19] In this light Europeans recognize that they are faced with strategic choices in formulating future relations with the United States. None of the European states, including the U.K. under Blair, wish to see the unrestrained continuation of American dominance and policy unilateralism.

Indeed, Blair has argued that in order to stem the tendency of the U.S. acting unilaterally it is necessary to engage Washington in friendly debate, rather than adopting antagonistic European policies without first consulting the Americans. Blair's policy has been to bandwagon with the U.S., seeking to maintain some influence on the margins. Blair was in attendance for President Bush's address to the joint meeting of the U.S. Congress after the 9/11 attacks. Turning to Blair, Bush said, 'America has no truer friend than Great Britain. Thank you for coming, friend'.[20] Later it was generally accepted that Blair was instrumental in persuading Bush to at least try to get a resolution through the United Nations Security Council to gain multilateral support for war against Saddam Hussein's regime in Iraq. In the end the UN was sidelined by Bush and Blair in the face of opposition from Germany, Russia and France, the latter two permanent members of the UNSC each threatening vetoes. Despite the clear differences on the Iraq issue between Britain and other countries of 'old' Europe, it should be noted that even before the Cold War ended British attitudes to Europe were changing. Britain was seen, for good reasons, as the reluctant European when the integration process first began gaining momentum after 1945. Winston Churchill, the former British war-time leader who coined the term the 'Iron Curtain', defined British foreign policy interests in terms of three circles: Europe, the United States and the Commonwealth. There was a 'good neighborly' aspect to relations with Europe, an 'emotional attachment' to the Commonwealth, but a 'special relationship' with the United States. The European circle was seen as the least important in terms of British strategic interests.[21] As Anthony King put it: 'Its preoccupations, its national interests, and its self-image…combined to keep Britain *apart* from Europe'. Psychologically Europe was 'over there, foreign, alien'.[22] The Iron Curtain gave added impetus for British political elites to foster the idea of a special relationship with the U.S., the world's most powerful state.

By the 1980s, even before the Cold War had ended, the changing political, economic, and strategic realities of Britain's position had led to a re-evaluation of its relationship with Europe. In the mid-1950s the European Community accounted for 25 percent of British foreign trade. By the mid-1990s this figure had reached over 50 percent. It was recognized by most politicians that Britain's interests lay in Europe, the key arena in which influence could reasonably be exercised. The Blair government, despite siding with the U.S. in the war on Iraq, has moved closer than any previous British government to accepting the idea of a common foreign and security policy for the EU.[23]

For Europe's other major powers, France and Germany, the emphasis has been on a more independent stance, seeking institutional strength in order to balance against U.S. military power (and its willingness to use it). The forthrightness of German foreign policy over the war on Iraq was another important manifestation of an already clear pattern that had emerged even before the Berlin Wall fell. In the 1970s West Germany's influence was critical in fostering East-West détente, and in the 1980s Bonn's diplomacy with the Soviet Union under Gorbachev was instrumental in triggering the peaceful reunification of Germany. Germany then played a key role in the break-up of Yugoslavia with the government unilaterally according official diplomatic recognition to the independence of Slovenia and Croatia. This was an assertion of Germany's national interests in the new geopolitical post-Cold War setting. No longer was Germany a 'semi-sovereign' state beholden to the U.S. in the conduct of its foreign and security policies. Germany was becoming a 'normal state', and as such its relationships could be conducted without being beholden to U.S. censure or restricted by historical complexes of a previous era. Over the issue of war in Iraq, Germany, like France, was asserting its own national interest, which put it on a collision course with the Bush administration.

Although successive British governments referred, much to the irritation of the French, to a 'special relationship' with the U.S., the reality was that during the Cold War period Germany was Washington's key strategic, military and political ally due to its location at the centre of Europe and its strong economy (the Federal Republic had the third largest economy after the U.S. and Japan). A senior U.S. official was quoted as saying that Chancellor Gerhardt Schröder's strident opposition to war in Iraq left Germany with no 'international voice', stating that 'it has sunk into insignificance'.[24] Yet in fact the opposite is the case. Germany is increasingly acting at the head of a broader Europe. As Schröder put it, Germany is 'coming of age'.[25] Schröder spoke of a 'coming of age' not just for Germany, but for all Europe, now 'emancipated', and able to pursue its own interests even where they are not symmetrical with those in Washington. Just one year after 9/11 a new government in Germany was elected on an anti-U.S. platform, as Schröder and the SDP pushed a strong and populist anti-war stance in the election campaign.[26]

The emergence of an understanding in Germany that its national interests do not always coincide with those of the hegemon has long been established in France, reflecting its Gaullist tradition of articulating a foreign policy focused tightly on the

French state. Even during the Cold War French diplomacy was openly designed to counter hegemony in international politics. Hubert Védrine, the French foreign minister, has stated that the '…entire foreign policy of France is aimed at making the world of tomorrow composed of several poles, not just a single one'.[27] Given the demise of an ideological and military bloc confronting the 'West', symbolized most graphically by the Berlin Wall, there is no longer any underlying existential requirement to maintain the idea of 'Western unity' at any cost. The idea of the 'West' disappeared along with communism, and the dominance of American power is increasingly being regarded in Europe as a threat to rather than a force for international stability.

Europe versus America?

Two important factors can be identified in the threats emanating from 9/11, international terrorism, the spread of WMD, and the dangers posed by Saddam Hussein's Iraq as well as other so-called 'rogue' states. First, these threats are perceived in significantly different ways by Europeans on the one hand and Americans on the other. Second, they do not constitute a universal threat that necessitates cohesion and solidarity amongst 'Western' states. 9/11 happened on American and not European soil, so it is understandable that threat perceptions between the two sides would differ. 9/11 was seen in the U.S. as a direct threat to U.S. global power, to America's position of global leadership, and to the global balance of power with Washington at the helm. It was not seen in Europe as a direct threat to the continent warranting a radical shift in strategic priorities. Whilst acknowledging the potent nature of the terrorist attacks of 9/11, most European states were accustomed to dealing with terrorism (witness, for example, the activities of the IRA in the U.K., the Basques in Spain, the Kurds in Turkey, and the Chechens in Russia). And although Europeans are concerned about the proliferation of weapons of mass destruction to states such as North Korea, they are more inclined than the U.S. to employ temperate diplomatic means in preference to aggressive confrontational approaches in order to counter this threat.

These differences were clearly manifested in the lead-up to the war on Iraq. Given the different perceptions between the U.S. and Europe about the nature of the threats from international terrorism, the proliferation of WMD, and 'rogue' states, it should not be surprising that there is an increasing tendency in Europe to promote *European* unity rather than *Western* unity. Of course, as other chapters in this book make clear, each individual country has its own national interest as a primary concern in formulating foreign and security policies. Nevertheless, influential actors in Europe are coming to see the value of fostering cooperation and closer harmony in these policy areas to add more weight to Europe's voice. And whilst 9/11 and the war on terror did not result in a cohesive CFSP being formulated by EU members, U.S. unilateralism has led many in Europe to recognize the potential advantages for European states in 'pooling' their diplomatic, economic, and political powers (if not their sovereignty) through the EU.

Using the EU as a vehicle when their interests do coincide, it may be possible for European states to influence, moderate, or oppose U.S. policies that are seen as detrimental to their goals. Indeed, France and Germany coordinated their consecutive roles as chair of the UN Security Council in an attempt to prevent the U.S. from instigating war on Iraq. Rumsfeld, in his depiction of an 'old' and a 'new' Europe, insinuated that the most recent members of the EU and NATO will be more 'realistic' and hence recognize more clearly that their interests coincide with those in the U.S. Speaking to reporters, Rumsfeld commented that '[Y]ou're thinking of Europe as Germany and France. You look at vast numbers of other countries in Europe. They're not with France and Germany on this. They're with the United States'.[28] However, it must surely be clear that the new members of the EU in Central and Eastern Europe have as an overriding priority complete and successful integration into the community of European nations. In the event of future serious rifts between 'old' Europe and the U.S., it is much more likely that 'new' Europe will ultimately see the necessity in avoiding a crisis in relations with its neighboring EU member states, and inter-European relations will take priority over transatlantic relations out of geopolitical necessity.

Britain of course was the important exception in the controversy over the war in Iraq, going out on a European limb in active support of the U.S. But it should be remembered that Blair acted against the wishes of the bulk of the British population. His policy on Iraq spawned massive anti-war rallies across the country, and vocal criticism from a substantial proportion of his own party in parliament. In addition there were resignations from junior ministers, as well as from former Foreign Secretary Robin Cook. Although the Spanish government supported the war, this was not reflective of public opinion, which was heavily opposed. The same was true in many countries across 'new' Europe. Polls in the U.K. in September 2002 found that more people saw George W. Bush as a threat to international security than Saddam Hussein.[29] It is difficult to believe, no matter what the final outcome of the war on terror and the question of post-war Iraq may be, that the vast majority of the governments in Europe would support a new military mission undertaken by the U.S. (for example against Iran or North Korea, the other two members of Bush's 'axis of evil').[30] The only conceivable rationale for such united action would be if one of these states directly threatened European interests or international security, perhaps by irrationally using WMDs. It is also the case that Tony Blair would not survive another military adventure in coalition with the U.S. against another 'rogue' state. In the event of another major international crisis with the involvement of U.S. unilateral military power, EU members are much more likely to rally together as they are to drift apart.

International institutions

Given the absence of sufficient military power to challenge the overriding military capabilities of the U.S., little willingness to make sufficient economic commitments to do so, and the lack of domestic support for such policies, Europe is left with only diplomacy and multilateral institutions as ways to influence, moderate, or balance

American power. A number of scholars have pointed out that the hegemony of the U.S. and its leadership of the West during the Cold War was by invitation, and that the Cold War institutions (for example, NATO, the IMF, and the United Nations) that the U.S. helped to establish not only successfully contained the Soviet threat, but also took on a dynamism of their own in forging a wider community of democratic states.[31] These international institutions, it is argued, served as a framework in which American power was exercised in partnership with others for the greater good of the international community and international security. The institutionalized process of consultation and joint decision-making moderated any temptation for the unilateral use of American power. The assumption was that these institutions would outlast the Cold War and provide multilateral means for managing global politics in a manner conducive to peaceful resolution of disputes. The neo-liberal argument is that 'co-binding', or 'sticky' international institutions serve to ultimately change state identities, which moderated state interests, and ultimately, state behavior.[32]

However these arguments overstate the role of institutions, for they are in essence the product of power, the instruments of strong states who are largely responsible for creating them in the first place. As power configurations change, so have international institutions changed, been adapted, abolished, or replaced with other institutions. William Wallace has noted that whereas in the Cold War period the United States used multilateral institutions, which legitimized policies and provided 'a narrative of common values shared by the "free world"', in more recent times the 'rhetorical justification' for U.S. unilateral policies is couched in realist discourse with reference to American national interests. Wallace states that this narrative, supporting policies that have no link to obvious global interests, is a 'central difficulty' for traditional allies of the U.S. in Europe.[33]

It is certainly the case that neither the United Nations nor NATO served to 'bind' the United States with other members of the so-called 'international community' or the Atlantic alliance in such a way as to influence or moderate its behavior in the war on terror. Indeed, in the case of the war on Iraq NATO was disregarded, whilst the UN was bypassed by the United States. At the same time the UN was being utilized by France, Germany, and Russia effectively as a realist instrument in an attempt to balance the power of the U.S. The case of Iraq demonstrates that major powers will ignore international institutions, and even ostensible alliance partners, where and when perceived vital national interests call for it. During such moments institutions and alliances are simply ignored, supposedly guiding norms are inconsistently followed, laws are broken, and unilateral policies are pursued even in the face of vociferous opposition from closest allies.

It is also clear that the idea that political identities change through participation in international institutions is overdrawn. As noted above identities in ideological terms during the 'East-West' Cold War were of some import in relation to the shaping of policy rhetoric through official justifications and rationalizations for both domestic and international audiences. But identity does not *determine behavior.* At various times the United States has undertaken protectionism, free trade, isolationism, unilateralism, multilateralism, and has allied with non-democracies of various types, including 'rogue' states in the Middle East, and with the Soviet Union in the war against fascist Germany. In the Cold War period the U.S. effectively sided with communist China in a deliberate attempt to balance the power of communist Russia in the 1970s. Indeed, some see that the present terrorist threats to the U.S. are linked directly to American policies of the second half of the twentieth century. American policies in the 1970s in support of anti-Soviet 'freedom fighters' in Afghanistan helped, for instance, to create the anti-Western Islamic fundamentalists of the 1990s.[34] During this time the U.S. remained a liberal democracy, and for the most part its Cold War institutions continued in place.

Conclusions

The key to understanding recent tensions in U.S.-European relations is the changes in the relative power capabilities of states. The end of the Cold War left the international system in turbulence, where the missions and futures of institutions that tied the Atlantic together were themselves in an uncertain state of flux. As Kenneth Waltz stated, the international system was abnormal, in the sense that no powers had joined together in the 1990s to balance the United States. This abnormality was due to the gross imbalance of power in the world. Waltz pointed out that 9/11 and international terrorism has not changed this basic fact of international politics.[35] Yet by reinforcing the basic fact of superior American power, and the consequent extension of a U.S. military presence in the world, 9/11 has nevertheless led to initial attempts to balance that power. One could state then, that despite the Europeans' immediate support for U.S. goals in punishing those responsible for 9/11, September 2001 marked a turning point in transatlantic affairs, where relations between America and Europe would become more tense and unpredictable. Just as 9/11 provided an impetus for Germany to continue its re-emergence as a 'normal' state, so too on the systemic level normality began to return.

In conclusion one can fairly easily identify the factors behind the divisions between Europe and the United States since 9/11 and the war on terror. As we have demonstrated these divisions were manifest long before September 2001, and are linked to questions of power and interests. During the second half of the twentieth century Europe and the United States had both geopolitical and ideological interests that were compatible in nature. Major strategic issues were centered in Europe. Since the collapse of communism and the end of the Soviet empire the strategic landscape has changed, and with the defeat of communism as an alternative to democracy and the market, there was no longer a requirement to maintain 'Western' ideological unity. As a result of these strategic and ideological shifts, the national interests of the Americans and Europeans started to diverge, even though the United States and Europe are now culturally closer than they were even during the Cold War. With the globalization of capitalism accompanying the end of the USSR, the so-called 'Third Way' in contemporary democratic politics has seen a closer convergence of European and American attitudes on economic issues, and on some matters of the welfare state and social capital. There are still differences on these matters, but they are not so great as in periods during the Cold War. Many in Europe do try and differentiate between a sophisticated Europe and a simplistic and often dangerous America. But this is simply the natural manifestation of envy, concern and frustration at living in a world of hegemonic American power. The point is that a Europe and an America that are converging politically, economically, and culturally due to the omnipotent processes of globalization, are nevertheless diverging markedly on issues of national and international security. In recent years, on issues as diverse as North Korea, Iraq, the Middle East, National Missile Defense, the Kyoto Treaty, the International Criminal Court (ICC), environmental issues, trade issues, and the role of international institutions – Europe and America have often been at loggerheads.

Differences in perceptions of threat are demonstrated by the language Europeans and Americans use to describe dangers to national security. Whereas the United States refers to 'rogue' states – and this terminology was employed by the Clinton administration, further revealing that transatlantic differences on this issue are not new – Europeans refer to 'failed' or 'failing' states. Divergences in threat perception also mean that Europeans are increasingly reluctant to accept American leadership on matters of international security. The idea that the United States can simply select coalitions among different European allies at different times depending upon the mission (defined by Washington) will become increasingly unacceptable to an expanding EU. Indeed, EU members will increasingly come to see that where their interests coincide, often diverging from those of the U.S., there will be clear advantages in European solidarity. As Javier Solana put it: the '...notion of ad hoc coalitions of docile followers to be chosen or discarded at will is neither attractive nor sustainable in the long run'.[36] 9/11 is likely to be seen in historical perspective as a further stimulus for Europeans to cooperate further in the realm of foreign, defense, and security policies. The United States began its 'war on terror' in September 2001 with practically the whole of the international community on its side. By the time it took this war to Iraq, it had very few supporters left. The fact that the most vociferous opposition to the war on Iraq came from member NATO allies in Europe is a portent for the future of U.S.-European relations.

Notes

[1]   See for instance Gompert, D. and Larrabee, F.S. (eds), *America and Europe: A Partnership for a New Era*, New York, Cambridge University Press, 1997.

[2]   See Mandelbaum, M., 'How the West is torn on dealing with Iraq', *The Age*, 12 February, 2003; and Kagan, R., 'Power and Weakness', *Policy Review*, no. 113, June-July 2002, pp. 3-28.

[3]   Mearsheimer, J., *The Tragedy of Great Power Politics*, New York, W.W. Norton, 2001.

4   See Nye, J.S., *The Paradox of American Power: Why the World's Only Superpower Can't Go It Alone*, New York, Oxford University Press, 2002.

5   From Kissinger, H., *Years of Upheaval*, Boston, Little Brown, 1982, p. 153. Two years earlier, in 1971, the Nixon administration had to fight hard to defeat the Mansfield amendment in the Senate, calling for a withdrawal of U.S. troops from Europe.

6   That arms control did not result in any radical reductions is evident by simply listing the numbers of nuclear strategic warheads for the USSR and the U.S. from the time of détente through to the late 1980s: in 1972 the U.S. had 7,601, the USSR 2,573; in 1976 the U.S. had 10,436, the USSR 3,477; in 1980 the U.S. had 10,608, the USSR 7,480; in 1988 the U.S. had 13,000, the USSR 10,834. Figures from the *SIPRI Yearbook 1991*, London, Brasseys/International Institute for Strategic Studies, p. 21.

7   There exists a huge literature on this topic. For a review of the arguments see Mandelbaum, M., 'The Democratic Peace', chapter 3 of his *The Ideas that Conquered the World*, New York, Public Affairs, 2002, pp. 241-276. Also: Ray, J.L., *Democracy and International Conflict*, Columbia, S.C., University of South Carolina Press, 1995.

8   Klein, J., *The Natural: The Misunderstood Presidency of Bill Clinton*, London, Hodder and Stoughton, 2002, p. 69.

9   Nye, J.S., *Bound to Lead: The Changing Nature of American Power*, New York, Basic Books, 1990.

10 Holbrooke, R., *To End a War*, London, Random House, 1999, p. 360.

11 Clarke, W.K., *Waging Modern War*, New York, Perseus, 2001, p. 35. It should be noted that Clark was also critical of the U.S. defense establishment in Washington, for its reluctance to countenance what Clark thought was imperative: the deployment of U.S. ground troops. See Clark, *Waging Modern War*, p. 425.

12 Joffe, J., 'Of Hubs, Spokes, and Public Goods', *The National Interest*, no. 69, Fall 2002, pp. 17-20.

13 Three years ago the Czech Republic, Poland, and Hungary joined NATO. Bulgaria, Estonia, Latvia, Lithuania, Romania, Slovakia, and Slovenia were invited to join the alliance in November 2002 at the Prague Summit.

14 Kagan, R., 'Power and Weakness', pp. 3-28. Kagan argues here that the Bush administration viewed NATO's historic decision to invoke Article 5 '...less as a boon than as a booby trap'. Kagan has extended (some would say stretched) his original thesis into a (slightly) larger text: *Paradise and Power: America and Europe in the New World Order*, London, Atlantic Books, 2003.

15 Quoted in Gordon, P.H., 'Reforging the Atlantic Alliance', *The National Interest*, vol. 69, no. 3, 2002, pp. 91-97, p. 91.

16 Quoted in Hirsh, M., 'Bush and The World', *Foreign Affairs*, vol. 81, vol. 5, 2002, pp. 18-43, p. 32.

17 Stephen Krasner, *Sovereignty: Organized Hypocrisy*, Princeton, Princeton University Press, 1999.

18 Ritter, S. and Pitt, W.R., *War on Iraq: What Team Bush Doesn't Want You To Know*, Crows Nest, New South Wales, Allen and Unwin, 2002, p.15. Also see Ritter, S., *Endgame: Solving The Iraq Problem – Once and For All*, New York, Simon & Schuster, 1999.

19 See, for example, relevant papers on the website of the *One Europe or Several?* programme funded by the Economic & Social Research Council in the U.K.: http://www.one-europe.ac.uk. In May 2003 proposals were put forward for a foreign minister to be appointed representing the interests of the EU. This is

perhaps unlikely to happen, at least in the short term, but it does reflect increasing recognition amongst influential elites in Europe that EU interests require more effective institutional representation.

20   Bush's speech can be found at: www.fas.org/irp/news/2001/09/gub092001.html.

21   Indeed, Churchill's favored vision was for a union of the United States and the English-speaking world. See Lukacs, J., *Churchill: Visionary, Statesman, Historian*, Melbourne, Scribe Publications, 2002, pp. 15-18. Some might see the coalition of the willing in the war on Iraq as the realization of Churchill's vision, with the three key players representing the English-speaking world across three continents: the U.S., the U.K., and Australia.

22   King, A., *Britain Says Yes: The 1975 Referendum on the Common Market*, Washington D.C., The American Enterprise Institute, 1977, p. 6.

23   On Britain's changing relationship with Europe see Shearman, P., 'Britain, the European Union and National Identity', in Milfull, J. (ed), *Britain in Europe: Prospects for Change*, Aldershot, Ashgate, 1999, pp. 91-102.

24   *The Economist*, 17 May, 2003, p. 44.

25   *The Economist*, 17 May, 2003, p. 44.

26   Or, as Karl Zinsmeister put it: 'Schröder scrambled back into Germany's top office...by planting his feet firmly on Uncle Sam's face', in his 'Old And In the Way', part of a special symposium on 'Continental Drift: Europe and the U.S. Part Company', *The American Enterprise*, vol. 13, no. 8, December 2002, pp. 4-9, p. 4. During the election campaign the SPD Justice Minister compared Bush to Hitler, whilst a leading parliamentarian compared him to a Roman emperor.

27   Quoted in Muravchik, J., 'The European Disease', *The American Enterprise*, vol. 13, no. 8, December 2002, pp. 24-27, p. 27. Muravchik comments: 'That makes American foreign policy enemy number one', p. 27.

28   Quoted in *The Australian*, 24 January, 2003.

29   Cited in Krauthammer, C., 'The Unipolar Moment Revisited', *The National Interest*, Winter 2002/03, pp. 5-17, p. 10.

30   Iraq was the third member of this axis.

31   See Deudney, D. and Ikenberry, J., 'The Nature and Sources of Liberal International Order', *Review of International Studies*, vol. 25, no. 4, 1999, pp. 179-196; and Lundestad, G., 'Empire by Invitation', *Journal of Peace Research*, vol. 23, no. 3, 1999, pp. 263-276.

32   Ikenberry, J., *After Victory: Institutions, Strategic Restraint, and The Rebuilding of Order after Major Wars*, Princeton, Princeton University Press, 2001.

33   Wallace, W., 'Living With The Hegemon: European Dilemmas', www.ssrc.org/sep11/essays/wallace.

34   See Johnson, C., *Blowback: The Costs and Consequences of American Empire*, London, Time Warner Paperbacks, 2002.

35   Waltz, K.N., 'The Continuity of International Politics', in Booth, K. and Dunne, T. (eds), *Worlds in Collision: Terror and the Future of the Global Order*, Houndsmills, Basingstoke, Palgrave, 2002, pp. 348-354.

36   Solana, J., 'The Transatlantic Rift: U.S. Leadership After September 11', *Harvard International Review*, vol. 34, no. 4, Winter 2003, pp. 62-66, p. 64.

Chapter 4

French Security After 9/11: Franco-American Discord

Rémy Davison

Introduction

Franco-American relations have traditionally been plagued by French exceptionalism in foreign policy, and the events of 9/11 have not altered the ground rules for international diplomacy. However, the key problem for French foreign policy makers is the fact that U.S. hegemony in Europe has been enhanced, not diminished, by September 11. U.S. investment in military R&D remains more than seven times higher than French expenditure, while EU defense spending as a whole was less than 50 per cent that of U.S. for the 1999-2001 triennium.[1] Significant increases in U.S. defense outlays are envisaged for 2003-2005.

The 'capabilities gap' between not only the U.S. and France, but the U.S. and the European NATO allies threatens French security in a number of respects. It reduces French influence in key areas of foreign policy, such as the Israeli-Palestinian conflict; the debate over the future of postwar Iraq; and, perhaps most significantly, NATO expansion. For the architects of French foreign and security policy, September 11 poses serious challenges to over a decade of planning for a pan-European security architecture, represented by the Common Foreign and Security Policy (CFSP). The events following 9/11, including the subsequent U.S.-led war in Iraq, overwhelmingly demonstrated the insignificance of both French and European defense policy. Even more glaringly, the marginalization of the European NATO members by the U.S.'s sidelining of its European allies in the war in Afghanistan and its preference for *ad hoc* coalitions in a wider 'war on terror' raises queries regarding the utility of the NATO alliance for anything but minor supporting roles in U.S. military campaigns.

French attempts at using international institutions as a means of 'multilateralizing' and diminishing U.S. power have also been victims of the post-9/11 period. The U.S.'s deployment of 'soft' power to quickly form a formidable global political alliance, and 'hard' power against the Taliban, saw America shift its strategy of 'aggressive unilateralism' from strategic trade policy to defense policy. As former Secretary of State Albright said, 'we will behave multilaterally when we can and unilaterally when we must'.[2] A U.S. Defense Department official underlined this point when stating 'the [Defense Secretary and the Defense Department] believe in unilateral American military power'.[3]

Even prior to September 11, French Foreign Minister Hubert Védrine argued that the U.S. was a 'hyperpower' and asserted that the 'entire foreign policy of France …is aimed at making the world of tomorrow composed of several poles, not just one'.[4] The hyperpower concept itself implies that the U.S. is a state far beyond an ordinary superpower and that its military capabilities have given the international system profoundly unipolar structural characteristics. It is the threat posed to global stability by a unipolar world order which has led French foreign policy elites to engage in diplomatic efforts designed to dilute American power by emphasizing the European pillar of the transatlantic alliance, while simultaneously demonstrating a strong commitment to UN operations and peace-keeping efforts.

The following section of the chapter commences with an assessment of French approaches to European security. The third section details French policy responses to the events of September 11. Section four examines French 'exceptionalism', while section five enlarges this discussion to include France's approach to varieties of proliferation. The impact of September 11 on domestic politics is considered in section six, which also discusses the nexus between national and international policy. Section seven contextualizes the French position in the post-Cold War system, while the concluding section considers the implications of French policy responses to American unilateralism.

France's approach to European security

The key to understanding French conceptions of European security is a comprehension of Gaullist foreign policy aims, these being the dual policies of German containment and limiting Anglo-American influence on the continent. The 1966 French withdrawal from NATO was partly a result of this refusal to accept U.S. domination of transatlantic security, and the conviction that the U.S. would never use its nuclear arsenal to defend Europe. The American refusal to share nuclear technologies with France, while arming the U.K., only served to increase French suspicions that the Americans would not allow France to play a leading role in West European defense and security.

The objectives of French security policy have remained remarkably consistent since the Fourth Republic's development of the European Defense Community (EDC) in 1952. Although the EDC failed to be ratified by the French National Assembly in 1954, it clearly signaled France's dual aims of containing West Germany and controlling West European security policy outside the confines of U.S.-dominated NATO. In this respect, French foreign policy exceptionalism predated de Gaulle by a number of years.

The clearest indication that France intended to develop a new European security architecture based on the EU, rather than NATO, emerged during the development of the Maastricht Treaty in 1989-91. The development of the Common Foreign and Security Policy (CFSP) as a pillar of the Maastricht Treaty gained unexpected support from the 1991 U.K. Defense White Paper which stressed the Western European Union (WEU) as a strong European pillar of NATO. However, the French position was that WEU should respond to European military tasks, and that its membership should be restricted to EU members. By contrast, the U.K. sought a WEU as NATO's European arm with membership not restricted to the EU. Under heavy diplomatic pressure from France, the Kohl government found itself caught in a conflict between French security interests and U.S. foreign policy. Ultimately, Germany opted to support France's 'Europeanization' of West European security, which meant German support for CFSP at the 1991 Maastricht Intergovernmental Conference (IGC).

The Maastricht Treaty's eventual promulgation in 1993 initiated the transformation of EU member countries from mere client states within NATO to an embryonic European defense community. Maastricht's endorsement of CFSP introduced qualified majority voting in the Council of Ministers on issues of defense. In 1992, Mitterrand spoke of an EU-based deterrence force, while in 1994, Prime Minister Balladur raised the prospect of a European army.[5] However, on assuming the French presidency, Chirac held WEU at arm's length, moving closer to the U.K.'s position on WEU as the European pillar of NATO. From 1997, the British position on an EU-based force had also altered, following the election of the Blair government. Conversely, the Major government had threatened to suspend the 1996 IGC and all EU activities – thus postponing some significant CFSP initiatives – unless the issue of British farm exports affected by mad cow disease was resolved. The completion of the 1996 IGC ultimately saw the amendment of Article 223 of the 1957 Rome Treaty to incorporate EU funding of the CFSP.[6] Although the 1996 IGC did not inaugurate the French project of an EU defense force independent of NATO, it laid the basis for the Anglo-French *entente* at St. Malo in December 1998. Previously, Chirac's attempts at enlisting Chancellor Kohl's assistance for a similar Franco-German proposal had been met with silence from the Clinton Administration. By essentially accepting the British position on WEU – its incorporation into the EU – Chirac and Blair could present a cogent and unified position at the December 2000 Nice European Council.

However, the improvement in Anglo-French relations has not masked policy divergence between France and Germany. While strains in the Franco-German relationship have been evident for some time, the events of 9/11 have further exacerbated foreign policy differences between the two. Following the European NATO members' invocation of Article 5 of the 1949 Washington Treaty for the first time, the Schröder government offered the use of German troops in UN-sanctioned anti-terrorist actions.[7] Irrespective of the use of the Bundeswehr for non-Article 5 operations outside NATO over the past decade, German forces are not equipped to engage in major actions in the Middle East or Afghanistan.

Nevertheless, the political implications of Germany's involvement in extra-European conflicts are considered a major problem by some French elites. Paramount among their concerns is that France has lost its pre-eminent political position in Europe. Although it was clear by the 1970s that France had ceded industrial and economic leadership in Europe to West Germany, the succession of war-time French and German leaders accepted *rapprochement* as the guiding principle of the relationship: a partnership enveloping both states' interests, but led politically and strategically by France. This was evidenced not only by the agricultural bargain underpinning the *acquis communautaire*, but also in military terms by the Franco-German Defense Agreement (1987) under French command. Promulgated at the same time as the wide-ranging Iklé-Wolhstetter Report on NATO, the Agreement quickly broadened into the Franco-German Brigade. In 1989, Mitterrand and Kohl launched the parallel IGCs which resulted in the incorporation of the Common Foreign and Security Policy (CFSP), which represented a French conception of European security, into the Maastricht Treaty.

However, as Heather Field notes, Clinton's Defense Secretary, William Cohen, cautioned the EU on consigning NATO to the status of a 'relic', and argued that what the EU needed was larger defense budgets, not 'institutions and alphabet soup'. Cohen's broadside was clearly directed at the French government, which he saw as undermining NATO's function and legitimacy in order to gain control over the military aspects of the European security agenda.[8]

This demonstrated the considerable divergence in the Franco-American positions, not in terms of their respective national interests, but with regard to the means which they used to secure them. From an American point of view, French attempts at using diplomatic leverage to secure non-proliferation and arms control agreements are pointless, as intelligence monitoring itself can only provide a very incomplete picture of a state's capabilities. It would misrepresent the French position, however, to speak only of the non-proliferation and counter-proliferation agenda, as France is committed to both the development of its defensive nuclear capability, as well as the European Security and Defense Policy (ESDP), which will deploy a 60,000-strong Rapid Reaction Force (RRF). However, the RRF has been delayed by a number of political and economic problems, including disinterest on the part of EU neutrals, such as Sweden, where green groups and anti-nuclear activists have attracted voter support. Logistical problems include RRF's employment of existing NATO infrastructure, which has led to disputes between Greece and Turkey over Turkey's role in decision making in the ESDP. Although the RRF was originally expected to be operational by 2003, the second Gulf War muddied the waters considerably following a German and French-led push to establish the RRF independently of NATO's security architecture.

The French response to 9/11

Chirac was the most senior foreign leader in Washington soon after the WTC attacks occurred. While Chirac supported NATO's invocation of Article 5, he carefully distanced himself from a number of Bush's statements. Prime Minister Lionel Jospin did the same. Like Blair and Schröder, Chirac and Jospin were careful not to offer the Americans *carte blanche* insofar as troop commitments were concerned. While Chirac offered the use of French forces, he made it clear that the military objectives had to be narrow and aimed at removing the perpetrators of the September 11 attacks, and not directed at the U.S.'s wider politico-strategic objectives.[9] The Bush-Chirac meeting on 18 September demonstrated that both Chirac and Jospin had agreed to a carefully-worded and common position on the commitment of France to any military engagements. Chirac told Bush that France would commit to military action, but that the French government had to be 'consulted in advance about the objectives and modalities of an action, whose goal must be the elimination of terrorism'.[10] However, Chirac refused to endorse the concept of a 'war' on terror.[11] While it is important not to overstate this point, it is clear that the French government considers 'war' implies that anti-terrorist solutions go beyond diplomatic activism.

Chirac's initial strongly-worded messages of support for the Americans – supported by similar statements by the British and German leaders – should not be interpreted in terms of a reassessment and reorientation of French foreign and defense policies. More accurately, the events of September 11 gave U.S. military objectives a resoundingly stronger focus, while simultaneously challenging the French-devised European security architecture, itself more than a decade in the making. The immediate French response to the WTC attacks was to initiate United Nations Security Council Resolution (UNSCR) 1368 on September 12, which condemned the terrorist attacks and sanctioned the United States' right of legitimate defense. However, Chirac simultaneously insisted upon a UN role in framing responses to the attacks.

The French government also moved quickly to freeze the assets of 'presumed terrorist movements and organizations',[12] although the question arises as to why suspected terrorists' resources were not seized or frozen earlier. Foreign Minister Hubert Védrine also suggested the U.S. would adopt French proposals to combat international money laundering, which the French government had pressed for prior to the September attacks. France has supported proposals aimed at curbing money laundering, particularly with regard to funds that could be used to fund terrorism. Védrine had previously presented a convention to the UN General Assembly on the financing of terrorism, arguing that the legal instruments to combat funding did not exist. The pace of implementation had been slow prior to September 11, although there has been a trend towards much speedier ratification of the Financial Action Task Force on Money Laundering (FATF) by the signatory countries.[13] Before the attacks, the U.S. had rejected the monitoring of offshore banking; after 9/11, the Americans largely adopted the French position.

President Chirac also stressed the European dimension of France's responses to the terrorist threats, being careful to emphasize the importance of European solidarity in the form of NATO and the role of the EU's Directorate-General covering

External Affairs. Védrine pointed to the EU Ministers' coordination of an integrated EU response under the auspices of the 'third pillar' of the Maastricht Treaty, Justice and Home Affairs. However, Védrine argued that both French and EU diplomatic efforts, in missions to Saudi Arabia, Syria, Pakistan and Egypt after 9/11,[14] were instrumental in securing support for subsequent UN, NATO and U.S. actions.

In this respect, Chirac, Jospin and Védrine followed the traditional French foreign policy approach of employing a number of non-military means to confront the threat of terrorism. Védrine argued that the struggle must 'not only be punitive but preventative...to fight against terrorism you must fight against its sources: finances, fanatical and destructive ideologies, situations and crises that provide militants to the terrorists'.[15] This was further emphasized by the French government's strong support for the use of the FATF to identify and freeze sources of finance to terrorist organizations. Acting upon a French initiative, the FATF met in Washington in an extraordinary plenary meeting on 29-30 October, 2001, moving to shift emphasis from the prevention of money laundering to establishing a special task force charged with combating terrorist financing.[16] While far-reaching in some respects, it should be noted that no Middle-Eastern states[17] or Asian states other than Japan – with the exception of intergovernmental organizations such as the Gulf Cooperation Council – are members of the FATF. Although membership is open to all states, it is likely that its effectiveness will be limited outside the OECD and other participant states.

Jospin implicitly placed some strict limitations upon the extent of French involvement in extra-European conflicts. In September, he said that France 'within Europe [,] will play her part'.[18] In a speech in November, he reiterated that France would play its 'full part' *on its national territory and within Europe*. In the same speech, Jospin emphasized the multilateral agenda, arguing that the struggle against terrorism was 'inseparable from an international battle for development and justice, since poverty and injustice are a breeding ground for radical ideologies and terrorism'.[19]

Sensitive to the prospect of domestic unrest in France as a result of the terrorist attacks, both Védrine and Chirac employed identical phrases in their attempts to deflect responsibility from the Islamic communities, warning that bin Laden had set out to 'trap' the West into a 'clash of civilizations'.[20] This sat uncomfortably with Bush's use of the term 'crusade' in his description of the 'war on terror'. According to Védrine, this 'reduction[ism] of terrorism to a "war" was simplistic', without acknowledging its roots – such as underdevelopment, poverty, injustice and the inhumanity of globalization. For Védrine, the 'war on terror' was an American approach which France 'cannot accept'.[21]

French action at the EU level has included a strong push for the finalization of the text of an EU arrest warrant in order to coordinate EU-wide information sharing on suspected terrorists. The development of a European arrest warrant was agreed at the 20-21 September 2001 EU ministerial meeting. Chirac called for the rapid establishment of a common judicial area.[22] Proponents of EU integration pointed to this as evidence of the EU's unity of purpose. However, it was quickly clear that nation states, not the EU, would take the lead in security policy making post-September 11. Chirac, Blair and Schröder did not attempt to coordinate their policy responses, despite their three-way meeting at the Ghent European Council on 19 October, 2001, which produced a public façade of unity, which was not supported by the triumvirate's subsequent actions.[23] In February 2002, French foreign ministry spokespeople accused the British government of 'reverting to type', by refusing to share its terrorist monitoring information with other EU intelligence agencies. The U.K.'s lack of 'transparency', according to the French government, allowed an extremely dangerous terrorist leader, Abu Kutada, to disappear.[24] In the wake of this incident, the French government urged the EU's Spanish Presidency to accelerate the arrest warrant process. By contrast, the French police acted quickly in December 2001 to arrest a French-Algerian al Qaeda liaison, Ahmed Laidouini, who was alleged to have involvement with terrorist cells based in Europe.[25]

However, the EU itself placed obstacles in the path of both the French national response to 9/11, as well as the cogency of the EU position. At the Ghent European Council on 21 September, Belgian Prime Minister Guy Verhofstadt said the EU supported only 'targeted' attacks against terrorists and their supporters, and that the EU would not be drawn into wider military conflict. At a stroke, Verhofstadt had automatically placed parameters upon the EU's involvement in wider military anti-terrorism activities. European Commission President Romano Prodi also adopted this position when stating that U.S. anti-terrorist plans needed a 'second look', although he argued there was no dilution of EU support for the U.S.[26]

The French government committed to the deployment of 2,000 personnel in Afghanistan for intelligence and reconnaissance tasks, as well as aircraft and warships. Ultimately, that figure grew to 4,500-5,000 personnel[27] in the Afghanistan campaign, which resulted in 31 strikes on targets by the French air force. This represented the only non-U.S. air strikes in the entire operation. However, as Jeremy Shapiro notes, French officers refused to attack some targets, due to the dangers they posed to the civilian population.[28]

Nevertheless, given the considerable size and expertise of French forces, some of which are particularly suited to fighting in the mountainous terrain found in Afghanistan, the U.S. failed to make any use whatsoever of those elements. Instead, a number of French units were given humanitarian assistance duties, while U.S. forces carried out the majority of the military tasks.[29] This was no different from the use of U.S. air strikes and ground troops in the Bosnian and Kosovo operations, where European troops were relegated largely to UN peace-keeping operations in the aftermath of the air war. From the U.S. point of view, the Europeans could not be trusted to carry out critical assignments given their procrastination on intervention in both Bosnia and Kosovo. For the Americans, the need to employ the Anglo-American wings of NATO in Kosovo demonstrated the utter uselessness of CFSP as a politico-military instrument, together with a dire lack of political and military will in the EU to take immediate and effective action against Belgrade.

The impact of French 'exceptionalism' and diplomatic activism

Védrine's 2000 statement that France 'cannot accept a politically unipolar world, nor a culturally uniform world, nor the unilateralism of a single hyperpower'[30] implied that French diplomatic efforts would be directed at the dilution of American power, not only in Europe, but also in other geostrategic areas. As a result, France made a point of criticizing U.S. support of Israel, while voting for the removal of economic sanctions against Iraq. Under Chirac, France also embarked on a strong diplomatic thrust into Asia, with over 90 ministerial-level visits to the region since 1997, compared to only five over the previous five-year period. The diplomatic effort since 1997 included three presidential visits (Japan, India and China), with two of these resulting in the Peking and Tokyo Agreements, both of which speak of 'global partnerships'.[31]

The French cultivation of China has a long history, with de Gaulle's establishment of diplomatic relations with the PRC in 1964, when China was diplomatically isolated by American non-recognition and the Sino-Soviet split. In recent years, France has abandoned criticism of China in the Human Rights Commission, unlike the U.S., which continues to make direct attacks. Premier Li Peng's visit to Paris included a lavish reception, which provoked condemnation of France's China policy in the National Assembly by former Prime Minister Laurent Fabius of Balladur and Chirac. This led Védrine to respond that the U.S. 'realist approach' to China had not produced 'concrete results'.[32]

In South Asia, following India and Pakistan's nuclear tests in 1998, the French government commenced dialogue on limiting testing with Pakistan and India, while the U.S. and China pushed for sanctions to be levied. Thus, France could claim that it had sponsored 'constructive engagement' which had kept diplomatic channels open when crisis forced the U.S. to incorporate Pakistan into the coalition against terror. Although U.S. officials are reluctant to admit the value of French diplomacy, France's dialogue with Pakistan following the 1999 coup opened the door to U.S. strategists who needed Pakistan's cooperation, first as a conduit for negotiations with the Taliban after 9/11, as well as the use of Pakistan's infrastructure and geostrategic position to assist in the blockade of Afghanistan's borders following the commencement of hostilities.

Despite France's non-recognition of the Taliban as the legitimate government of Afghanistan since the mid-1990s, the French government continued to receive diplomatic missions from the Taliban after September 11, and it was the only state with a *chargé d'affaires* in regular contact with Kabul prior to the commencement of hostilities. The links with the Taliban allowed the French to have intelligence officers on the ground in Afghanistan prior to the WTC attacks, which produced important contacts with the Northern Alliance, who partnered U.S. forces during the campaign. Shapiro describes the Northern Alliance contacts established by the French as 'critical' to U.S. efforts to remove the Taliban and destroy al Qaeda training camps.[33]

French responses to proliferation

French governments have traditionally had a poor record in the area of nuclear non-proliferation and testing, having exploded new devices in the South Pacific (1995) prior to the promulgation of the Comprehensive Test Ban Treaty (CTBT) in 1996. France was not a party to the 1969 Anti-Ballistic Missile (ABM) Treaty, leading to France's development of a number of anti-missile sites, while the USSR retained two and the U.S. only one (which was later closed). In the area of proliferation, Khomeini's Iran came close to obtaining French nuclear technology in 1979 as a result of a contract signed by the Shah, a situation which emerged out of the complacency of both the U.S. and French governments. Nor was France a signatory to the 1987 Intermediate Nuclear Forces (INF) treaty between Moscow and Washington, which eliminated an entire class of missiles from the East and West European theatres.[34] Throughout the 1980s, France remained a staunch critic of Reagan's Strategic Defense Initiative (SDI), and strongly opposed the Clinton Administration's reactivation of SDI in the form of the National Missile Defense (NMD) project in 2000.

According to Michael Gordon,[35] the American view is that NMD dilutes the effectiveness of the relatively small French nuclear deterrent. However, Vaïsse argues that French objections to the Clinton-Bush NMD system are based around three points.[36] First, non-proliferation treaties, while not wholly effective, are important agreements designed to control the spread of chemical, biological and nuclear weapons. Second, French strategists asserted that Western – particularly American[37] – assessments of the offensive capabilities of 'rogue states', such as Iraq and North Korea were overstated, and that the technological capacity required to deliver offensive nuclear and non-nuclear weapons capabilities to these states would have developed over a longer time frame than that envisaged by the U.S. Védrine's assessment of the threat capabilities of 'rogue states' was that they were 'not very serious', and that the threats themselves were 'theoretical'.[38] Vaïsse concurred with this contention, asserting that such weapons constituted a risk, and not a threat. Third, French defense plans stressed the importance of Theatre Missile Defense (TMD) utilizing short and medium-range missiles, with French defense budget papers including provision for the development of a TMD system in their spending to 2005. The French view this as a useful means of defending Europe's southern flank, although TMD does not provide a 'shield' capacity in the way the NMD is designed to. Chirac argued against the concept of NMD, stating that where there was a 'struggle between sword and shield, there is no instance in which the shield has won'.[39] Rather than pursuing NMD, Chirac has persistently called for more active support for non-proliferation efforts, forming what he calls a 'virtuous circle of the non-proliferation of weapons and disarmament' under the CTBT. 'On all these issues', Chirac said, 'the EU and U.S.A, driven by their common values of humanism, must combine their efforts to point the way to a peaceful world'.[40]

The key French security concerns with NMD since September 11 have been the acceleration and legitimation of the U.S. project, with the abandonment of the ABM Treaty (with grudging Russian acquiescence) and the increase in the NMD budget. French strategists suspect the outcome of NMD will be to create a 'domino effect' among nuclear powers, with the consequence that China, Russia, India and Pakistan will increase the pace of their ballistic missile programmes in order to close the perceived missile and capabilities gaps. In the medium to long term, French strategists argue that German and Japanese[41] insecurity will force them to adopt nuclear capabilities, as they may be threatened directly by medium-range ballistic missiles launched from the Middle East, or China/North Korea, respectively.

French concerns regarding NMD surfaced well before the September 11 attacks, but the accelerated development of NMD since then has exacerbated transatlantic tensions. French concerns are based around three key issues. First, Paris perceives that NMD will reduce the U.S.'s commitment to European defense; second, that the U.S. has abandoned diplomatic efforts at non-proliferation in favor of missile defense; and third, that NMD will provide security for the U.S., while creating instability in other regions, threatening the interests of U.S. allies.[42]

Védrine and Chirac shared broadly similar views on NMD, with both expressing reservations about its destabilizing effects. The French position was driven largely by two overlapping reports, both issued in 2000, commissioned by the National Assembly and the Senate. The former focused upon weapons of mass destruction and the proliferation of chemical and biological weapons, while the Senate reported on the impact of NMD systems. The Senate report argues that the benefits of NMD are unclear, regardless of whether NMD is directed at deterring nuclear strikes by China, Russia or smaller states such as North Korea. As Vaïsse argues, while the economic costs of NMD will be borne by the U.S., the political consequences of the programme will be shared by the entire international community.[43] For the French government, the implementation of NMD runs the risk of introducing an arms race, with little prospect of controlling proliferation, particularly in the absence of an ABM Treaty and/or effective CTBT and NNPT treaties. As Kissinger pointed out in 1986, arms races with no ceilings on stockpiling are pointless, and make nuclear deterrence obsolete. In this respect, Kissinger encouraged future U.S. administrations to move away from the concept of TMD – a cornerstone of French deterrence strategy – and towards NMD:

> 'Strategic defense [SDI] is the only idea that points the way from the excessive reliance on weapons which threatens strategy with paralysis and arms control with triviality... [B]y the end of the century, several Third World countries will have acquired nuclear weapons. Some will thereby

acquire a vast capacity for blackmail because they could make the threat of suicide more plausible than the superpowers'.[44]

The French strategic shift to a 'flexible response' posture over the last decade is particularly striking, as the U.S. has made a similar *volte face* towards inflexible response since around 2000. While U.S. policy in Europe was based upon flexible response for most of the Cold War period, the French and NATO preference – if not always the practice – was for inflexible response. For French governments, the first response was also the last resort. When Mitterrand was asked whether he would launch nuclear strikes if Soviet troops crossed the French border, he replied 'by then, it would have been too late'.

The fundamental point is that NMD reduces the effectiveness of French TMD and the EU's RRF, and that both nuclear and non-nuclear proliferation dilutes the impact of an independent French deterrent. This is why Chirac has argued against the U.S. NMD project which, almost inevitably, will drive regional arms races and, possibly, as Yost suggests, 'could cause Germans to question the long-established advantages of retaining non-nuclear-weapon-state status'.[45]

The domestic impact of 9/11

Tensions in the Franco-American relationship which pre-dated 9/11 and were exacerbated by George W. Bush's election in 2000 included issues such as abortion, capital punishment and the U.S.'s support for hardliners in successive Israeli cabinets. While 73 per cent of French voters in a poll taken one week after September 11 supported the use of military action (a ratio of support second only to Britain in Europe), as well as their own country's commitment to the use of force,[46] 75 per cent of voters in another poll said that U.S. foreign policy was to some extent responsible for the rise of Islamic extremism.[47] This has significant implications for French domestic stability and internal policy, given that over 4 million Muslims live in France. In the 2002 presidential elections National Front leader Jean-Marie Le Pen received only minor support from voters after he blamed rising crime upon migrant populations and called for the cessation of immigration. But the dual themes of the impact of globalization on French society and economy, together with the perception that the U.S. has embarked on an anti-Islamist crusade, has been blamed for anti-semitic activities by some French Muslims. The fact that an overwhelming majority of French Muslims polled (92 per cent) condemned the attack on New York suggests little support for bin Laden's call for Muslim peoples to rise up against host countries.[48] Nevertheless, French elites were uncomfortable with Washington's soft line on Israel during the 2002 Israeli-Palestinian conflict, which some officials blame privately for recent domestic violence. Although the French government has consistently backed a Palestinian state, its simultaneous support for the U.S.'s actions in Afghanistan means it appears to be a supporter of U.S. policy, however tacitly. The question some voters and elites are asking is whether France can coexist securely with Islam in a period of strong antipathy towards Muslim extremism.

The difficulties in accommodating the electoral demands of France's domestic Muslim and Jewish constituencies have significant external implications, not only for French foreign policy in the Middle East, but also in terms of the Franco-American relationship. This is at least partly why Chirac urged Bush to confine military activities to Afghanistan and to avoid civilian casualties as far as possible. Although the issue of French support (or lack of it) was decided by the time much-anticipated American strikes were launched against Iraq, U.S. officials had much recent history to suggest that France would not be its most reliable ally in the region. Until the last hours of Desert Shield, the French foreign ministry sought a diplomatic solution with Iraq to the Kuwaiti crisis, although ultimately France provided the third-largest force on the ground in the Gulf War, and supplied invaluable air support. However, both the Mitterrand and Chirac administrations – however reluctantly – consistently sided with China and Russia in the UN Security Council on the issue of lifting economic sanctions against Iraq, an action which proved successful only after more than a decade.

French security in the post-Cold War system

The outcome of the post-Cold War international system has produced a unipolar structure, characterized by the emergence of the U.S. as a 'hyperpower'. Despite the application of this term by French Foreign Minister Védrine to the U.S. prior to September 11, the expression was widely viewed as hyperbolic, given that most analysts argued that the international system had reverted to strategic multipolarity, with the U.S. facing a series of military and economic challenges to its hegemony from China, Japan and the EU.

Contrary to pessimists' expectations, who predicted 'another Vietnam' as a consequence of the U.S.'s engagement in Afghanistan, America emerged virtually unscathed from the September 11 attacks, the war against the Taliban and al Qaeda, and most recently in Iraq, with its globally preponderant position consolidated. The U.S. has now moved far beyond what Charles Krauthammer called 'the unipolar moment' during the 1990s. Not even the intensity of the 2002 Israeli-Palestinian conflict challenged to the U.S.'s ability to impose solutions in regional disputes.

The end of the Cold War system, and with it, strategic bipolarity, meant that the French strategic and diplomatic positions were weakened considerably. Although it was not immediately clear that a significant structural shift had taken place – from a bipolar[49] to a unipolar system – what was clear was that the Franco-European position had altered markedly. First, the demise of bipolarity consigned France's independent nuclear deterrent to strategic irrelevance in the European theatre; second, it reduced the importance of France's strategic position as the leader of the 'third force' (the EU) in international affairs between the U.S. and USSR; and third, the end of the Cold War consolidated and confirmed the U.S.'s position as the dominant power in world politics. All of these factors served to marginalize the impact of French diplomatic exceptionalism.

France's position was marginalized still further by its inability to convince its EU partners to adopt a coherent and consistent response to intervention in Iraq. The EU fractured into three camps, with France and Germany opposing a war without UNSC authorization; Britain supporting intervention, backed by Spain, Italy, Denmark, the Netherlands and 2004 EU members Bulgaria, Poland, the Baltic republics, Hungary, the Czech Republic, Slovakia, Romania and NATO member Turkey; and the traditional neutrals, represented by Austria, Ireland and Sweden. Chirac angrily lectured the new East European members of the EU, castigating them for their 'bad manners'. Similarly, Prodi was unhappy with the EU's failure to present a united front, just as he was clearly uncomfortable with his compatriot, Italian Prime Minister Silvio Berlusconi, who volubly supported the U.S.-led 'coalition of the willing'.

The Iraq question in 2002-2003 brought Franco-American tensions to a head. France's support for UNSC Resolution 1441 in 2002 exemplified its legalistic approach to WMD proliferation.[50] However, neither Chirac nor Foreign Minister Dominique de Villepin would countenance unilateral action against Iraq, arguing instead for the resumption of UN arms inspections. Following the unanimous adoption of UNSC 1441, Chirac noted that 'The message of the international community is clear. It is united in telling Iraq that it is now time to cooperate fully with the United Nations'. The resolution 'offer[ed] a chance for Iraq to disarm in peace'.[51] But 1441 presaged closer Sino-Franco-Russian solidarity, not support for the U.S. position. Russian President Vladimir Putin echoed the French legal position, arguing that Iraq should comply with UNSC resolutions 'in accordance with the principles and norms of international law'.[52]

1441 was a watered-down document, at the insistence of the French, Russian and Chinese governments. The U.S. and U.K., as co-drafters, deliberately sought to provoke Saddam into rejecting the resolution by inserting terms that were thought to be unacceptable to the Iraqi government. However, the final draft of 1441 was much less stringent, and it requested inspections on a basis which Saddam could accept. Chirac adopted a two-stage position at this point. The first was embodied in 1441 which requested the resumption of inspections; the second was a requirement that action in the event of Iraqi non-compliance would require a second UNSC resolution. Chirac's plan gained approval from Chinese Foreign Minister Zhu Rongji following a meeting with the French premier. The Elysée also said that Chirac and Putin had agreed to cooperate closely on the Iraq question,[53] further evidence that the Paris-Moscow-Beijing axis was hardening its opposition to the Anglo-American strategy.

The initial drafts of 1441 authorized the use of military force in the event of non-compliance. This was unacceptable to the French and the Russians, who said they would only accept a resolution which stated that only the UNSC could authorize military action. The gulf between the French and the Anglo-American positions widened over the next few weeks, despite the return of the inspectors to Baghdad.

Blair and Bush interpreted 1441 to mean the UN had authorized military action against Iraq if Saddam failed to comply with the resolution. Blair stressed: 'Defy the UN's will and we will disarm you by force'. Similarly, Bush was in no doubt that 1441 authorized the use of force in the event of non-compliance: 'If Iraq fails to fully comply', Bush said, 'the United States and other nations will disarm Saddam Hussein'.[54] Bush and Secretary of State Colin Powell argued that the coalition's invasion of Iraq was authorized under Resolutions 678, 687 and 1441. However, the French reaffirmed their position in March 2003: 'We cannot accept an ultimatum or the automatic recourse to force. Before any decision the inspectors must come back before the UN Security Council to make their report and it is up to the council to decide', Chirac's spokesperson said. The Elysée's position further ruptured cross-Channel relations, with Blair's spokesperson accusing the French of 'poisoning' diplomacy.[55]

There is little doubt that Iraq had successfully sought to cultivate French support in order to produce divisions within the UNSC since the early 1990s. Iraq's position was bolstered by its traditional alliance with Russia, which benefited considerably from higher world oil prices as a result of the economic sanctions placed upon Iraq from 1990. China had also had close links with Saddam's regime in the late 1980s, selling Iraq a significant amount of defense materiel, including tanks, armored vehicles and fighter aircraft. Moreover, although French loans to Iraq amounted to only $U.S. 5 billion by 2002, and two-way trade totaled only 0.2-0.3 per cent of French GDP, potentially lucrative contracts with Iraq in the event of the removal of economic sanctions provided a significant incentive to French governments and business to preserve ties with Saddam.[56] A war which would leave the Americans and British in control of Iraq would be a significant blow to French commercial interests within the region. The rapid advance and occupation of Iraq in March 2003 by Anglo-American-led forces in the wake of French, Russian and Chinese obstruction in the UNSC caused considerable damage to the Franco-American relationship, with members of the Bush Administration warning that France would face 'consequences' for its actions. It was clear that the Washington hawks saw France as the leader of both the anti-U.S. faction within the UNSC, as well as the force behind negative EU attitudes towards the U.S.

The repercussions for France are unclear at this stage, although the exclusion of France from NATO's governing North Atlantic Council has been mooted as one diplomatic snub Washington may visit upon Paris. In March 2003, Paris attempted to employ the North Atlantic Council as a vehicle to block NATO from defending Turkey in the event of war with Iraq.[57] The move forced the Council to convene an extraordinary meeting and may have been behind Ankara's eventual decision to forbid coalition troops from using Turkey as a launching pad for their operations in northern Iraq. Trade retaliation by the U.S. against France may also follow, although consumer sentiment in the U.S. saw some businesses cease stocking French goods, leading to a small, but significant downturn in the sale of French products throughout the U.S. Following the coalition's occupation of Baghdad, Powell said France would face 'consequences' due to its actions prior to the war.

Speaking at the Evian G8 meeting in May 2003, Powell said that: 'There has been a review of some of the activities that take place between the United States and France on a bilateral basis. Some of our military activities, joint military activities are being looked at in light of the changed circumstances'.[58] The French acceptance of the Anglo-American occupation of Iraq was reflected, however, in the 14-0 vote in favor of the removal of sanctions in the UNSC in May 2003. However, as Powell continued to speak of 'consequences' for France, Germany and Russia during his visit to the Evian G8, Chirac provocatively insisted upon the 'full implementation' of the Kyoto Protocol and argued that 'other measures' must be applied until the treaty was fully in force.[59]

However, American opprobrium for outspoken opponents of its Iraq policy has not been confined to France; in May 2003, the U.S. Trade Representative, Robert Zoellick, implied that the U.S.-New Zealand Free Trade Agreement (FTA) negotiations would 'go to the back of the queue' due to the New Zealand Prime Minister's outspoken criticism of the Bush Administration. Although the Prime Minister apologized, no such treatment was meted out to Australia, which is also negotiating an FTA with the U.S. In marked contrast with its trans-Tasman partner, Australian leaders were fêted in Washington and Camp David, as Australian troops represented the third-largest coalition force in Iraq. Ironically, this was France's position during Gulf War I. Franco-American and Russo-American relations were more conciliatory at the Paris G8 meeting in May-June 2003, where Bush met Chirac and Putin privately, but not Schröder. The rift in German-American relations appeared wider, despite Defense Secretary Rumsfeld's declaration that relations were 'unpoisoned' in November 2002. Germany's unequivocal solidarity with France on the Iraq issue in early 2003 clearly 'repoisoned' relations between the two, particularly as Washington insiders reported that comments from Schröder's ministers during the 2002 German elections – which compared Bush's Iraq policies to those of Hitler – infuriated the U.S. President.[60] As Germany does not occupy a permanent seat on the UNSC, it is unlikely Washington will seek reconciliation with Germany as quickly as it will with France and Russia, both of which can place considerable legal obstacles in the path of U.S. foreign policy. But this assumes that the U.S. will continue to view the UNSC as the appropriate forum for peace enforcement; victory in Iraq is much more likely to encourage Washington to be less inclined to take the UN seriously. In this respect, the UNSC has become very much like a legalistic Maginot Line for the U.S.: cumbersome, slow and inappropriate. Unable to overcome the strictures imposed by the prospective French, Russian and Chinese vetoes on a second UNSC vote to authorize military action against Iraq, the Americans simply circumvented it.

Military dominance is only one aspect of American power. What Joseph Nye terms 'soft' power also constrains and affects the ability of America's allies to have a meaningful place in world politics. The overwhelming influence of the U.S. in international institutions such as the IMF (chaired for the first time by a German, not a Frenchman), the UN Security Council and NATO, as well as America's successful export of globalization, consigns other states to cheerleader status, with little opportunity to affect global policies. However, this has often only served to harden French governments' resolve to pursue regional and global policies opposed to those of the U.S. Traditional explanations of French antipathy towards U.S. policies assert that France, like Britain, was a global power, and finds it difficult to adjust to middle-power status. Both seek recognition as great powers and each state's elites view global governance quite differently. As Philip Gordon notes, 'nearly all French leaders and experts seem to believe that multipolarity is the healthiest formula for the management of the international system, whereas many Americans tend to think that system functions better with a single leader'.[61] Bush's January 2002 speech made this latter point explicit: 'You are either with us or with the terrorists. There is no third way'.

Conclusions

The May 2002 bombing of a bus in Karachi containing French citizens may not have been directed at France, but the incident heightened the perception of insecurity felt by the French both domestically and abroad. In this respect, French elites fear that unless French foreign policy – articulated both in national policy and in EU policy via the CFSP – is not discernibly, if subtly, different from U.S. policy, then American unilateralism will endanger French policies of constructive engagement, partnership and multilateralism.[62] More importantly, the U.S.'s war on terror may result in increased insecurity in European states if they are faced with extremist terrorist threats themselves. Indeed, given the ethnic composition of French society, with between 4-5 million Muslims and several hundred thousand Jews, it is possible that France has become much *less* likely a target for terrorist attacks, given that it opposes the U.S. on a wide range of international security issues. Nevertheless, potential terrorists would be ill-advised to assume that because France is 'against' the U.S. on certain issues, that it is 'with' the terrorists on others. From the French perspective, there is a third way.

Due to the U.S.'s dominance of the organization, France cannot enunciate a multilateral security dialogue through NATO, where it is not even a member. Instead, Chirac is likely to develop a distinctive European security framework which will draw some important contrasts with the Bush doctrine. As a middle-ranking power, France will be unable to do this alone and will require German – and to a lesser extent British – cooperation. This poses not only serious challenges for Franco-German relations, where Chirac and Schröder, in contrast to the Mitterrand-Kohl alliance, have never been close, but also for French policy towards the EU as a whole, a challenge made even more difficult by the EU's complex enlargement process over the next decade.

The fact that the transatlantic community shares similar, but not identical, interests cannot be dismissed lightly. While neither the French nor the EU will rupture transatlantic relations, unipolarity and its consequences, including increased American unilateralism, may jeopardize U.S. foreign policy initiatives in the longer term and lead to both France and Europe developing security regimes which could result in reduced involvement of the Europeans in American military 'adventurism'. This means that in regions where French and EU interests are threatened by U.S. military activities, such as the Middle East and East Asia, that Franco-European policy will be highly sensitive to the negative outcomes arising as a consequence of U.S. security policy. French elites perceive the insecurities of post-Cold War international politics have arisen from the U.S.'s unwillingness to restore the equilibrium of the Yalta system, and that the rise of international terrorism, of which September 11 is a concomitant part, is a result of the inability of state-based actors to resist American unilateralism.

Opinion is split over what is commonly viewed as a 'new', more aggressive form of American foreign policy. Although it is true that the 2003 war in Iraq divided Europeans into pro and anti-American camps, it is incorrect to assume that French or European opposition to U.S. foreign policies is a recent development. French attempts at balancing U.S. power by coalition-building in Europe and with China have had currency since at least the 1950s, the most recent example being the CFSP. However, some commentators, such as Vaïsse, argue that the Bush Administration – as a direct result of September 11 – was transformed from a conservative government to a force for change in the international system.[63] This may be the case, but it does not account for the economic cold wars and security policy divisions which have broiled for decades between the EU and the U.S.: over agricultural policy; the bitterly-fought WTO dispute over the EU banana regime; European inactivity over Bosnia; the Anglo-American liberation of Kosovo; and the Doha Round. Lukewarm U.S. support for French-led European security initiatives suggests to French policy elites that American administrations have no interest in European security beyond the expansion of NATO to Russia's borders.

It is important to assess Franco-American tensions in view of the post-Yalta system, and to recognize that French diplomatic exceptionalism is discrete from French commitments to military engagements where France perceives both national interests and a sense of *noblesse oblige* that is intrinsic in great power status. The Gulf War and Afghanistan represent two instances of this, while Bosnia and Kosovo compel U.S. strategists to doubt the commitment of France to European, let alone global, security. But American administrations cannot complain about the level of the French military commitment to the two major conflicts they have fought in the last 10 years; it is the persistence of French diplomatic exceptionalism which continues to raise suspicions in Washington and reflects Kissinger's dictum: 'who are we going to call in Europe?'

As a result, the net effect of France's global and regional diplomacy post-September 11 may be a unilateralist America, which finds itself increasingly isolated in its efforts in the war on terrorism. By default, the U.S. has, to some extent, placed itself in this position, by insisting upon fighting the war in Afghanistan largely on its own. Failing to incorporate NATO into the anti-terrorist coalition in more than a symbolic sense is a policy failure on the part of the Bush Administration. However, this policy represents a prevalent view in the U.S.

Defense and State Departments in both the Clinton and Bush Administrations: that the Europeans, particularly the French, as Richard Perle put it, cannot be trusted.[64]

If the U.S. persists with a unilateralist and interventionist foreign policy – which appears likely – this will drive France, Germany and Russia, and possibly China, closer still, as they attempt to balance the American hyperpower. However, cooperation will be difficult for these states as they identify very different national interests, and their common antagonism towards American unilateralism may be insufficient for them to mark out anything other than defensively positional stances on key areas of international security. Moreover, the U.S. has demonstrated in the past and in the present that it is increasingly willing to link security with trade issues, which the EU, with its burgeoning trade surplus with the U.S., but a strengthening Euro, will be keen to avoid. But if Vaïsse is correct in his prediction that Afghanistan and Iraq are merely the first battles in the U.S.'s long struggle against international terrorism,[65] then Franco-American relations are likely to experience long-term turbulence. In turn, the Franco-German tandem, the dominant partners in the EU throughout its history, will be forced to become closer, despite the lack of personal trust between their leaders, Chirac and Schröder.[66] However, the divisions between EU members will persist. If the British had plotted to divide the EU on security policy and destroy CFSP, they could hardly have planned it better.

French multilateralist approaches to security and institution-building will remain at significant variance with Anglo-American approaches to the post-September 11 terrorist threat. It is also no longer possible to speak of a 'European' position on significant questions of international security. The net result has been an uneasy transatlantic relationship, exacerbated by the behavior of the SPD-Green coalition during the 2002 German elections, and French prevarication over the wording of UN Security Council Resolution 1441/02. However, the 2003 Franco-Russian capitulation to U.S. demands for a UN resolution on the cessation of sanctions on Iraq, as well as *de jure* recognition of the Anglo-American forces as the sole occupying powers in Iraq demonstrated not only the relative power of the U.S. in the post-September 11 environment, but also the comparatively limited policy influence French governments have, despite their UNSC veto. In Washington, the multilateral security agenda pursued by France is viewed with distrust, not only because it is aimed at diluting U.S. power, but also because French activism presents a divided front to anti-Western forces. As long as France retains reservations about American motives in the Middle-East, French and U.S. policy is likely to remain distrustful and controversial. This represents an historical continuum in Franco-American relations, and the impact of September 11 is not likely to bridge the chasm of policy divergence between the two uneasy allies.

Notes

[1] Figures from *SIPRI Yearbook 1998*, London, Brasseys/International Institute for Strategic Studies, 1998; and *The Military Balance 1998–1999*, London, Brasseys/ International Institute for Strategic Studies, 1999.

[2] Cox, M., 'American Power Before and After September 11: dizzy with success?', *International Affairs*, vol. 78, no. 2, pp. 271-276, p. 276.

[3] *The Observer*, 10 February, 2002.

[4] Védrine, H., *Les Cartes de la France à l'heure de la mondialisation*, Paris, Fayard, translated by Gordon, P.H., *France in an Age of Globalization*, Washington, D.C.: Brookings Institution, 2001, pp. 26-38.

[5] *Le Monde*, 9 December, 1994.

[6] European Parliament, 'Conférence intergouvernementale: la politique étrangère et de sécurité commune (PESC)', Brussels: Office for Official Publications, 21 March, 1997.

[7] The German offer should not be given undue emphasis. As Forster and Wallace note, only France and Britain, among the European NATO allies, possess the capacity to project and sustain forces for any considerable length of time outside the European theatre; for example, in the Persian Gulf. It is highly unlikely without considerable long-term restructuring that a German force could be deployed effectively beyond western, central and southern Europe. See Forster, A. and Wallace, W., 'What is NATO for?', *Survival*, vol. 43, no. 4, 2001/02, pp. 107-122.

[8] Field, H., 'Problems of Enlargement, Security and Foreign Policy in Europe', paper presented to the National Europe Centre Workshop, Australian National University, Canberra, 8 December, 2000.

[9] 'Jacques Chirac annonce la participation des forces françaises', *Le Monde*, 7 October, 2001.

[10] 'Jacques Chirac réaffirme à Washington l'offre de coopération de la France', *Le Monde*, 19 September, 2001.

[11] Chirac, Washington press conference, 18 September, 2001.

[12] Chirac, Speech to the Future of Europe Regional Forum, Montpellier, 4 October, 2001.

[13] These are principally OECD member countries. The FATF was a French initiative in 1989 and a French official chaired the intergovernmental organization for its first two years. The FATF's presidency revolves annually and it has identified a number of states, such as Nauru, as money-laundering centers since September 11.

[14] Interview by LCI with Pierre Moscovici, Minister Delegate for European Affairs, 1 October, 2002.

[15] Quoted in *Le Monde*, 'Le monde entier reconnaîtra que les Etats-Unis sont en situation de légitime défense', 18 September, 2001.

[16] Financial Action Task Force on Money Laundering (FATF), press release, 30 October, 2001.

[17] Including Israel.

[18] Prime Minister Jospin, Speech at the Memorial Ceremony Honoring the Victims of the Terrorist Attacks in the United States, Paris, 19 September, 2001.

[19] Jospin, Speech to the Préfets, Paris, 20 November, 2001.

[20] Chirac said 'Above all, we must not confuse these fundamentalist, terrorist and fanatical groups with the Arab or Muslim worlds. That would be a cardinal error, would be profoundly unjust and above all result in us falling into the very trap set

for us by the terrorists, those seemingly seeking what's been called the 'clash of civilizations' and is the world of the absurd', whereas Védrine stated 'falling into the diabolical trap that the terrorists wanted to set, that of a 'clash of civilizations'. See Chirac, statement at Joint Press Conference with the UN Secretary General, 19 September, 2001; and Védrine, *Le Monde*, 'Le monde entier reconnaîtra que les Etats-Unis sont en situation de légitime défense,' 18 September, 2001.

21 *France Inter*, interview with Hubert Védrine, Question Directe, Paris, 6 February, 2001.

22 Chirac, speech to Future of Europe Regional Forum, Montpellier, 4 October, 2001.

23 Heibourg, F., 'Europe and the Transformation of World Order', *Survival*, vol. 43, no. 4, 2001, pp. 143-148, p. 146.

24 Statement by the Ministry of Foreign Affairs, France-diplomatie, 1 February, 2001.

25 Shapiro, J., 'The Role of France in the War on Terrorism', Washington D.C., Brookings Institution, Center on the United States and France, May, 2001.

26 CNN, 'Terror to dominate EU Summit', 18 October, 2001.

27 Not including French special forces, for which deployment numbers remain confidential.

28 Shapiro, 'The Role of France in the War on Terrorism'.

29 Shapiro, 'The Role of France in the War on Terrorism'.

30 Védrine, H., *Les Cartes de la France à l'heure de la mondialisation*.

31 Dorient, R., 'Un septennat de politique asiatique: quel bilan pour la France?', *Politique étrangère*, vol. 67, no. 1, 2002, pp. 173-88.

32 Védrine, *Les Cartes de la France à l'heure de la mondialisation*, p. 147.

33 Shapiro, J., 'The Role of France in the War on Terrorism', Washington D.C., Brookings Institution, Center on the United States and France, May 2001.

34 Note that the INF Treaty did not involve the dismantling of any warheads and removed predominantly the ageing SS-18s and Pershing II classes of missiles.

35 Gordon, M.R., 'Moscow Signaling a Change in Tone on Missile Defense', *New York Times*, 22 February, 2001.

36 Vaïsse, J., 'French Views on Missile Defense', Washington D.C., Brookings Institution, Center on the United States and France, April 2001.

37 This was the conclusion of the 1998 Rumsfeld Commission. See Gordon, P.H., 'Bush, Missile Defense and the Atlantic Alliance', *Survival*, vol. 43, no. 1, 2001, p. 17.

38 Ministry of Foreign Affairs of the French Republic, 'Entretien du Ministre des Affaires Etrangères M. Hubert Védrine avec la Revue Trimestrielle Politique Internationale', press release, November 2000.

39 'Joint Press Conference by Jacques Chirac, Tony Blair and Lionel Jospin during the Franco-British summit at Cahors', 9 February 2001.

40 Chirac, '2010: The Challenges to Global Security', *Jane's Defense Weekly*, 22 December, 1999.

41 Japan has previously renounced the development of nuclear weapons, although a strong nationalist domestic constituency, together with elements of the Liberal-Democracy Party, may force it to reconsider, particularly if the U.S. ceases to actively promote non-proliferation.

42 See Vaïsse, 'French Views on Missile Defense', Washington D.C., Brookings Institution, Center on the United States and France, April 2001.

43 'U.S. Making Little Headway with Allies on NMD', *BASIC Press Release*, May 2000.

44   Quoted in *The Australian*, 14 January, 1986, p. 6.

45   Yost, D., 'Transatlantic Relations and Peace in Europe', *International Affairs*, vol. 78, no. 2, 2002, p. 296.

46   'Jacques Chirac annonce la participation des forces françaises', *Le Monde*, 7 October, 2001.

47   *Le Point*, 27 September, 2001. Global opposition to the war prior to March 2003 was reflected in opinion polls throughout the Western world, including an overwhelming 92 per cent of French voters who supported Chirac's stance in March 2003. Following the lightning American victory in Iraq, public support for Chirac quickly slumped to a mere 50 per cent, compelling him to stage a mild *volte-face*. See CNN, 'Huge Support for Chirac', 20 March, 2003.

48   Laurence, J., 'Islam in France', Washington D.C., Brookings Institution, Center on the United States and France, December 2001.

49   See Waltz, K., 'The Stability of a Bipolar World', *Daedalus*, vol. 93, 1964, pp. 881-909.

50   El Khatib, F., 'Counter-Proliferation Policy and France's New Government', Washington D.C., Brookings Institution, Center on the United States and France, September, 2002.

51   *Agence France Presse*, 'UN Security Council Votes to Disarm Iraq', November 9, 2002.

52   *The Age*, 'U.S. drums up support for tough resolution', 28 September, 2002.

53   *The Age*, 'U.S. drums up support for tough resolution'.

54   *Agence France Presse*, 'UN Security Council Votes to Disarm Iraq'.

55   CNN, 'Chirac Reaffirms France's Rejection to Ultimatum on Iraq', 15 March, 2003.

56   Gordon, P.H., 'Getting Paris On Board', Brookings Institution, Center on the United States and France, 18 October, 2002.

57   CNN, 'Chirac, Putin: No Need for War', 10 March, 2003.

58   U.S. Secretary of State Colin Powell, press conference, French American Press Club, 22 May, 2003.

59   CNN, 'G8 Meeting Tests Post-Iraq Unity', 22 May, 2003.

60   *The Washington Post*, 'Washington and Berlin Healing Rift', 11 November, 2002.

61   Gordon, P., 'The French Position', *The National Interest*, vol. 68, Fall 2001, pp. 85-96.

62   *France Inter*, interview with Hubert Védrine, Question Directe, Paris, 6 October, 2001.

63   Vaïsse, J., 'La Nouvelle Politique Étrangère Américaine', *Politique Internationale*, vol. 92, 2003, pp. 22-23.

64   Gordon, P., 'The French Position'.

65   Vaïsse, J., 'La Nouvelle Politique Étrangère Américaine'.

66   Klau, T., 'France and Germany: A re-marriage of convenience', Washington D.C., Brookings Institution, Center on the United States and France, January 2003.

Chapter 5

German Security After 9/11

Franz Oswald

Introduction

The terrorist attacks on New York and Washington D.C. of September 11, 2001 had a significant but limited impact on German security policies, which continued trends visible since the end of the Cold War, German unification in 1990, and the disintegration of the Soviet Union in 1991. Over the last decade, Germany has developed political prerequisites for a new role in the international system without, so far, developing corresponding military capabilities. Plans to develop a capacity for long distance intervention, together with NATO and EU partners, predate September 11, 2001, and are connected with NATO's Strategic Concepts of 1991 and 1999.

After September 11, Germany provided political support to the U.S., contributed to anti-terrorist law enforcement and intelligence efforts, and participated to a lesser extent in military action. Germany's institutional framework for law enforcement and domestic intelligence has been retained, but in response to September 11, legislation to expand the powers of these institutions has been adopted (Security Packages I and II). Parliamentary debates showed broad support for the U.S. campaign against terrorism. However, this support was also fragile. Within the centre-left government coalition of Social Democrats and Greens, support for military action was conditional upon the concurrent search for political solutions for post-Taliban Afghanistan and other regional conflicts. German politicians shared European concerns about U.S. interpretations of the antiterrorist campaign as a 'crusade', and a willingness to widen the scope of action. By 2003 this had culminated in Germany's rejection (together with France and Russia) of U.S.-led moves to topple Saddam Hussein's regime in Iraq.

The post-1991 context

There is a tendency amongst analysts to identify the events of September 11, 2001 as marking a sea-change in German foreign policy. According to Philip H. Gordon, Germany's Chancellor Schröder sought to 'end the post-war pattern' of standing on the sidelines and avoiding military risks, instead adopting a 'new conception of German foreign policy'.[1] In terms of the renewal of Germany's long-term strategic outlook, however, it is more precise to place this in the post-1991 context since Schröder also emphasized that the 2001 contribution would not have been possible without the changes in Germany since 1991. The normalization of German foreign and security policy had begun in 1990-1991, resulting in the engagement of German armed forces 'out of area' beyond the territorial defence of NATO. This occurred, for instance, in the employment of German airpower in Kosovo during 1999, and Germany's participation in IFOR and SFOR peacekeeping operations in former Yugoslavia. Moreover, Germany took a lead role in the conflict in Macedonia. This, as Jackson Janes notes, was 'a far cry from where Germans were ten years ago during the Gulf war... Germany's role as a secondary player on the world stage, according to the Chancellor, now belongs to the past'.[2]

Solidarity with qualifications

Total solidarity with the U.S. was initially expressed after 9/11 by the German executive and parliament. Chancellor Schröder, in a statement on September 12, 2001, declared that Germany would be involved in the campaign against terrorism and was willing to take various necessary risks. He also signalled that Germany did not want to be dragged into 'adventures', and that he expected the U.S. response to be proportionate. In a multilateral context, the FRG contributed to gestures of political support for the USA by the EU and NATO. At the EU summit of September 14, heads of state and heads of government offered symbolic solidarity. And, although it did not have relevant military capabilities, the EU was in a position to contribute to the law enforcement aspects of the campaign against terrorism. Since the Schengen agreement of 1985, a growing number of EU countries had shared responsibilities for border control, and since the Treaty on European Union (TEU) of 1992 the field of Justice and Home Affairs had become one of the three pillars of the EU treaty framework. Germany had participated from the beginning in the Schengen agreement, and in the cooperation of law enforcement agencies following from the TEU. The Schengen Convention (Schengen II) of 1990 envisaged the establishment of the 'Schengen Information System...linking relevant databases in participating states'.[3] These earlier developments made cooperation between EU member countries easier after 9/11. At the same time, 9/11 made EU countries more willing than before to share information. On 16 October 2001, EU justice ministers discussed a common definition of 'terrorism', in order to facilitate a cooperative application of national criminal codes. They also agreed on procedures for a common European arrest warrant facilitating the detention and extradition of terrorist suspects.

As a member of NATO, the FRG backed the declaration that the terrorist attack of September 11 constituted an attack on a NATO member country, invoking Article 5 of the Washington Treaty of 1949. There were, however, differences between European governments regarding the practical implications of these statements. For Great Britain, significant military support for the U.S. was an obvious conclusion. Belgium and the Netherlands, on the other hand, understood NATO expressions of solidarity as not necessarily implying military action, but rather as a means of influencing the U.S. in order to prevent overreactions.[4] The German response can be located in between: The FRG contributed a small military contingent while, at the same time, attempting to exercise a moderating influence on U.S. decision-making.

Visits to the U.S. by German leaders also signalled solidarity with qualifications. Foreign Minister Fischer and Chancellor Schröder traveled to Washington on 20 September and 1 October respectively. Yet, as Sebastian Harnisch and Wolfgang Braumer have pointed out, this 'did not mean that Berlin would be willing to engage in "adventures" a barely veiled reference to the possible extension of U.S. military action in Iraq'.[5] Thus the expressions of solidarity by German leaders combined promises of political and military support with an interest in moderating U.S. policies. These German (and European) arguments were highlighted by American commentators sharing some of the European concerns:

> Even traditional U.S. allies have been concerned about the concentration of power in U.S. hands and Washington's penchant for unilateralism, and they have searched for ways to constrain U.S. freedom of action... they resent Washington's tendency to impose its will on others and worry that it will use its power unwisely.[6]

Differences of interpretation: clash of civilizations or surgical action?

Germany's government, like other European nations, agreed with the Bush administration on the need to take decisive action against the al Qaeda network and against the Taliban government harboring this organization in Afghanistan. There were differences, however, regarding the nature of the threat and the scope of action to be taken. German leaders shared a European emphasis on non-military responses and a concern about 'root causes' of terrorism such as regional conflicts and the inequality inherent in the North-South situation. They demanded that any military response be limited, precise and proportionate, and argued against the use of provocative terms such as 'crusade' and 'war'. While expressing solidarity with the U.S. they also warned against exaggerated responses exacerbating the situation into a clash of civilizations, instead of isolating the terrorists. U.S. President Bush, on the other hand, used the terms 'crusade' and 'war' implying the need for larger scale military measures in, as he put it, a conflict representing what he called 'civilization's fight'.[7]

Bush's approach did, however, find some support in Germany. Analysts like Joachim Krause, for example, warned against transatlantic misunderstandings and rifts. Krause pointed out that U.S.-German policy divergence over the interpretation of the level of threat from terrorism, and the strategies employed to deal with it, would result in damage to the cohesion of NATO. In Germany and the U.S., he noted, these differences had quickly solidified:

The events of September 11 are mainly understood [in Germany] as terrorist acts being directed against the U.S...the terrorist acts are perceived as something between the U.S. and a transnational terrorist organization. In the U.S., on the other hand, the fight against terrorism has turned into a war against an informal network of Islamic fundamentalist extremists, whose primary goal is to throw out the U.S. and her allies from the Middle East and to erect some kind of fundamentalist Islamic rule in the Islamic world.[8]

According to Krause, 'the German debate is characterized by a lack of awareness of such strategic implications'. Although Germany provided assistance to the U.S. as a NATO member and in an *ad hoc* coalition, Krause still asked whether the nature of the threat had really been fully understood in Germany. This critique of the German government's position was also shared by Edmund Stoiber (Christian Social Union), premier of Bavaria and the (unsuccessful) candidate for the chancellorship in the 2002 German elections, who expressed unqualified support for Bush's approach during a visit to the USA.[9] However, domestic tensions sparked by Washington's intention to invade Iraq ultimately resulted in a negative public perception of the CSU's stance. In the elections that followed, voters turned against Stoiber and back to Schröder, who successfully played upon popular anti-American sentiments in order to regain the Chancellorship.

Efforts to create consensus in the government coalition

All parties represented in the Bundestag showed broad consensus in their condemnation of the terrorist attacks of September 11. However, parliamentary debates revealed significant differences in the government coalition regarding the appropriate response and the German contribution to this response. These differences required efforts by government and parliamentary leaders to create sufficient cohesion in the coalition of Social Democrats and Alliance 90/Greens.

While Schröder's first declaration of solidarity with the U.S. was widely supported in the Bundestag, the proposal to offer a German military contribution created divisions within the government coalition. The Schröder government could normally rely on disciplined majority support from the two parties forming the government, the SPD and Alliance 90/Greens. However, on this issue the distribution of support and opposition in the Bundestag did not follow usual patterns. The centre-right Christian Democrat Union (CDU/CSU) and Free Democratic Party (FDP) supported military action; the left-socialist Party of Democratic Socialism (PDS) was opposed. Within the centre-left government coalition of SPD and Greens, a minority was opposed to any German military contribution. The Schröder government faced potential embarrassment given that it could not find majority support in the Bundestag without having to rely on opposition parties to compensate for government defectors. In the U.S. presidential system it is not uncommon for the executive to rely on shifting cross-partisan majorities. In the German parliamentary system, however, defections from the government could be interpreted as signs of instability, which was especially problematic for the government in an election year.

To avoid this embarrassment Schröder linked the proposal for military action with the question of confidence in his government. This raised the threshold for parliamentarians considering a 'no' vote since a defeat would have brought down the government and brought forward new elections. Schröder's actions forced the CDU/CSU and FDP to vote 'no' although they supported the proposed German participation in military action. It also forced a sufficient number of opponents of military action in government ranks to vote 'yes' in order to preserve the coalition government.

In the end, the government motion was supported by 336 and opposed by 326 Members of the Bundestag (MdBs). In reality, support for the action was much larger since the centre-right opposition parties CDU/CSU and FDP unanimously supported military action although they voted against the motion linked to a question of confidence in the government. The narrow outcome of the vote in the Bundestag was thus doubly deceptive. As Hans Maull put it at the time: 'The actual support for deployment in parliament is considerably stronger than the tally suggest, while the state of the coalition in fact is rather less healthy than the clear majority might suggest'.[10]

Unity in the government coalition was achieved not only by the linkage of military action and the question of confidence but also by a joint motion of both coalition parties articulating numerous concerns and qualifications held amongst SPD and Green parliamentarians. While this joint motion may not have had many consequences in terms of military action, it was necessary to produce domestic political prerequisites for action. The resolution was also an indicator of possible limits of transatlantic consensus. A position paper by eight Green MdBs pointed out that their support had been conditional on joint coalition action, and a similar view was put forward by members of the SPD:

> The government clearly underestimated the number of parliamentarians of their own parties opposing this shift... In an oral declaration after the vote, 15 members of the SPD unequivocally declared in the Bundestag that they would have rejected the decision had it not been for the rescue of the coalition.[11]

German participation in the campaign against terrorism was favoured in the government coalition only if attacks remained limited to precisely defined targets, if a broad coalition or UN resolutions legitimized action, if military means were not the only instrument used, and if the campaign included the search for political solutions. These concerns were shared, to some extent, by other European leaders, and they were broadly compatible with similar 'liberal internationalist'[12] positions in the U.S. The need to create parliamentary consensus also highlighted Germany's emphasis on the need for political solutions after the war in Afghanistan. Without the Petersberg conference in December 2001, hosted by Germany, parliamentary support for German participation in military action might not have been sustained.

Impact on the party system: the fragility of Alliance 90/Greens

The Bundestag controversies over Germany's military contribution had ramifications for the party system and for the viability of future governments. Opposition leader Edmund Stoiber (CSU) used a visit to the USA to present himself to the German public as an unhesitant supporter of Washington's campaign against terrorism and as a decisive leader, in contrast to the incumbent, Chancellor Schröder,[13] whose coalition of SPD and Greens came close to disintegration over the issue. Of the government parties, the larger SPD was less likely to be affected by disillusionment amongst left Social Democrats with pacifist leanings than the smaller Alliance 90/Greens party. In reality, the 'loss of cohesion of the coalition under the pressure of international events' helped to demonstrate the importance of the Greens in the German polity. This was because Green party officials, especially Foreign Minister Fischer, initiated a '"civilian response" to the terrorist attacks, stressing diplomatic and humanitarian aspects of Germany's anti-terror policy', which was instrumental in solidifying domestic support for the government's position.[14]

Fischer had many years of experience of shifting the Greens towards a more pragmatic approach to politics. As leader of the 'Realo' wing, he persuaded the party in the 1980s to accept the compromises required to join government coalitions at a regional level. Before the 1998 national elections, Fischer had readied the Greens for the coalition with the SPD at the federal level. Without the willingness of the Greens to abandon or postpone demands for the abolition of NATO, it would have been impossible to form the SPD/Green coalition and for Fischer to become Foreign Affairs Minister. Fischer's experience in reducing the influence of less accommodating pacifist and environmentalist Green politicians had also been useful in 1999, when he succeeded in persuading the NATO-sceptic wing of the Greens to accept NATO action against Serbia as humanitarian intervention.

Nevertheless, the tensions between pacifist Green traditions and its role as a government party after September 11 were likely to affect party membership and electoral support. This could benefit the Party of Democratic Socialism whose opposition to German military contributions could 'probably win over principled pacifists from the Alliance 90/Greens and the SPD, thereby broadening its meagre electoral base' in the former West Germany.[15] Yet at the same time it also posed a potential future danger in that it could undermine the coalition of SPD and Alliance 90/Greens. Should Green electoral support weaken, the party would not be able to gain the 5 per cent required to be re-elected to the Bundestag. Differences over foreign and security policy also impeded the SPD/Green coalition after the 2002 election. In this situation, the SPD could find a coalition with the centre-right Free Democrats more attractive. The Greens, on the other hand, would find themselves in the wilderness, not pacifist enough compared to the PDS nor pragmatic enough for inclusion in government. Threatened by an existential crisis resulting from a failure of the government coalition, even reluctant Green parliamentarians decided on November 14, 2001, to vote for Germany's military contribution linked with the question of confidence in Chancellor Schröder.

This discussion of domestic party politics has shown that the fragile German consensus could be threatened if the campaign against terrorism was widened to include military action against targets other than al Qaeda. As Harnisch and Braumer presciently argued in early 2002:

> The current consensus could come under pressure if the U.S. government should decide to expand the war on terrorism, e.g. to military action against Iraq. Military action in Iraq... is clearly beyond the current policy consensus in Germany. Thus, if U.S. action occurred (especially without European explicit approval), this could seriously damage transatlantic relations.[16]

Military action and German public opinion

A military contribution by Germany to the war in Afghanistan met with majority approval by the public. However, the majority was not as large and support was not as deep as in France or Britain. This was not due to any sympathies for al Qaeda or any widespread anti-Americanism but due to Germany's 'amilitary' political culture,[17] due to the lasting impact of World War II and forty years of West German experience as a trading nation using 'chequebook' diplomacy rather than military means between 1949 and 1990.

Yet German foreign policy culture has not been predominantly pacifist. Hans Maull argues correctly that otherwise the formation of the Bundeswehr in the mid 1950s and its subsequent growth would have been impossible, although there was, admittedly, a pacifist movement of some significance, reaching a peak of influence in the mid 1980s and leading to the formation of the Green party. Thus, German public opinion 'continues to be rather skeptical about the utility of force in solving political problems'. Nevertheless, 'pacifism is not a dominant theme of overall German public opinion...rather, Germany's foreign policy culture could be called "pacificist" – ie., inclined towards negotiated political solutions to conflict, rather than imposition through military force'. Military actions will be supported 'as long as these are perceived by the public as legitimate and appropriate...In short, German foreign policy culture of reticence vis-à-vis the use of force has not (yet?)

changed fundamentally, and it continues to differ substantially from that of America, France or Britain'.[18]

Despite the fact that German political culture is more concerned with diplomacy than pacifism *per se*, it is nonetheless evident that given the German population's reluctance to endorse the use of force, German governments have to take public sentiment into account. In practice this meant combining an acceptance of coercive intervention in support of the U.S. with the important proviso that any military action ought to be legitimate and proportionate.

Terrorism as matter for law enforcement

According to Barry Posen 'much of the war [against terrorism] will look a lot like conventional law enforcement by the government of cooperative countries'.[19] In contrast to Germany's rather limited military role, U.S. commentators expected Germany 'to take the lead in dealing with other dimensions of the fight against terrorism, particularly in dealing with the extensive network of financial support and money laundering, a good deal of which takes place in Germany'.[20] Besides pragmatic arguments for law enforcement measures, there was also the view articulated by Jurgens Habermas, and widely shared among Social Democrats and Greens, that terrorist attacks were a crime rather than an act of war. In early 2002 Habermas argued that the decision by the Bush administration to declare 'war' on terrorism was 'a grave mistake, normatively as well as pragmatically. Normatively, these criminals are raised to the status of combatants in a war, and, pragmatically, one cannot conduct a war against a hardly palpable network'.[21] From this perspective, law enforcement was perceived to be the most appropriate response, whereas a 'war against terrorism' unnecessarily elevated the status of what were simply common criminals.

a) Legislation to strengthen domestic security institutions

Since the FRG had an appropriate institutional framework for domestic security, there was no need to discuss the creation of an 'Office of Homeland Security' as in the USA. A variety of institutions existed in Germany's federal structure, at the federal and the regional levels, concerned with policing and domestic intelligence, including coordination mechanisms. Nevertheless, legislation covering these institutions was modified in response to 9/11. The existing institutional framework for police and intelligence response included, at the federal level, the Bundeskriminalamt (Federal Office of Investigation). the Bundesgrenzschutz (Federal Border Protection), and the Bundesamt für Verfassungsschutz (Federal Office for the Protection of the Constitution). At the state level, there was a Landesamt für Verfassungschutz (State Office for the protection of the Constitution) in each state, as well as the Landespolizei (State Police), supervised by the Interior Minister. The state level institutions were coordinated by the committee of the Interior Ministers of the states, while the federal institutions were coordinated by the Coordinator of Security in the Office of the Chancellor (Sicherheitsbeauftragter im Bundeskanzleramt).[22]

German authorities had some experience with terrorism from the 1970s and 1980s, when the Baader-Meinhof Gang (also known as the Red Army Faction) was responsible for kidnapping and murdering politicians and business leaders. However, the events of 9/11 posed the problem of terrorism on an unprecedented scale. The immediate response involved police raids in Hamburg and other cities where some of the perpetrators and collaborators connected to the September 11 attacks had lived and studied. Thus German authorities could provide useful intelligence about the background and the connections of the terrorists. Beyond these immediate responses, Interior Minister Otto Schily presented legislation meant to facilitate the work of law enforcement authorities in his Security Package I and Security Package II.

b) Conservative critiques of SPD/Greens government

The law enforcement approach of the SPD/Greens government was criticized by conservatives as too soft, and by civil rights lawyers as too authoritarian. The shock effect of 9/11 contributed to the outcome of the state elections in Hamburg (23 September, 2001) when a long period of government by the SPD ended. A right-of-centre government coalition of CDU and FDP also included the PRO (Partei Rechtsstaatliche Offensive), a new law-and-order party which attracted almost 20 per cent of voters due to the reputation of their leader as a tough former judge. Conservative analysts regarded government policies after September 11 as deficient:

> The Red-Green Coalition is adamantly against deploying air-defense units at nuclear power stations. The other taboo is the civil rights of foreigners. Although federal authorities are now entitled to start investigations against associations of foreigners which are pursuing goals directed against international peace and mutual understanding among the peoples, these legal possibilities are a far cry away from realistically tackling the issues connected to the presence of more than 31,000 Muslim extremists living in Germany. So far, the possible expulsion of foreigners living in Germany as followers of fundamentalist organizations that have a hostile attitude against the Western democratic order is out of the question – something that eventually might raise some serious concern among our U.S. allies.[23]

Leading CDU/CSU politicians also criticized the response of the government as insufficient. Edmund Stoiber suggested patrols by the Bundeswehr in the streets as a method of preventing terrorism.[24] Social Democrats and Liberals, on the other hand, insisted on the customary separation between the tasks of police and the military.

c) Security Packages I and II

In comparison to Stoiber's expectations, the SPD/Greens government took a more restrained approach in the two legislative packages proposed by Interior Minister Otto Schily. As part of Security Package I, the Bundestag changed laws pertaining to associations and clubs (Vereinsrecht). These banned 'religious groups... deemed to be extremist'. The laws also introduced a new Section 129b in the anti-terror paragraph of the criminal code, and federal authorities 'toughened air travel and banking security regulations, bolstered security for public buildings... and allowed for access by the police to personal information gathered by government agencies'.

Only a few weeks later, on October 27, 2001, the coalition government endorsed Security Package II (Sicherheitspaket II), which included revisions to laws related to the powers of government agencies in order to more effectively coordinate anti-terror policies.[25] This legislation was criticized by civil liberties lawyers. Martin Kutscha, for example, argued that the legislation hollowed out the 'rule-of-law characteristics of police law', gradually replacing them with 'elements of a state of emergency'. While the perception of a massive threat 'created acceptance', the result according to Kutscha was a 'loss of legally guaranteed restraint of state power'.[26]

Terrorism and its impact on military thinking

a) Reorientation of FRG military since 1991

Due to changes in foreign and security policy throughout the 1990s, Germany was politically ready but did not yet have the military capabilities to play a prominent role in the campaign against terrorism. Germany's military response to September 11 was shaped by earlier adaptations following the historic changes of 1990-1991, which encompassed German reunification, the end of the Warsaw Pact, and the disintegration of the Soviet Union. In this respect, September 11 was an event illustrating the scenarios expected under the post-1991 strategic concepts of NATO, and Chancellor Schröder's statements on the events of September 11 in the Bundestag have repeatedly and explicitly referred to changes since 1990-1991. During the first Gulf War of 1990-91, Germany's role had been limited to financial support. Since then German contributions to U.S. and NATO campaigns have developed beyond money, from logistic backup to the provision of non-combat personnel and, finally, the deployment of combat troops. This gradual 'normalization' of German foreign policy after regaining full sovereignty, and in contrast to the restrictions of 1949 to 1989, required fundamental changes to the 'amilitary' German political culture, and the creation of political and military prerequisites for domestic acceptance of 'out of area' military power projection.

Changes to German foreign and defence policy coincided with a similar reorientation of the entire NATO alliance, characterized by the 'Strategic Concepts' adopted by NATO summits in Rome (1991) and Washington (1999). A parallel development also occurred in European institutions, beginning with the adoption of the 'Petersberg tasks' of 1992 by the WEU, which included peace keeping and peace enforcement into its catalogue of future tasks of European security policy. Thus, both NATO and EU/WEU had conceptually adjusted to the end of the bipolar international system with its well-defined unidirectional threats replaced by a greater variety of multifaceted and multidirectional threats.[27] This adjustment, however, did not necessarily incorporate acceptance of U.S. hegemony in international security affairs. Disagreements over the appropriate strategy for dealing with emergent threats persisted, eventually reaching a peak during the split within NATO over the U.S.-led war in Iraq. This resulted in acrimonious debate between Washington and Berlin that threatened the continued cohesion of the transatlantic alliance.

b) German contributions to NATO 'backfilling'

Yet prior to these events NATO had in fact acted swiftly in response to the threat of terrorism. On September 12, 2001, NATO invoked Article 5 of the Washington Treaty and declared the terrorist acts an attack on a NATO member requiring the support of other members of the alliance. But beyond this expression of political solidarity, NATO structures were not involved in the military intervention in Afghanistan although individual NATO members participated.

A key problem here was that the U.S. made very specific and rather limited demands for NATO contributions. The U.S. was disinclined to prosecute the campaign in Afghanistan under the banner of NATO, yet at the same time Washington hoped 'to make more of Article 5 than a symbolic commitment'. As Philip Gordon notes, in early October the United States 'presented the allies with a request that they take eight specific measures...to support the American campaign'. NATO allies agreed to U.S. requests on October 4. The steps included:

- enhanced intelligence sharing
- blanket overflight clearances
- increased security for U.S. facilities in Europe
- backfilling certain allied assets in the NATO area that might be required elsewhere for the campaign against terrorism
- access for the United States and other allies to ports and airfields on NATO territory
- the deployment of standing NATO naval forces to the Eastern Mediterranean

- the deployment of NATO airborne early warning-and-control systems (AWACS) to U.S. airspace so that American AWACS could be used abroad.[28]

Germany contributed to these 'backfill' measures. At the time initial U.S. requests were 'for rather marginal German military activities – the dispatch of multinational AWACS planes for the control of the continental North American air space was the most conspicuous one'. Even the longer set of requirements listed above 'ultimately still demands rather little of the Bundeswehr. This reflects the fact that the German military has only little to offer in that conflict'.[29]

Germany's military contribution to the campaign against terrorism was smaller than one might have expected after the initial expressions of solidarity by government and parliament. There was, indeed, 'rather less than meets the eye in Germany's posture of forceful support for the American fight against terrorism'.[30] In mid November, the Bundestag contributed 3,900 combat personnel to the actual intervention in Afghanistan. As Germany's Bundeswehr suffers from a shortage of Special Operations Forces, these troops were utilized for back-up operations.

On 21 December, the Bundestag approved a government proposal to send another 1,200 German soldiers to Afghanistan as part of ISAF, the International Security Assistance Force led by Great Britain. These 1,200 peacekeepers were deployed in addition to the 3,900 soldiers committed to the campaign by the decision of 14 November. In line with Germany's emphasis on political solutions, the contribution to ISAF was justified as 'an essential contribution by Germany to the implementation of the national reconciliation process in Afghanistan started in Petersberg opening the road to reconstruction of the country after more than twenty years of war and civil war'.[31]

c) Limits of capabilities

Germany has, a decade after the end of the Cold War, still not developed the military attributes of a 'normal' state in the post-1991 international system. The political normalization of German foreign and security policy may be well advanced but it has not yet been translated into corresponding military capabilities. Indeed, it is widely recognized that 'only the United States (and to a much lesser degree Britain) had the types of forces... that would be useful in the early stages of the campaign.'[32] From the perspective of raw material capabilities then, one should not be surprised that the Bundeswehr was not called upon by the U.S. to undertake a more active role in Afghanistan.

German experts generally agree that Germany lacks the military means to play a major part in a war against terrorism. With domestic political and economic issues still being prioritized by the German government, the Bundeswehr has undergone little enlargement since reunification. Here, Maull argues that 'any significant change in security policy would therefore have to start with the budgetary allocation for the Bundeswehr'. This assessment blamed the present government coalition of SPD and Greens as well as the previous government under Chancellor Kohl (CDU) for this deficiency. On the other hand, a similar attack on the government by CDU defence spokesman Volker Rühe in his platform for the 2002 election campaign neglected the fact that, even before the 1998 change of government, the Bundeswehr budget had been affected by the costs of German unification. The budget discipline connected with the introduction of the common European currency was an important problem in this regard.[33]

The transformation of the Bundeswehr, envisaged by defence planners since 1992 and discussed in official policy reports published in 1998 and 1999, will take ten to fifteen years to be implemented. U.S. analyst Jackson Janes sees the need for the FRG to make significant adjustments, claiming that 'if it wants to graduate to a primary player, it needs to have a primary defense capability. For Germany, that will require a stronger and larger commitment to defense, and possibly the involvement of the KSK Special Force'.[34] Clearly, in late 2001 or even 2002, Germany was not ready for a more significant military role in Afghanistan. If the war against terror broadens to incorporate Germany as a target of al Qaeda and other disaffected groups, it is reasonable to assume that significant domestic pressure will be brought to bear on the government. This will be done either to accelerate the process of normalization in the military sphere, and/or for Germany to play a much more central role in diplomatic efforts, such as coalition-building, to address new areas of threat.

Crisis prevention: Political solutions as condition for German consensus

Germany hosted the UN Talks on Afghanistan, a conference of Afghan politicians (Petersberg, 27 November–5 December 2001) searching for a post-Taliban solution. This conference resulted in the formation of a temporary Afghan government and the deployment of the International Security Assistance Force (ISAF). It also outlined a process leading to a more permanent settlement, including the convocation of a representative through Loya Jirga – a meeting of Afghan elders representing main tribes in order to reach agreement on the future of Afghani politics. Hosting the conference also contributed to the maintenance of consensus in the government coalition since parliamentary support for military action had been conditional upon a concurrent search for political solutions.

In contrast to the Bush administration's focus on military responses to September 11, German politicians demanded that the root causes of terrorism be tackled, such as the Israel-Palestine conflict which, if unresolved, would remain a source of motivation for future terrorists. German criticism of Israeli incursions on Palestinian territory differed from U.S. support for the Sharon government's actions. Government ministers of the centre-left SPD as well as opposition parliamentarians of the centre-right CDU and FDP described the conduct of Israeli troops as shocking. Far from accepting Israeli leader Sharon's argument that he was fighting terrorism in his attacks on Palestinian territory, CDU spokesman Karl Lamers argued that, for the sake of Israel's security, Sharon had to withdraw, claiming: 'This policy of the present Israeli government could lead to a catastrophe, first for Israel, but then for the region and the West'. To underline this, in early April 2002, Germany suspended weapons sales to Israel. This move signalled 'a growing impatience with Israel and an unexpected echo here of widespread European revulsion at current Israeli policy'.[35] Although Edmund Stoiber, then the conservative front-runner to become Germany's next Chancellor, felt European support for Arafat was 'not coordinated with the U.S.' and 'cannot lead to success',[36] criticism of Bush's support for Israeli PM Sharon was shared widely by German politicians from the centre-left and centre-right.

In an indirect response to President Bush's earlier call for a 'crusade' against terrorism, German Foreign Affairs Minister Fischer advocated a dialogue between the West and Islam. Fischer's call for intercultural dialogue intended to prevent an extension of the conflict with one terrorist network and one government harbouring it into a much larger conflict involving Muslims in many countries. Whereas Bush's use of the term 'crusade' could have had the unintended effect of helping Osama Bin Laden to broaden his support base among Muslims, Fischer's approach was meant to contribute to the isolation of the terrorist network or would, at least, not motivate recruits to join al Qaeda. German criticism of Bush's term 'axis of evil', including Iraq, Iran and North Korea, also signalled a reluctance to agree to military action against these countries as part of the campaign against terrorism.

Conclusions

The initial German response to September 11 included military contributions to the U.S. led campaign against terrorism, but placed greater emphasis on law enforcement measures. German leaders were also inclined to prioritize the search for political and economic solutions to regional conflicts. The political response to September 11 also demonstrated the fragility of the SPD/Greens government coalition. At the same time, parliamentary debates and public opinion showed broad majority support for solidarity with the USA and for a German military contribution. Germany was well prepared for a response in terms of law enforcement and domestic intelligence. The institutional framework for police and intelligence was not changed but the restrictions on their actions were eased. There was no need for any new 'Homeland Security Office' although the capabilities of existing institutions were enhanced by legislation (Security Packages I and II).

The reform of the German military was driven by the changes in the security environment at the end of the Cold War. Without the events of 1990-1991 and the subsequent 'normalization' of foreign and security policy, Germany would not have been ready for any military contribution in Afghanistan. The structural reform of the Bundeswehr, building a capability of power projection and crisis intervention, will still be guided by NATO's strategic concept and held back by the limitations of the federal budget. The events of September 11, 2001 increased the operational costs of the Bundeswehr, thereby making allocations for new initiatives even more difficult.

Germany's offer of solidarity with attached qualifications illustrated prevailing attitudes to transatlantic relations. Compared to Britain, Germany made a significantly smaller military contribution. Compared to France, Germany articulated less criticism of U.S. policies. While French foreign minister Hubert Védrine stated that the transformation of the unipolar international system dominated by the USA into a multipolar system was a guiding strategic objective for France, German politicians never expressed this degree of distancing from the United States, even at the height of disputes over U.S. plans to invade Iraq. The combination of solidarity with the USA, cautious criticism of President Bush's rhetoric, and firm desire to avoid the entanglement of Germany in a wider war on terror indicate that German leaders have continued to emphasize 'soft power' as an extension of the approaches pursued during the 1949-89 period, while learning to make use of Germany's new, and still rather limited, military capabilities to participate in long distance crisis intervention.

The U.S.-led war in Iraq further demonstrated Germany's emergence as a 'normal' state, a process it had been undergoing since reunification. German criticisms of Washington's policy were more vociferous than during the intervention to unseat the Taliban in Afghanistan, leading to consternation from Bush administration officials, and speculation that the transatlantic alliance was being jeopardized by the divergent interests (and policy paths) of American and European protagonists in the debate over war. But the key point to note is that Germany played an increasingly independent role, adding weight to the perception that Berlin is gradually gaining both the will and the means to assert itself more overtly in world affairs.

Notes

1   Gordon, P.H., 'NATO after 11 September', *Survival*, vol. 43, no. 4, 2001-2002, pp. 1-18. The quote appears on p. 3.

2   Janes, J., 'Transatlantic Relations', *German Foreign Policy in Dialogue*, Newsletter, Issue 5, 23 November 2001, p. 8.

3   Dinan, D., *Ever Closer Union? An Introduction to the European Community*, 2nd ed, New York, Lynne Reiner, 1999, p. 442.

4   Wijk, R. de, 'The Limits of Military Power', *The Washington Quarterly*, vol. 25, no. 1, 2002, pp. 75-92, p. 81.

5   Harnisch, S. and Brauner, W., 'The German Response to the September 11th Terrorist Attacks: A Shift in the Domestic Political Debate and Party Politics?' *German Foreign Policy in Dialogue*, Newsletter, Issue 5, 23 November, 2001, p. 17.

6   Walt, S.M., 'Beyond Bin Laden: Reshaping U.S. Foreign Policy', *International Security*, vol. 26, no. 3, 2001/02, p. 60.

7   Gordon, P.H., 'NATO after 11 September', p. 7. For Bush's statement see his address to the joint sitting of Congress on September 20, 2001, available at www.whitehouse.gov.

8   Krause, J., 'The Consequences of September 11 2001 for transatlantic relations', *German Foreign Policy in Dialogue*, Newsletter, Issue 5, 23 November, 2001, p. 10.

9   Schmid, J., 'A new vision for Germany', *International Herald Tribune. The IHT Online*, 8 April 2002, pp. 1-2.

10 Maull, H.W., 'The Guns of November? Germany and the Use of Force in the Aftermath of 9/11', *German Foreign Policy in Dialogue*, Newsletter, Issue 5, 23 November, 2001, pp. 13-15.

11 Harnisch and Brauner, 'The German Response', p. 20.

12 Posen, B.R., 'The Struggle against Terrorism: Grand Strategy, Strategy, and Tactics', *International Security*, vol. 26, no. 3, 2001/2002, pp. 39-55 (p. 53).

13 Schmidt, J., 'A New Vision for Germany', p. 2.

14 Harnisch and Brauner, 'The German Response', p. 21.

15 Harnisch and Brauner, 'The German Response', p. 20.

16 Harnisch and Brauner, 'The German Response', pp. 21-22.

17 Hyde-Price, A., 'Of Dragons and Snakes: Contemporary German Security Policy', in Smith, G., Paterson, W.E. and Padgett, S., *Developments in German Politics 2*, Houndsmills, Basingstoke, Macmillan, 1996, p. 178.

18 Maull, H.W., 'The Guns of November', p.14.

19 Posen, B.R. 'The Struggle Against Terrorism', p.43.

20 Janes, J., 'Transatlantic Relations', p. 8.

21 Habermas, J., 'Fundamentalismus und Terror', *Blätter für deutsche und internationale Politik*, vol. 47, no. 2, 2002, p. 172.

22 An interesting comparison of institutions dealing with domestic intelligence and law enforcement is provided in this survey: United States General Accounting Office, 'Combating Terrorism: How Five Countries Are Organized to Combat Terrorism', Report to Congressional Requesters. GAO. Washington D.C., April 2000.

23 Krause, J., 'The Consequences of September 11, 2001 for transatlantic relations', p. 11.

24 Wedemeyer, G., 'Anfällig für Sündenfälle', *Stern*, no. 4, 2002, p. 34.

25 Harnisch and Brauner, p. 16 and p. 18.

26 Kutscha, M., 'Anti-Terror-Paket, Fortsetzungslieferung', *Blätter für deutsche und internationale Politik*, vol. 46, no. 11, 2001, p. 1301.

27 NATO, 'The Alliance's Strategic Concept', Rome, 8 November 1991. http://www.nato.int/docu/basictxt/b911108a.htm.

28 Gordon, P.H., 'NATO after 11 September', p. 5.

29 Krause, J., 'The Consequences of September 11 2001 for transatlantic relations', pp. 10-11.

30 Maull, H.W., 'The Guns of November', p. 14.

31 Deutscher Bundestag. 'Beschluß des Deutschen Bundestages vom 21. Dezember über die Beteiligung bewaffneter deutscher Streitkräfte an dem Einsatz einer Internationalen Sicherheitsunterstützungstruppe', documented in *Blätter für deutsche und internationale Politik*, vol. 47, no. 3, 2002, p. 384.

32 Gordon, P.H., 'NATO after 11 September', p. 5.

33 See Maull, H.W., 'The Guns of November', p. 15; and Rühe, V., 'Zukunft der Bundeswehr-Zehn Thesen', 21 March, 2002. Available at www.cdu.de/ueber-uns/buvo/ruehe/040802bw.pdf.

34 Janes, J, 'Transatlantic Relations', p. 8.

35 Finn, P., 'In Germany, harsh words for Israel', *International Herald Tribune: The IHT Online*, 10 April, 2002, pp. 1-2.

36 Schmid, J., 'A new vision for Germany', p. 2.

Chapter 6

9/11 and Russian Perceptions of Europe and NATO

Alexey D. Muraviev

Introduction

The end of the Cold War dramatically changed the geopolitical situation in Europe at the start of the 1990s. The East-West strategic confrontation was replaced by cautious and slow but steady growth in cooperation between former adversaries. One of the most crucial concerns for Europe was how the former Soviet states, especially Russia, would relate to their Cold War adversary, the North Atlantic Treaty Organization (NATO), which effectively became the centerpiece of the immediate post-Cold War European security system. The importance of NATO's new role meant that East-West security relations in Europe were consequently focused around Russian-NATO dialogue.

The main threat to regional equilibrium, from Russia's perspective, has been NATO's eastward expansion. It was widely perceived in Moscow that NATO's new role was that of Europe's policeman. This seemed to be borne out by NATO actions in Bosnia, Kosovo and Macedonia, and the expansion of the alliance into Central and Eastern Europe. Russian policymakers feared that further enlargement to encompass Russia's traditional sphere of geopolitical influence would re-establish old patterns of confrontation, and would lead to the disappearance of the window of opportunity for integrating Russia into the post-Cold War European security system. Yet despite continuing disagreements, the events of 9/11 united Russia and NATO in the common struggle against international terrorism.

The changes in the nature of Russian-European security relations after 9/11 must be analysed in the broader context of the evolution of Russia-NATO security relations throughout the 1990s. By the end of the Cold War strategic standoff in Europe it seemed that the reasons for the division of Europe into two antagonistic parts had ceased to exist. The Warsaw Pact (WP) had been disbanded, the Berlin Wall had come down, and the Soviet Union had collapsed in December 1991. Newly independent states appeared in the post-Soviet space and in Central and Eastern Europe. But NATO remained, and in fact enlarged itself, starting in 1991 with the addition of a reunified Germany under the NATO banner. Since 1994, when NATO expansion was placed firmly on the U.S. policy agenda by the Clinton administration, Russian analysts articulated the fear that NATO was fixated on expanding its sphere of influence eastwards, rather than seeking to engage in a reorganized European security architecture that would incorporate Russia. The perception that NATO was moving inexorably closer to its borders was highlighted by NATO's new round of expansion in 1999, when it invited three new countries to join: the Czech Republic, Hungary and Poland (the so-called Visegrad Group).

Russia-NATO relations before 9/11: Failure to overcome Cold War legacies

(a) Geo-strategic consequences of NATO's first wave of expansion – Russian perceptions

Russia failed to prevent the first wave of NATO's eastward expansion despite making its displeasure clear on repeated occasions. Analysts within the academic community and the Russian government itself emphasized that the expansion of the alliance contributed little to the European security system. At the same time, liberals in the fledgling Russian democracy worried that expansion would fuel popular mistrust of the West, which would be played on by domestic nationalists and 'red-brown' hardliners. To most observers it was clear that Russia's geopolitical situation was worse than it had been at any time during the Cold War. With the break-up of the WP, the collapse of the Soviet Union, and the withdrawal of Russian troops from Eastern Europe and the Baltic states, Russia's geo-strategic position in Europe had seriously deteriorated, and its military power in the strategically important western direction had been considerably reduced.

It may be argued that with the end of the Cold War, the geo-strategic imperative for admitting new members into the NATO alliance had all but disappeared. This may have been the case for the smaller former Soviet republics and former communist East European states, many of which have sought membership of the alliance. But it was not the case for Russia. Despite progress towards stability and cooperation in Europe, the provisions of the 1949 Washington Treaty outlining the goals of the alliance as a military-political union remained largely unchanged. After the break-up of the USSR, this role of the main potential 'threat' was automatically transferred to Russia – in effect, as John Duffield argued, the former Soviet threat had not vanished but become a 'residual' threat posed by Russia's dwindling (yet still significant) military power.[1]

Russian experts remained concerned about the effects of admitting Poland, the Czech Republic, and Hungary into the alliance, since the move extended the NATO zone of control up to 750 kilometers to the east, thus incorporating part of the European strategic space left in a vacuum after the Warsaw Pact's self-liquidation. Before the expansion, NATO outnumbered the armed forces of the Russian Federation by 2.8:1; incorporating the Visegrad group, the gap had grown to 3.7:1 by 1997 and has continued to grow, thus dramatically shifting the balance of forces in Europe in NATO's favor.[2] According to the Russian military, by 1999 NATO's fighting strength and capability to wage operations in the European strategic military theatre had been exponentially enhanced.[3]

The most damaging military effect of NATO expansion, from the Russian point of view, was the increased capacity of NATO to carry out potential airborne strikes deep into Russian territory.[4] According to assessments made by the Russian General Staff, the inclusion of the Visegrad group enabled the majority of NATO tactical aircraft to reach targets in Russia. This had not been possible during the Cold War, when NATO's borders had been further to the west.[5] In the opinion of General Viktor Barynkin, NATO aircraft were now able to hit targets 'as far deep into the Russian territory as Smolensk, Bryansk and Kursk by taking off from Polish airfields'.[6]

The Russian military regarded Poland's admission into NATO with greater concern than any other new member, partly as a result of historical precedent,[7] but also because Poland was considered (by strategists on both sides of the old Cold War divide) as an ideal base from which to conduct combined land, naval and air operations against European Russia.[8] In addition, it was feared, the use by NATO of strategically positioned Polish naval bases would considerably impair freedom of movement for the Russian Baltic Fleet, as NATO's naval forces would have access to the Polish Gdynia and Hel bases in the Gulf of Danzig (Gdansk). Consequently this could directly impact on the operational capabilities of the Russian Navy based at Baltiysk, also situated at the Gulf of Danzig.[9]

While the admission of the Czech Republic gave NATO a chance to improve its defensive capabilities in the Central European zone, the incorporation of Hungary into NATO also provided the alliance with an opportunity to increase its influence in Southern Europe.[10] The excellent communications radiating from Budapest would permit NATO forces to easily penetrate into Romania in the east. Thus, with or without Romania's future membership, NATO would now be able to project its military power all the way to the shores of the Black Sea.[11]

By using Hungarian territory NATO forces were now also able to access the northern parts of the former Yugoslavia, via the Pannonian Plain that spans the Hungarian-Slovenian border up to Belgrade, about 100 miles south.[12] Hungary's strategic value for the alliance was demonstrated during NATO's air campaign against former Yugoslavia, when flights were mounted from Hungarian southern air bases, including the Pecs air base, which was explored by the U.S. military for possible use as early as 1996.[13]

The improvement of NATO's geo-strategic position in Europe was complemented by qualitative improvements in force capabilities and alliance infrastructure on Europe's north western and south western flanks – in Norway and Turkey – which are NATO member states each sharing borders with Russia. These developments could not have resulted in a passive Russian response since in both cases NATO's qualitative edge and increased activity on Europe's flanks collided overtly with Russia's national interest in securing the post-Soviet geopolitical space.[14]

(b) After the first wave: Russia unconvinced

NATO officials have maintained that there are basically two reasons to expand: to achieve stability in the region, and to bring democracy to new member states. This policy was based on an assessment by NATO historians of a causal link between the formation of NATO and the relative peace and democracy that has prevailed in Western Europe since that time. But NATO was created in 1949 as a military-political organization to defend democracy against communist expansion, not to install the democratic system (as latter-day revisionists would have it). Democracy in Europe was achieved through economic assistance, which stimulated trade and peaceful cooperation. Central and Eastern European nations need not rely on NATO to give them lessons in democracy and stability.[15]

However, the problem is not simply a result of the new security situation. Membership in the alliance by the Czech Republic, Hungary and Poland, and later other Central and Eastern European states (including the three Baltic states) hardly poses an immediate military threat to Russia's security, and NATO's offensive capabilities toward the east can be limited through multilateral agreements and inspections. The main source of concern is elsewhere, concealed in the reasons why NATO expansion was proposed in the first place. Russia's negative reaction to expansion proceeded from the concern that the West had not provided an unambiguous answer to the question: why does NATO need to move closer to Russia? Official statements to the effect that the Eastern and Central European countries would be admitted to safeguard their security were not convincing enough, since it was unclear who threatened these countries – unless it was Russia itself.

While not denying the fact that NATO should occupy an important place in the system of European security, Moscow proceeds from the premise that such a security system must be comprehensive, utilizing the resources of other intergovernmental European security organizations (such as the Organization for Security and Cooperation in Europe, or OSCE) and ensuring the security of all European states, including neutral as well as non-aligned countries.

For Russia, NATO expansion remains a central theme of its foreign policy in relation to Europe. Russia has argued against NATO enlargement, taking the position that NATO is a military-political alliance, which is not truly pan-European, and thus cannot claim to be the main institutional vehicle for European security. Russia regarded expansion as a threat to its security not from the danger of direct military intervention of NATO joint forces against Russia, but from the potential of 'power-pressing' on Russia as a result of NATO's increasing proximity.[16] It was feared in Russia that the geographic relocation of NATO could be used in times of crisis as an instrument with which to influence Russia's political and military decisions.

There was, in fact, a window of opportunity to legitimize Russian participation in an expanded NATO and provide new rationales for deeper cooperation. This was the main purpose of the Founding Act, adopted and approved by NATO and Russia in 1997, and leading to the creation of the Permanent Joint Council (PJC). However, the creation of this institution represented little more than a concession to the Yeltsin administration, rather then a serious attempt to establish a viable and inclusive European security organization. As Oksana Antonenko has argued, 'while the Permanent Joint Council was a place to express disagreements, it could do little to resolve them'.[17] Russia was given a 'voice', but not a 'veto' in the alliance, and thus was in effect still marginalized. In addition to security considerations, NATO enlargement also had ideational consequences for Russia. Since the collapse of the USSR and the demise of communist ideology, internal debates focused upon Russia's future world role and its post-Soviet identity. Liberals called for Russia to be integrated into a wider European community, whereas other, more conservative groups saw Russia as a unique civilization separate *from* the West. Liberals identified Russia as part of the West. Conservatives saw the West still as the 'other', hence fostering a Russian identity that would more likely be hostile to Europe. By moving the alliance eastward during the 1990s NATO was feeding into these internal debates. In a sense, NATO was defining Europe's new borders, leaving Russia on the outside. It is not surprising therefore that the manner in which NATO enlargement proceeded in the first post-Cold War decade was perceived in a negative light and with hostility by both liberals and conservatives in the Russian Federation.

(c)   From hostility to pragmatism: the 'Kosovo syndrome' and Russia's change of heart

NATO's military operation against Serbia, in response to then Serbian President Slobodan Milosevic's ethnic policies in and around Kosovo, had a dramatic impact on Russian attitudes towards the alliance, and resulted in the most dangerous development in East-West relations since the Cold War. Indeed, the Kosovo phenomenon contributed to the consolidation of Russia's anti-NATO stand to a greater extent than the entire vociferous anti-enlargement campaign.[18] However, in June 1999 Moscow contributed to the political settlement designed by NATO, and signaled it would participate in the IFOR troop deployments in Kosovo, perceiving that to take more serious action (other than strongly worded protests) would cut it out of future decisions shaping the Balkans. The surprising subsequent deployment of Russian paratroopers from Bosnia to Pristina airport on 12 June, 1999 led to an escalation of tensions between NATO and Russia that nearly turned into open confrontation. At the time there seemed to be strong evidence that Kosovo would become a long-term irritant, overshadowing any new initiatives aimed at improving the Russian-NATO relationship. A new Cold War seemed to be in the making.

However, contrary to such widespread expectations, the Kosovo syndrome in Russia's negativism towards NATO turned out to be surprisingly short. In 2000 the relationship moved from a total freeze to the normalization of exchanges between Brussels and Moscow.[19] By mid-2001 the NATO-Russia dialogue had practically resumed in full. Both sides re-launched the programme of developing the relationship that was put on hold during NATO's intervention in Kosovo. The tone of Russia's comments on NATO significantly lightened, and meetings between officials and representatives on both sides became more frequent.

One interpretation for Russia's apparent change of heart has focused upon the pragmatic foreign policy approach taken by Russia's President Vladimir Putin. While Russia would certainly have preferred some alternatives to NATO, it has clearly been necessary to act on the basis of existing realities rather then re-entering a period of confrontation, which Russia, in its weakened state, could ill-afford. From first taking office in 2000 Putin's goal had been to consolidate Russia's position as a centre of influence, especially in Europe, in what his administration has stressed is an emerging multipolar world. To achieve this aim Putin has demonstrated an understanding of the importance of integrating Russia into Europe's security and other structures, which has included building stronger links to NATO.

Nevertheless, it is evident that despite significant improvements in the relationship between Russia and NATO in 2001, the post-Cold War attempt to create an effective mechanism for security cooperation in Europe was unsuccessful. As noted above, this was for three primary reasons:

- The failure to provide the established PJC Russia-NATO with a notable role (where the original format 19-plus-1 in reality became 19-*versus*-1).
- NATO's actions in former Yugoslavia.
- The adoption of a new strategic concept by NATO at its 50th anniversary summit in Washington. Russia also maintained its overall negative position in regard to NATO's further eastward expansion.[20]

9/11 and the possibility of change

(a) A renewed strategic partnership?

September 11, 2001 brought with it a shift in the international security environment generally, including a radical shift in East-West relations. This reorientation has had important consequences for Russia's relations with both Europe and the United States. News of the attacks on U.S. cities was met in Russia with a great deal of sympathy and understanding. Indeed, the destructive power of terrorist attacks was something with which the Russians were all too familiar. After major acts of terrorism in the first half of the 1990s, largely associated with the first Chechen war, in 1999 the country was suddenly shaken by the indiscriminate bombings of apartment blocks in Moscow, Volgodonsk and Kaspiysk, causing hundreds of deaths. The media and government sources quickly implicated Chechen insurgents as the most likely culprits. In fact, terrorism and religious extremism were identified as one of the major threats to Russia's security in the twenty first century under the provisions of the Military Doctrine adopted in 1999.[21] The Russian government had also already identified terrorism as a principle threat to global security two years before 9/11.

Nearly 100 Russian nationals died when the towers of the World Trade Centre collapsed. President Putin was the first foreign leader to contact President Bush, promising that Russia would do whatever was necessary to help the United States. On 17 September, Russian Defense Minister Sergei Ivanov discussed possible avenues of cooperation with his American counterpart, Donald Rumsfeld, and U.S. National Security Adviser Condoleeza Rice. The advent in New York and Washington D.C. of a new era of super-terrorism brought swift pledges from Russia of full intelligence cooperation with the U.S. to defeat terrorism.[22] In a show of goodwill and an understanding of U.S. security sensitivities at the time, Russia also cancelled large-scale exercises involving its strategic bomber force in the Far East.

The security structures of the Commonwealth of Independent States (CIS) were mobilized in response to the attacks. On 12 September, members of the CIS Collective Security Treaty (CST) issued a statement condemning the attacks and expressing willingness to cooperate with the United States and other countries in a common struggle against the growing threat of international terrorism.[23]

On 24 September 2001, Putin publicly outlined Russia's position and its involvement in the mounting international campaign against the Taliban and al Qaeda in Afghanistan. Russia's stance also reflected the combined position of other members of the CIS CST. The main provisions of Russia's involvement in the anti-terrorist coalition included:

- A promise of full cooperation in the gathering and sharing of intelligence information.
- Authorisation for American and NATO aircraft to fly over Russian territory in pursuit of 'humanitarian and support missions' in Central Asia.
- An offer of assistance with search-and-rescue missions in Afghanistan, if needed.
- Backing for any decision by Central Asian states to offer air bases and other military infrastructure to support U.S. operations in Afghanistan.
- An offer of military-technical support to the Northern Alliance.[24]

Although Russia was reluctant to commit combat troops to the U.S.-led operation in Afghanistan, it did bolster the strength of its troops in the neighboring former

Soviet republic of Tajikistan.[25] Apart from military supplies to the anti-Taliban coalition, Russia promised significant humanitarian aid to the Afghan population.[26]

A combination of immediate motives and longer-term reasons formed the policy shift that accelerated Russia's rapprochement with the West after 9/11. For the first time since the battles of the Second World War Russia and the Western world were united in a struggle against a common threat. Since the late 1980s, Russia had faced a growing problem of countering the rise of nationalist and extremist movements, mostly Islamic in origin, in the south of the (then) Soviet Union. After the USSR's collapse, Russia was forced to intervene in a number of low-level local and regional conflicts that erupted in the southern periphery of what had recently been Soviet space, in an attempt to halt the spread of Islamic extremism across post-Soviet Eurasia, whilst simultaneously facing the growth of terrorism within its own borders.

Russia has been particularly concerned by the spread of Islamic terror along its southern periphery, and blames the secessionist insurgency in Chechnya on Islamic radicals, some of them allegedly trained, funded, or equipped by Osama bin Laden and the Taliban regime in Afghanistan.[27] Following the overthrow of the Rabbani Government in Afghanistan by the Taliban in the mid-1990s, Russia had stepped up military aid to the Central Asian republics, and was preparing to fight advancing Taliban forces that had clear intentions of invading ex-Soviet Eurasia.[28] At the same time, Russia was one of only a few countries providing the Northern Alliance in Afghanistan with political, military-technical and intelligence support, which was one of the key reasons why the anti-Taliban forces were able to survive and continue their struggle. As early as 2000, Putin had suggested to the U.S. government that a joint Russian/U.S. campaign of air strikes and special forces operations should be employed against the Taliban regime after it had refused to deny sanctuary to bin Laden.[29] A year later, Russia mobilized its regional security organizations in an attempt to foster the struggle against the Taliban and Afghanistan-based terrorist groups.[30] It was in Russia's interests to see the overthrow of the Taliban regime and the destruction of the al Qaeda network in Afghanistan (and elsewhere). The thinking amongst Russian planners was that this would stabilize the military-political situation in the southern periphery of ex-Soviet Eurasia and would be a serious blow to Chechen separatists due to their strong links with both the Taliban and al Qaeda. In this context, a combined Russian/Western effort was regarded as a useful mechanism to legitimize Russia's prolonged campaign in Chechnya, as well as fostering a new spirit of cooperation that would aid Russia's attempts to join the World Trade Organization (WTO) and Europe's economic structures.

In the immediate aftermath of 9/11 the West, and especially the United States, quickly realized that Russian cooperation was of crucial importance in the global anti-terror campaign. The United States needed Russia's assistance more than NATO for Operation Enduring Freedom in Central Asia, due to Russia's geopolitical position in the area and its experience in fighting the *Mujaheddin* and the

Taliban in Afghanistan. As a result of its long standoff against the Taliban, Russia was able to develop a robust intelligence operation in Afghanistan and Central Asia, as well as a powerful military grouping comprising the 201st Division and thousands of border guards stationed in Tajikistan. Russia was in a position to assist the Northern Alliance, and its voice was decisive in allowing American and NATO forces into Central Asia to encircle Afghanistan.

While not committing any ground troops, aircraft or other military assets to Enduring Freedom, Russia played a key role during the U.S.-led military offensive in Afghanistan through direct military aid to the Northern Alliance, and providing the Americans with intelligence and logistical support.[31] Moscow also became actively involved in humanitarian relief operations on the ground by dispatching large personnel contingents from the Ministry of Emergency Situations to Kabul and other major cities.

Following the events of 9/11, Russia-NATO security contacts, which were already improving after Putin's decision to adopt a more pragmatic approach to engagement with the West, received an additional stimulus when the Russia-NATO Permanent Security Council condemned the attacks on the World Trade Centre and Pentagon in a rare joint statement on 13 September 2001. Russia and NATO announced they were 'united in their resolve not to let those responsible for such an inhuman act go unpunished' and agreed to closely cooperate in the field of counter-terrorism.[32] Russia and NATO also intensified consultations on other subjects, such as problems of proliferation of weapons of mass destruction and missile defense, a dialogue initiated by the 3 October 2001 meeting in Brussels between President Putin and NATO's Secretary General Lord George Robertson.[33]

After 9/11, Russia and NATO also began discussions on changes to the basic structure of their relationship to give Russia ground-level participation in formulating common policies on security and defense issues. Russia sought to use the positive developments in the East-West strategic relationship to enhance its involvement in NATO's structures and gain a stronger role in the alliance. Initially, officials in Brussels were cautious about a closer relationship with Moscow and were reluctant to alter the '19+1' mechanism. As one NATO official commented: 'we are interested in any practical and concrete programs, but we feel there is nothing wrong [with the existing partnership]'.[34] This position sparked negative reactions in Moscow,[35] but after an intensive period of meetings and discussions Russia and the NATO Secretariat decided to initiate a new phase in the security relationship.[36] Both parties agreed to form a new joint council, the 'Council of 20', which in comparison to the JPC had legislative rather than mere consultative functions. Russia's new security relationship with NATO was formalized by the Rome Declaration, signed by Putin and Robertson on 28 May 2002. Under the new provisions, Russia was to be treated as an equal member, especially when discussing common problems (for example, joint counter-terrorist or peace-keeping operations). However, Russia was still left without a veto on key matters such as the alliance's decision to expand further eastward. The Rome Declaration further stated that Russian-NATO security cooperation was to focus on the following problems:

- Combating terrorism.
- WMD proliferation.
- Non-strategic missile defense.
- Crisis settlement.
- Cooperation between defense agencies and industries.
- Confidence building measures.
- Arms limitations monitoring.
- Search-and-rescue operations at sea.
- Joint reaction to non-military emergency situations.
- Joint educational programs.[37]

Although the warming relationship between Russia and NATO reinforced discussions about possibilities of eventual Russian membership of the alliance,[38] the idea seems unlikely to be realized in the foreseeable future. One report concluded:

> Privately, there were suggestions that Russia would eventually like to join NATO. While the idea caused a stir of interest in alliance think-tanks, most rejected it. The allies ultimately concluded that even to start a study on Russian membership would be a mistake, for it might lead Moscow to think entry was an eventuality, thereby reducing its incentives to reform and become more transparent.[39]

While increasing cooperation with the U.S. and NATO in efforts to combat terrorism, Russia at the same time has demonstrated that it can cope with this new threat independently of the West through its regional security structures. After September 11, Russia intensified contacts with other members of the CIS CST, and the Shanghai Organization, formed between Russia, China, and post-Soviet states on Russia's southern periphery, partly in order to foster multilateral security dialogue, but also stressing the need for a multipolar (as opposed to the U.S.-dominated unipolar) world order. For a week in April 2002, military and security forces of eight CIS states conducted a large-scale anti-terror exercise codenamed 'South-Antiterror-2002' on the territory of Kyrgyzstan and Tajikistan. The operations of the multi-national forces were coordinated by the new CIS Counter-Terrorist Centre, with its headquarters in Bishkek.[40] On 15 May 2002, during the Moscow summit of defense ministers of the Shanghai Five, it was decided to concentrate future efforts on combating terrorism, separatism and extremism, three major problems that threaten the security of its members.[41] In June 2002, members of the CIS CST staged another large-scale anti-terror exercise in Kyrgyzstan and Kazakhstan codenamed 'Southern Shield of the Commonwealth-2002'. Upon the conclusion of the exercise it was announced that members of the CIS CST would intensify joint efforts to combat regional terrorism and armed extremism, and would develop joint counter-terrorist strategies for the Central Asian theatre.[42] Russian officials used the occasion to reinforce their position that Russia would continue its active involvement in Central Asia, maintain its military presence in the region, and preserve the means and structures to carry out independent security and defense policy, regardless of strengthened ties with the United States and NATO.

(b) The persistent obstacle of expansion

In spite of the obvious breakthrough in relations between Russia and the United States and NATO as a result of 9/11, a number of disagreements have remained. Russia has been especially concerned about U.S. plans to expand its counter-terrorist operations to focus on states as well as non-state actors. Along with France and Germany, Russia played a leading role in European (not to mention global) opposition to Washington's invasion of Iraq. The 10-year economic cooperation plan approved by Russia and Iraq in August 2002, when it was already clear that war was likely, provided a clear indication that Russia had its own strategy, and that Moscow's cooperation with the United States within the framework of the anti-terror coalition was contingent on their interests coinciding. Given that most European nations, including NATO members, opposed military intervention in Iraq, it was not surprising that Russia and Europe found common ground in exercising a united policy.

Unresolved problems have also remained in Russia-Europe/NATO relations. Europe's condemnation of Russia's actions in Chechnya, although not as vehement as before 9/11, remains a sore point. Moscow's assistance to the United States forced Washington to tone down its criticism of Russia's handling of the campaign, but NATO's position remains unchanged: to quote Robertson, the alliance is not prepared to 'turn a blind eye to unacceptable Russian behaviour, in Chechnya or elsewhere'.[43] Yet in October 2002 NATO's response to the ending of the Moscow theatre hostage crisis was mute. Putin ordered the storming of the theatre and the use of poisonous gas, resulting in many deaths among the hostages, as well as the Chechen terrorists.

The most serious test of future security relations between Russia and NATO will be connected with the second wave of the alliance's expansion. Putin's softened rhetoric regarding further NATO expansion was mistakenly interpreted in the West as a fundamental change in Moscow's stand on the matter. However, the Kremlin had clearly identified the conditions underlying Russia's position. During his October 2001 trip to Brussels, Putin stated:

> NATO is transforming. If it takes on a different shade and becomes a political organization, of course, we would reconsider our position with regard to such expansion – so long as we feel involved in the process.[44]

Moscow has argued that even after the establishment of the new framework between Russia and NATO, the alliance has not changed significantly since the Cold War era. Indeed, the format of the new 'Council of 20' leaves Russia with little power to influence key decisions NATO can make in relation to European security. It seems unlikely that the war on terror and the current East-West anti-terrorist alliance will stop or even slow down the process of expansion. As long as the alliance retains a fundamentally military-security character, Russia will feel suspicious about its intentions and actions.[45]

The principal issue now concerns how the reaction to the events of 9/11 and the war in Iraq will affect the tempo of NATO's enlargement. The three Baltic states: Lithuania, Latvia and Estonia, plus Slovakia, Slovenia, Bulgaria, Romania, Macedonia and Albania were all aspirants for the second enlargement round due to be formalized in 2004. At the Prague summit in November 2002, NATO members decided that most of these applicants would be offered membership. The admission of Romania will bring NATO's zone of responsibility to the borders of the two former Soviet states of Ukraine and Moldova.[46] Russia will dislike NATO firmly establishing its presence in the Black Sea region, but it will be even more concerned if future waves of enlargement embrace the Baltic states, complemented by the alliance's increased activity in the Transcaucasus and Central Asia.

Whilst critics of further NATO expansion argue that it is particularly important to take Russia's concerns into consideration after September 11, when Russia's role in the global anti-terrorist campaign is crucial, its supporters argue that NATO's eastward enlargement is even more necessary than ever. Robertson stated at the end of 2001: '...September 11 has reinforced the logic of NATO enlargement. The broad coalition that we need to respond to the scourge of terrorism makes the notion of "ins" and "outs" less and less relevant'.[47] Consequently, the supporters of enlargement argue that the addition of former Soviet Baltic states into NATO's security system will only help to strengthen European security and unite it against a new common enemy, without necessarily endangering Russia's security, or isolating it from the rest of Europe.[48]

Transcaucasus and Central Asia   In the early 1990s, the West's ability to influence developments in the Transcaucasus and Central Asia was limited. NATO's military cooperation with CIS states increased greatly between 1994-97. Bilateral assistance programmes were set up with Caucasian and Central Asian states before the U.S. and NATO's increased interest in the region after September 11.[49] The main instrument that allowed the U.S. and NATO to engage with regional states was the Partnership for Peace (PFP) programme, with other multilateral activities playing only a minor role. While two Caucasian states – Georgia and Azerbaijan – showed increasing commitment to fostering links with NATO, Central Asian states exercised a more cautious approach for fear of repercussions from Moscow.[50]

After 9/11 the situation changed. Prior to the commencement of military operations against the Taliban and al Qaeda forces, U.S. and NATO attention was fixed on Uzbekistan, which played a key support role in the anti-terrorist campaign in Afghanistan.[51] To a lesser extent, the U.S. and its European allies bolstered strategic links with Kyrgyzstan, Tajikistan and Turkmenistan.[52] In early 2002, some reports suggested in the very near future the United States may deploy a significant military contingent to Kazakhstan.[53] The United States and NATO also expanded their defence ties with Azerbaijan, known for its pro-western orientation following domestic resentment of Soviet actions during the conflict with Armenia.[54]

At the same time, Georgia's strategic importance has grown in the eyes of Western political and defense officials. Georgia is among several CIS states that have attempted to broaden military contacts with NATO with the aim of counteracting Russian pressure. Tbilisi has been active in both NATO's PFP programme, and in the GUUAM group, a regional multilateral effort by a number of ex-Soviet republics to establish a security and economic framework independent of Russia.[55] In January 2000, Georgian President Eduard Shevardnadze said he would be applying to join NATO by 2005, which caused a storm in the Russian media at the time, and remains a sensitive topic in relations between the two former Soviet republics.[56] The Georgian government's decision to allow several hundred members of U.S. special forces ('instructors') to train local security forces in March 2002[57] prompted a delayed, but fairly hostile response in Moscow. At the end of July, already strained Russian-Georgian relations were further damaged after a large group of Chechen guerrillas attempted to infiltrate the Russian-Georgian border.[58] Moscow accused Tbilisi of harboring international terrorists and threatened military action.[59]

Russian opinion remains divided on the issue of Western strategic cooperation with CIS states. On the one hand, some Russian observers suggest that the United States now recognizes Russia's right to its traditional dominance on the former Soviet space, but others are wary of an increased U.S. influence in the Transcaucasus and Central Asia, as a consequence of the anti-terrorist campaign in the region. The military campaign in Afghanistan involved the United States and NATO deeply in a region which was previously peripheral to their core interests. Russia's influence with the former Central Asian republics facilitated their decision to allow more intensive cooperation with the U.S. and NATO forces. And while increasing U.S. and NATO involvement in the region presented Russia with a number of near-term strategic benefits, there are fears in Russia that the United States and its European allies, once drawn into ex-Soviet Eurasia, may stay there.

For a number of years, Russians referred to the region as part of Russia's 'near abroad', an area that occupied a special position in the hierarchy of Russian foreign policy priorities. It is still asserted by leading Russian officials that Russia has a distinctive and pre-eminent if not exclusive set of economic and security interests in the region, which other foreign powers should accept. The tendency to see

Western engagement in the region in zero-sum terms, whereby any gains for the United States automatically meant a loss for Russia, has resulted in considerable efforts devoted to blocking or limiting Western political, economic, and military involvement in Central Asia.

The Baltic Republics   As noted throughout this chapter, there remains strong Russian sensitivity to NATO's planned expansion into post-Soviet states, but Russia's opposition to the eventual involvement of the three Baltic states into NATO will be much stronger than in the case of the three ex-WTO members. In addition, the issue is particularly sensitive on the domestic political level, since popular disenchantment with NATO reached a high point once the question of the Baltic states joining the alliance was formally raised in NATO discussions.

Indeed, the most important concern for future Russia-Europe relations is the question of the Baltic states' incorporation into NATO. The states in themselves do not threaten Russia's security. Their desire to become NATO members, however, in the view of Russian experts, will create 'an explosive situation, which will be the inevitable result of attempts to bring NATO military structures close to St. Petersburg and Pskov'.[60] A NATO military force in the Baltic states would be considered by the Russian military a threat to Russia. It would be seen as an aggressive strategic deployment of forces in peacetime with only one purpose – to support future land, air and naval offensive operations against Russia. The membership of the Baltic states will provide NATO with an additional 400 kilometers of border with Russia, with the alliance's zone of responsibility lying just less then 200 km from St. Petersburg.[61] Military experts have estimated that the range of NATO's tactical aircraft will extend as far as the Petrozavodsk-Yaroslavl-Belgorod line if operating from Baltic airfields. Additionally, because Russia considers the region to be of vital importance to its security, it would probably react by military means if foreign forces perceived hostile to Russia were to be stationed in the region.

A separate but related problem concerns Russian access to the Kaliningrad enclave,[62] which has no land routes connecting it to the rest of Russia. Short-term agreements have allowed Russia to transit via Belarus and Lithuania to Kaliningrad, but since much of Russian material crossing this route is of a military nature, Lithuania has raised objections to extending these agreements, whilst attempting to tie any further agreements to its efforts to enter NATO. In this context the geo-strategic reconfiguration of the Baltic Sea maritime theatre may become another cause of concern for Russia.[63] Finally, there are strong tensions between Russia and the Baltic states about the treatment of Russian ethnic minorities.[64] It is feared that Baltic membership in NATO may result in unwelcome changes in Russia's security relations with Europe and the United States, potentially ushering in a new 'Cold Peace'.

Conclusions

One of the most important foreign policy issues in Europe concerns relations with Russia, Europe's largest and geo-strategically most important neighbor. The common interests linking Western Europe with Russia have been highlighted by 9/11. What consequences will September 11 have on Europe-Russia relations and the international system? Immediately after 9/11, European nations and Russia expressed their solidarity with the United States and immediately began to draw up a plan of action to combat terrorism.

Prior to September 11, expanding NATO eastward undermined Russian security in the minds of its policymakers, and threatened to indefinitely divide the European continent. Two factors are essential in this respect. First, the alliance is still often perceived as a challenge to Russia's security interests, even if only a potential one. Second, Moscow seeks to prevent the central security role in Europe from being played by a structure in which Russia does not and cannot play a key role.

The events of 9/11 and the subsequent wars in Afghanistan and Iraq are unlikely to either slow down or speed up the enlargement process significantly. There is no doubt that NATO will use the 'carrot' of membership to enforce its expanding internal security agenda in Central and Eastern Europe. At the same time, the alliance is also finding that Russia is an essential partner in fighting the new security threats of terrorism and disorder. 9/11 brought the liberals and conservatives in Russia together in support of a war on terror that required cooperation with Europe and the U.S., and NATO enlargement was no longer the salient issue. However, if NATO continues to expand to the east and foster links with Transcaucasus and Central Asian states, then Russia's influence in this region will be reduced. And if the West persists in treating Moscow as its main rival in the post-Soviet space, refusing to include it in its security institutions as a full-fledged member, Russia will find itself surrounded by potentially unfriendly states. As a result, Russia's strategic relationship with the West, especially its future engagement with Europe, may undergo significant change. It should be noted though, that in the aftermath of the divisions between parts of Europe and the United States over the war in Iraq, that the future of NATO is once more open to question. This perhaps provides a timely opportunity for serious discussions about the future of Russia within a broader European security architecture.

One alternative is in the elaboration of a unified European security system that would protect the interests of all parties to it. To implement this, it will be necessary for Russia to seek firm guarantees, the aims of which would be to facilitate Russia's rapprochement with NATO, even after the next wave of expansion. Such guarantees might include a promise of non-deployment and storage of nuclear weapons and large stockpiles of conventional armaments on territories of new NATO member states (especially the Baltic states), a pledge that NATO's military infrastructure would not be extended to these territories, and guarantees of Russian participation in NATO's decision-making mechanisms on issues concerning European security. The most desirable outcome of the current changes in the European security landscape would be a fundamental change in the nature of NATO, which would turn it into more of a political club and less of a military-political union, embracing all European nations, including Russia. So far, however, NATO has failed to develop a policy that would enable the alliance to embrace Europe under its security umbrella without isolating Russia. While the establishment of the Russia-NATO Council of 20 creates an opportunity to overcome this deadlock, whether this mechanism will be more effective than the 19+1 formula remains to be seen.

It should also be kept in mind that Putin's Russia in the new millennium differs from Yeltsin's Russia in the 1990s. Given the political disarray of the Yeltsin era, when the country found itself struggling to survive as a united nation, trying to cope with dramatic crises in the economic and military spheres and internal struggles by political elites for domination, it was hard to imagine that Russia could effectively counter the West's policy in Central and Eastern Europe, and the former Soviet space. Russia under President Putin is different. As a strong leader, he was able to unite the nation, calm the internal political situation, and arrest the economic and military decline. Tough actions in Chechnya and strong decisions designed to foster economic recovery have demonstrated Putin's determination to rebuild Russia's great power status. While slowly recreating ties with old Soviet allies and clients in the Asia-Pacific, Middle East and elsewhere, Putin has shown, at the same time, a flexible and pragmatic approach in Russia's relations with Europe and the United States.

Overall, Russia's future strategic relations with Europe will continue to be closely linked to Russian-NATO and Russian-U.S. relations. Matters such as the alliance's future eastward expansion, strategic arms limitation and reduction treaties, and Russia's recognition as a great power and respect for its traditional sphere of influence by Western powers will play a determining role. In particular, the Russian Government has softened, but not dropped, its hostility to NATO's expansion up to Russia's borders, as the prospect draws closer of another group of former WP members and even former Soviet republics (the Baltics) joining the alliance. The degree of Russia's future involvement in and commitment to any anti-terror coalition will also depend on the above-mentioned factors, in addition to future international initiatives by the United States and its allies. While the military campaign against Iraq seemed initially to result in a major revision by Moscow of its involvement in the global war on terror, statements by the Russian government soon after the fall of the Saddam regime have stressed that the Iraq issue has not altered the Kremlin's long-term policy of engagement with the U.S.

The realities of a new European security are finally taking shape, unifying the continent and hopefully bringing stability and peace. The Russian dimension remains, nevertheless, problematic. Russia has supported U.S. and NATO policies and actions in the fight against terrorism in areas where it did not have significant national interests at stake. Russia-Europe and Russia-U.S. relations have improved since 9/11, but there is a chance that they may deteriorate if (and when) NATO expands further eastward. In the current climate it is important to exploit the positive momentum in Europe-Russia relations and develop a comprehensive security system that would embrace and benefit all nations from Gibraltar to the Ural Mountains.

Notes

[1]   Duffield, J.S., 'NATO's Functions After the Cold War', *Political Science Quarterly*, vol. 109, no. 5, 1994-95, pp. 763-787. The quote appears on p. 766.

[2]   Nelan, B.W., 'Present Danger', *Time*, 7 April 1997, p. 49.

[3]   With the admission of Poland, the Czech Republic and Hungary the alliance's combined force was reinforced with 11 divisions and 38 brigades; the total pool of main battle tanks grew by 24 per cent, armored vehicles by 22 per cent, artillery systems by 18 per cent, combat fixed wing aircraft by 17 per cent and combat helicopters by 13 per cent. The Russian side also underlines that NATO command has received more than 100 stationary surface-to-air missiles (SAMs), a network of 290 airfields of different classes, highways (over 280,000 km), railways (over 44,000 km), pipelines (over 5200 km), up to 550 warehouses with weapons and hardware, fuel and lubricants and other material-technical suppliers, and 33 testing ranges which will considerably increase the operational scale of the European strategic theatre and give NATO a possibility to quickly deploy its troops there (in expert opinion, within 30 days). See Ivashov, L., 'Europe Needs a New Security System', *Military News Bulletin*, vol. 2, February 1997; Israelyan, V., 'Russia at the Crossroads: Don't Tease a Wounded Bear', *Washington Quarterly*, vol. 21, no. 1, 1998, pp. 53-54; and Pishchev, N., 'NATO: Myths and Reality', *Krasnaya Zvezda*, 4 January, 1997.

[4]   Russian military experts think that the initiation of hostilities by using solely air forces is most likely. See Prudnikov, V., 'Mains Lines of Air Defence Development in Russia', *Military Parade*, July-August, 1996.

[5]   Pishchev, N., 'NATO: Myths and Reality'.

[6]   Barynkin, V., 'Russia's Stand on Plans for Enlargement of NATO', *Military News Bulletin*, vol. 5, May, 1996.

[7]   The armies of Napoleonic France and Nazi Germany invaded Russia via Poland in 1812 and 1941 respectively, and, during World War I, in 1915 German forces started a major offensive campaign against Russia near Gorlice (southern Poland) which led to disastrous consequences.

[8]   Like the rest of the Central European countries, Poland has a well developed system of communications, in particular an extensive railway network. In general, its geographic advantages and well-developed communications make Poland an ideal place for the concentration of large groups of troops; extensive plains give enough space for maneuver, and large forest areas allow the concentration and movement of troops in secrecy.

[9]   Due to Poland's relatively significant navy, Russians expect an increase of NATO's joint naval forces in the Baltic Sea by 18 per cent by including Polish warships, and by 50 per cent regarding naval aviation. 'Contrary to Common Sense', *Military News Bulletin*, vol. 1, January, 1997.

[10]   Hungary's distinctive geopolitical position, as a basically flat country the borders of which lie along hilly or low mountain regions of branches of the Alps and the

Carpathians, and along the Danube and its tributary, the Drava, has made it pivotal in terms of transportation. The country stands at the crossroads of Central Europe, the Balkans, and the Near East, and controls the lines of communications in all of these strategic directions.

[11] France is pushing for membership for Romania. According to former French Defence Minister Charles Millon, 'Romania lies in a leading geostrategic position for the alliance'. See his article in *Jane's Defence Weekly*, 11 June, 1997, p. 112.

[12] In fact, this is the only easy way into the expanse of the former Yugoslavia, because the border with Bulgaria is mountainous, the Adriatic coast is rugged, and most of the former Yugoslavian territory is well protected by the extensive mountain core.

[13] 'U.S. Plans Military Base in Hungary', *The Times*, 3 July, 1996. Pecs is one of Hungary's largest air bases, and there is little doubt why the Americans were interested primarily in its facilities.

[14] When Norway joined the alliance, it did not allow any NATO military exercises or troop deployments in the north of the country near the Russian border. In the 1990s the situation changed. Norway is still considered in NATO as a bridgehead for intelligence gathering operations against Russia. Furthermore, the country has revised its defense strategy by shifting the emphasis from protecting both northern and southern frontier approaches to defending only the northern zone. While reducing the number of its military units and personnel, since 1992 the Norwegian army began its largest modernization of land forces. This modernization will significantly improve the combat efficiency of the Norwegian Army, raising concern in Russia due to Norway's geographic proximity to Russia's strategically important Kola Peninsula in the country's north. NATO's unprecedented naval activity in the Black Sea is regarded by Russia as another factor damaging the nation's security, apart from NATO's expansion. The southwestern flank has always been of great concern to Russian strategists and military planners due to its crucial significance in defense strategy of the mainland, plus its growing economic importance. Besides NATO's growing presence in the Black Sea, Russia is also concerned about the growth of Turkey's military power. Since 1992, the Turkish Armed Forces have been carrying out a major reorganization, which has already transformed it into one of the largest and most powerful forces in Europe, the Transcaucasus and the Middle East.

[15] The fear of a resurgent and expansionist Russia is the strongest motive for Central and Eastern European applications for NATO membership rather than any expected gains in democracy and stability. In spite of proclamations of friendly relations, Russia is still regarded with suspicion. Consequently, while Central and Eastern Europeans together with NATO initiated the enlargement based on what was initially only a perceived threat, Russia responds to the alliance's eastward expansion as a hostile act.

[16] Makarenko, B. (Deputy Director of the Centre of Political Technologies), in 'Where Does the Potential Threat to Russia Come From: The West or the South?', *Moskovskiy Komsomolets*, 15 October, 1996.

[17] Antonenko, O., 'Russia, NATO and European Security After Kosovo', *Survival*, vol. 41, no. 4, 1999-2000, pp. 124-144, p. 130.

[18] Antonenko, O., 'Russia, NATO and European Security After Kosovo', pp. 130-31.

[19] In particular, the *Kursk* submarine tragedy provided an additional forum for the resumption of high-level discussions between Russian and NATO military officials.

20   While meeting his Spanish counterpart on 19 June 2001, Russia's Chief of General Staff General Anatoliy Kvashnin, reinforced Russia's views that since NATO has declared Russia its partner, not an enemy, the need for any further enlargement is no longer in demand. 'Protivniki ili Partnery' [Enemies or Partners?], *Nezavisimoe Voennoe Obozrenie*, no. 22, 2001, p. 1.

21   While officially the 1999 Military Doctrine is considered a revised edition of the initial 1993 edition, it is in fact a conceptually new document.

22   'Moskva Gotova Delitsya Informatiei s Vashingtonom' [Moscow is Ready to Share Information with Washington], *Krasnaya Zvezda*, 19 September, 2001, p. 1.

23   'Ekho Tragedii' [Echo of the Tragedy], *Krasnaya Zvezda*, 15 September, 2001, p. 3. In 1992, members of the CIS (Armenia, Belarus, Kazakhstan, Kyrgyzstan, Russia and Tajikistan) decided to form a joint defense alliance and signed a Collective Security Treaty in Tashkent.

24   See Putin's official statement in *Krasnaya Zvezda*, 26 September 2001, p. 1.

25   Soon after September 11 attacks, the Russian 201st Motor Rifle Division stationed in Tajikistan was reinforced with some 1,500 personnel. See Golts, A. and Novichkov, N., 'Putin Outlines Cooperation', *Jane's Defence Weekly*, 10 October, 2001, p. 3.

26   In 2001, the Russian Government allocated 102.5 million rubles to support humanitarian assistance to Afghanistan. 'Rossiya Pomozhet Naseleniu Afganistana' [Russia Will Help People of Afghanistan], *Krasnaya Zvezda*, 5 October, 2001, p. 1.

27   Some reports suggest that in 2000 as many as 2,500 Chechen guerrillas were undergoing combat training and were fighting in Afghanistan under Taliban control. See Davis, T., 'Putting Pressure on Kabul', *Jane's Defence Weekly*, 20 December, 2000, p. 17.

28   Russian border guards stationed in Tajikistan were engaged in routine encounters with Talibs and their agents who tried to smuggle narcotics and weapons through the Afghani-Tajik border in Central Asia, Russia and Europe.

29   Davis, 'Putting Pressure on Kabul', p. 17.

30   For example, on 5 January 2001, leaders of four Central Asian nations met in Almaty (Kazakhstan) to discuss joint efforts to combat terrorism in the region and expansion of Talibs in Central Asia. On 19 April 2001, members of the regional security organization, known as Shanghai Five – Russia, China, Kazakhstan, Kyrgyzstan and Tajikistan – met in Bishkek (Kyrgyzstan) to discuss similar matters. Both meetings were supervised by Russia's senior officials. See Davis, A., 'Afghanistan Top of Central Asia Security Agenda', *Jane's Defence Weekly*, 17 January 2001, p. 16; and also his, 'Shanghai Five Step Up War on Terrorists', *Jane's Defence Weekly*, 2 May, 2001, p. 17.

31   In 2001, the overall volume of Russian armaments supplies to the Northern Alliance amounted approximately $U.S. 30-45 million. See Novichkov, N., 'Putin Pledges to Supply Equipment to UF', *Jane's Defence Weekly*, 24 October, 2001, p. 5.

32   Bennet, C., 'Aiding America', *NATO Review*, Winter, 2001-2002, p. 6.

33   'An Attack on Us All: NATO's Response to Terrorism', *Military Technology*, vol. 25, no. 11, 2001, pp. 5-16.

34   Hill, L., 'NATO Responds, Rivalries Remain', *Jane's Defence Weekly*, 17 October 2001, p. 4.

35   'New Russia-NATO Relationship off to Rocky Start', *Jane's Defence Weekly*, 2 January, 2002, p. 2.

36   Hill, L., 'War on Terrorism Spur Closer NATO-Russia Ties', *Jane's Defence Weekly*, 12 December, 2001, p. 2.

37   See the special report of the Russia-NATO working group in *Nezavisimoe Voennoe Obozrenie*, No 13, 2002, pp. 4-5; 'Rossiya-NATO: Novy Format' [Russia-NATO: New Format], *Krasnaya Zvezda*, 15 May, 2002, p. 1; Korotchenko, I., 'Putin Dazhe ne Vspomnil o Rasshirenii NATO' [Putin Didn't Even Remember About NATO's Expansion], *Nezavisimoe Voennoe Obozrenie*, no. 17, 2002, p. 1; Galeotti, M., 'The View From the Kremlin', *Jane's Intelligence Review*, vol. 14, no. 7, July, 2002, p. 16.

38   While the idea still meets strong opposition, particularly from the Central and Eastern Europe members and potential candidates for admission (whose desire to join the alliance was largely driven by the so-called 'Russian threat'), it finds growing support in the western community. For example, see the discussion with James A. Baker III in, 'Russia in NATO?', *The Washington Quarterly*, vol. 25, no. 1, 2002, pp. 95-103.

39   Hill, L. and Golts, A., 'NATO Fails to Warm Putin', 7 November, 2001, p. 21.

40   Streshnev, R., 'Sovmestno Protiv Obshchei Ugrogy' [Together Against Common Threat], *Krasnaya Zvezda*, 19 April, 2002, p. 3.

41   'Ukreplaya Bezopasnost v Azii' [By Strengthening Security in Asia', *Krasnaya Zvezda*, 16 May, 2002, p. 1.

42   Streshnev, R. and Zhagiparov, S., 'Shchit Sotruzhestva Derzhit Udar' [Shield of the Commonwealth Holds the Strike], *Krasnaya Zvezda*, 18 June, 2002, p. 1.

43   'An Attack on Us All: NATO's Response to Terrorism', p. 16.

44   Lake, 'Putin Outlines Cooperation', p. 3.

45   Russia's decision not to attend NATO's November meeting in Prague demonstrated that Russia continued to oppose enlargement.

46   Luke Hill, 'NATO Set for "Big Bang"', *Jane's Defence Weekly*, 17 April, 2002, p. 21.

47   'An Attack on Us All: NATO's Response to Terrorism', p. 15.

48   Gordon, P.H., 'NATO After 11 September', *Survival*, vol. 43, no. 4, 2002, pp 1-18.

49   Toward the end of the 1990s, NATO began reassessing its strategic policy toward the Transcaucasus and Central Asia and expressed desire to be more actively involved in regional affairs. See the brief article of then NATO Secretary General Javier Solana's visit to Central Asia in March 1997 in *NATO Review*, no. 3, May-June, 1997, p. 15. Also see de Witte, P., 'Fostering Stability and Security in the Southern Caucuses', *NATO Review*, no. 1, Spring, 1999, pp. 14-16.

50   For more discussion about NATO's involvement in the region see Bhatty, R. and Bronson, R., 'NATO's Mixed Signals in the Caucasus and Central Asia', *Survival*, vol. 42, no. 3, 2000, pp. 129-145.

51   Davis, A., 'Uzbekistan Emerges as Key to Allied Effort', *Jane's Defence Weekly*, 10 October, 2001, p. 3.

52   American and NATO limited military contingents were deployed so far to five Central Asian air bases: Manas (Bishkek) in Kyrgysztan, Karshi, Kulyab (Tajikistan), Koraidy, and Termes in Uzbekistan. Initially, intended for use as logistic support bases, some of the above-mentioned facilities are being converted into strike bases with the deployment of tactical combat aircraft. See Khodarenok, M., 'Ozherelie iz Amerikanskikh Baz' [A Necklace Out of American Bases], *Nezavisimoe Voennoe Obozrenie*, no. 10, 2002, p. 4.

53   In particular, the U.S. may deploy a 5,000-strong infantry brigade to the Karaganda region and gain access to major air bases in Chimkent and Lugovoi.

See Khodarenok, M., 'Amerikanskiy Desant v Kazakhstane' [American Landing Party in Kazakhstan], *Nezavisimoe Voennoe Obozrenie*, no. 11, 2002, p. 3.

54

'Pomoshch SSHA' [America's Help], *Nezavisimoe Voennoe Obozrenie*, no. 11, 2002, p. 3.

55

GUUAM comprises Georgia, Ukraine, Uzbekistan, Azerbaijan, and Moldova.

56

A possibility that NATO may establish a permanent presence in the former Transcaucasus remains a nightmare scenario for Russia's political and military leadership.

57

'Amerikanstsy v Gruzii' [Americans Are in Georgia], *Nezavisimoe Voennoe Obozrenie*, no. 7, 2002, p. 1.

58

On 27 July around 60 armed Chechens attempted to enter Chechnya via the Russian-Georgian border but were surrounded by Russian border guards and paratroopers. After several days of heavy fighting the insurgent group was destroyed. 'Itum-Kalinskiy Proryv' [Insurgency Near Itum-Kali], *Nezavisimoe Voennoe Obozrenie*, no. 26, 2002, p. 2.

59

Russian officials claim that the area of Pankissa Valley near Russian border was effectively transformed by Chechen rebels into a training and recreation base. Sergei Ivanov in particular argued in favor of a Russian preventive military operation against Chechen rebel forces based in Pankissa. See Soloviev, V., 'Po Stsenariu Chechenskikh Boevikov' [According to Chechen Guerrillas Scenario], *Nezavisimoe Voennoe Obozrenie*, no. 26, 2002, p. 1.

60

Hill, 'NATO Set for "Big Bang"', p. 21.

61

Hill, 'NATO Set for "Big Bang"', p. 21.

62

For detailed discussions about the Kaliningrad problem see Galeotti, M., 'Kaliningrad at the Crossroads', *Jane's Intelligence Review*, vol. 14, no. 9, 2002, pp. 50-51.

63

The independence of the Baltic states does substantially reduce the naval facilities available to Russia in case of war. The ports in the St. Petersburg area are limited and vulnerable to blockade by an enemy power. Kaliningrad is also isolated and possibly not supportable in wartime from Russia proper. With a port easily subjected to enemy blockade, Kaliningrad is not seen by the Russian military as significantly adding to Russia's naval capacity in the Baltic Sea. In case of war Russia would need the ports of the Baltic states – if for no reason other than to deny their use to an enemy power.

64

Kuzio, T., 'NATO and the Baltic States', *Jane's Intelligence Review*, vol. 12, no. 11, 2000, p. 17.

Chapter 7

New Lines in the Sand: 9/11 and Implications for British Policy in the Middle East

Peter Hinchcliffe

Introduction

Live television coverage ensured that few people escaped the immediate impact of the devastating attacks of 9/11 on the United States. Americans experienced a direct sense of terrifying vulnerability (although several hundred non-U.S. citizens died in the World Trade Centre), yet the shock waves were felt worldwide; in the United Kingdom (U.K.) as much as anywhere. Of those killed fully one hundred were British, and the media reaction in the U.K. reflected much of the sensational comment elsewhere in the world. The instant judgment on the terrorist attacks was that 'it changed everything'.[1] The twentieth-century tradition of nation states in conflict had been, at a stroke, transformed into the twenty-first-century prospect of a new world disorder – with the evil forces of fanatical trans-national terrorism challenging the established basis of civilized society on an unprecedented scale. In this instance, the shadowy network of al Qaeda, controlled by Osama bin Laden, represented the major challenge to the West (as represented principally by the United States of America), enshrining both 'civilized values' and 'democratic traditions'. As a fundamental part of the 'West', and as one America's closest allies, this would have appeared to apply to the U.K. more keenly than to most other nation states.

The 'Islamic connection' assumed from the outset also resonated strongly in the U.K., with its historical connections with the Islamic world, now accentuated by the presence of a large resident British Muslim community, mostly from the Indian sub-continent.[2] The U.K. may have shed an empire throughout the last half of the twentieth century, but there remains, amongst the professional classes at least, an intense and (unlike in the U.S.)[3] generally well-informed interest in international affairs.[4] In the narrower field of engagement with the Islamic world, historical links with the Middle East, in particular, are reflected by the expertise on this region within the British Diplomatic Service. Only the U.K. and France, amongst Western countries, routinely appoint diplomatic heads of mission in the Arab world from a cadre of Middle Eastern Arabic speaking specialists. And it is worth recalling that Britain and France between them, as part of the colonial carve up of the Middle East in the immediate aftermath of the First World War, created most of the now independent Arab states. Moreover, the foundation of Israel and the consequent misfortunes of the Palestinians were consequences of Britain's inability to manage those responsibilities that it awarded itself under the terms of the League of Nations Mandate for Palestine. This was a blatantly neo-colonial device, which enshrined the provisions of the 1917 Balfour Declaration promising British support for a Jewish national home in Palestine.[5] It is clear then that political elites and the diplomatic corps in the U.K. would have a strong interest and stake in the American response to 9/11, and any subsequent initiatives for dealing with the wider Middle East problems. This was especially true in relation to the key questions of Palestine and the Arab-Israeli dispute. Given British history and interests in the Middle East, the fact that many British citizens perished during the 9/11 attacks, and given Britain's very close relationship with Washington, the U.K. was certain to play a major part in the war on terror. This was reflected in the pro-active diplomacy of British Prime Minister Tony Blair immediately after 9/11.

The 'War on Terror': U.K. dimensions

Since 9/11 public interest in the U.K. has focused on the 'war against terrorism'. Prime Minister Tony Blair's immediate and high profile political support for the United States, and subsequently for British military involvement in the war against the Taliban in Afghanistan caught the public mood. Blair's international travels in support of U.S.-led efforts to encourage the formation of a coalition of like-minded states to combat the new threat dominated the national agenda throughout the autumn of 2001. Inevitably there was some domestic opposition to Blair's peregrinations from those who felt that he should concentrate on important domestic problems such as health, transport and education, rather than posturing on the world stage. Such critics tended to brand Blair as an errand boy for President Bush, rather than a statesman espousing an independent British foreign policy that reflected the real interests of the United Kingdom. Public interest was rekindled by the dispatch in March, 2002 of 1,700 British combat troops to Afghanistan to reinforce U.S. forces hunting the remnants of the Taliban and al Qaeda followers in remote mountainous areas.[6] Some twelve months later the Bali terrorist bombings in October 2002 (in which 30 young Britons died), reminded the British public that international terrorism was still a force to be reckoned with.

Popular focus is not confined to events overseas, and the threat from 'the enemy within' has caused domestic concern. British Muslims, perhaps a few hundred, are known to have fought with the Taliban in Afghanistan. At least six were captured and imprisoned by the Americans in 'Camp X-Ray' at Guantanamo Bay, an American base in the southeast of Cuba. There is evidence of a U.K. connection with some of the perpetuators of the hijackings in September. A Briton, Richard Reid, a Moslem convert of Caribbean descent was foiled in an attempt to blow up an American Airways plane out of Paris on 22 December 2001, using explosives concealed in his shoe. He admitted to being an al Qaeda operative. About 100 arrests were made in police raids on suspected terrorist cells, and although most of those arrested were subsequently released for lack of evidence the police have been quoted as saying that there are about 200 al Qaeda 'elements' in Britain.[7] Popular suspicions of terrorist activities by British Muslims, or sympathies for their cause, sparked off episodes of 'Islamaphobia', some involving verbal abuse and physical assaults on members of the Asian community. Several tabloids called for British Muslims to put loyalties to their country before any commitment to Islam, or risk being branded as traitors. British citizens of Asian background seen at anti-war demonstrations, as the campaign against the Taliban got underway, fuelled such sentiments. Ironically, in most cases the majority of anti-war demonstrators were white and middle class professionals. Many of these demonstrators were drawn from those causes dear to the 'New Left' such as anti-globalization and radical 'Green' politics. Nor were the demonstrations themselves particularly well supported, and they soon subsided as military action became both inevitable and very quickly successful. But worries remained about the attitudes (and therefore the loyalties) of many members of this, the biggest ethnic minority in Britain and how anti-government sentiments could be aroused by any future involvement by the U.K. in military action against another Muslim country. These worries appeared to be warranted leading up to the war on Iraq in 2003, with Muslim communities openly opposing any British involvement. Indeed a large anti-war-in-Iraq demonstration, involving over a quarter of a million people, took place in London in October 2002. A large Jewish pro-Israeli rally in early May 2002 also demonstrated that the views of the U.K.'s 300,000 or so Jews must be considered when formulating the U.K.'s Middle East policy. The mass rallies in many British cities opposing war on Iraq was not, however, a reflection of local Muslim anti-Western rage, but rather perhaps an example of a multicultural society participating in the democratic process to articulate its views. In the end, as with the war on the Taliban, so with the war on Iraq, the conflict was quickly won by the U.S.-led coalition, in which Britain played the important second-lead role. Although a number of radical Islamists and al Qaeda operatives were still known to be resident in the U.K., the war on Iraq did not result in a mass outpouring of anti-government sentiment among British Muslims as the terrorists might have hoped. Indeed, many Iraqi exiles in the U.K. rejoiced at the ouster of Saddam Hussein's totalitarian regime.

Developments since 11 September: Afghanistan and the Middle East peace process

Before looking at British interests in the Middle East, we need first to put them into the context of not just what happened in the U.S. on 9/11, but what has occurred since. A crucial factor remains the mood in Washington. As *The Economist* in its edition '*Six Months On*' put it: 'Since September, Americans have thought differently about their vulnerability, their power and the need to use that power in faraway places in order to feel safe at home. Because America has changed, the world has changed too'.[8] The greatest change with major implications for all nations' policies is the new feeling of confidence and almost triumphalism in Washington, springing from the success of the initial stages of the 'war against terrorism' and the war on Iraq. Despite other terrorist attacks since 9/11, such as those in Bali, Riyadh and Casablanca, this mood of confidence is still palpable.

Some degree of self-congratulation is in fact not out of place. The U.S.'s rapid removal of the Taliban regime from Afghanistan with negligible loss of American lives was a remarkable achievement. This was achieved despite concern that the U.S. and its allies could, like the Russians before them, be sucked into a long, bloody and eventually futile campaign in which victory was impossible (the proverbial 'quagmire'). It is probable that a low intensity guerrilla war against elusive opposition will continue in the more remote mountain fortresses of Afghanistan. But with the ejection of the previous regime and the installation of a new broadly based interim government, the main task was achieved. Osama bin Laden also lost out on a wider front. Despite his appeals, there were no uprisings against moderate Muslim regimes with close links to the West, stigmatized as being part of a 'Zionist-Crusader alliance'. The *Jihad* (loosely: 'holy war') never materialized. The anti-Western demonstrations in a number of Muslim countries were less in both quantity and qualitative fervor than bin Laden must have hoped. In general, official as well as popular criticism was more muted than many Western commentators expected, and this was noted in Washington.

Success on the Afghan front emboldened President Bush to widen his campaign. The 'axis of evil' reference to Iraq, Iran and North Korea in his State of the Union address jarred many ears, and was widely ridiculed for its jingoistic presentation. But this was not just chest thumping. Rather, it contained a serious message. The epithet: 'Axis of Evil', reminiscent of President Reagan's memorable description of the former Soviet Union as an 'Evil Empire', together with deliberate leaks of a U.S. Pentagon hit list of nuclear targets in a number of 'rogue', or potentially rogue states[9] signaled Washington's determination to deal harshly with any government that it believed presented a serious threat to its security. This could either be by overt or covert support for organizations such as al Qaeda. Or it could be by being in possession of weapons of mass destruction (WMD), which, because of the nature of the regimes in question, could find their way, deliberately or negligently, into the hands of terrorists in the mould of Osama bin Laden. As President Bush made clear on 11 March 2002, the war would not be over when the terrorist networks were 'disrupted, scattered and discredited' but when the sources of the weapons of mass destruction they were seeking to obtain had been removed as well. The war against Iraq was justified in these terms.

Washington's language was consistently stark and uncompromising. 'You are either with us or against us' has been the message to the international community since 11 September.[10] Friendly governments will be assisted. Soon after 9/11 U.S. military personnel were helping to battle home grown terrorists in the Dominican Republic, Georgia, Indonesia (where the October 2002 massacre of Western tourists in Bali lent a new sense of urgency) and the Philippines; with similar involvement in the Yemen and Pakistan. The U.S. government was also (initially at least) anxious to build and maintain a long-term international alliance against terrorism. Once the Taliban had been routed, the Iraqi President Saddam Hussein, and his regime, was framed in policy circles and the media as the next primary target on the U.S. list of 'rogue states'. President Clinton's policy of containing Iraq was replaced with one of active and aggressive confrontation. And much as the U.S. would like to carry a respectable body of international support with them, especially in the Islamic world, the bottom line appears to be that if their traditional friends cannot or will not help them (or if the UN is unwilling or unable),[11] they will do the job themselves. And given the mood in Washington it was clearly unwise to assume that the Americans were bluffing. The carnage in Palestine and slaughter in Bali complicated the equation, but these only temporarily put Iraq into the background.

A significant casualty of the 9/11 attacks and the subsequent U.S. response was what then remained of the Middle East peace process (MEPP). By September 2001 the second Palestinian uprising or *Intifada* was into its second year. Palestinian violent resistance to the continued occupation of the West Bank, and the hopeless stalemate in the MEPP was met by increasingly aggressive Israeli military actions that led to unprecedented (and mostly civilian) casualties. Palestinian suicide bombers were becoming a familiar phenomenon, inflicting horrific carnage – acts that inevitably led to instant military retaliation.

After 9/11 the Israeli government, sensing a major tactical advantage, was quick to align Israel with the U.S. in the war against terrorism, categorizing Palestinian attacks as being on a par with those carried out by al Qaeda. Israel, and the powerful Israeli lobby in the U.S., enthusiastically embraced and endorsed a simplistic view prevalent mostly on the American (and Israeli) Right that indiscriminately lumped together all kinds of dissident elements, mostly with Islamic connections, and for the main part, Arabs. As Camille Mansour has put it 'Sharon immediately concluded that the new situation allowed him to claim that he was in the front line against terrorism. He now had *carte blanche* to set the rules of the game in the Palestinian-Israeli sphere...while loudly proclaiming that Arafat was Israel's bin Laden'.[12]

The most striking manifestation of Prime Minister Sharon's post-9/11 policy was his efforts to marginalize Chairman Arafat and to degrade his security apparatus. Later he tried to drive him into exile. From December until early May 2002 Israeli tanks besieged Arafat, confining him to his office complex in Ramallah. Punitive air strikes targeted his security forces and destroyed much of the Palestinian Authority's infrastructure. At the same time the Israelis demanded that the neutered Palestinian authorities rein in radical elements like Hamas and Islamic Jihad, whose leaders and lesser Palestinian militant luminaries became prime targets for Israeli assassination attacks. In pursuing these tough tactics Ariel Sharon appeared to be acting with U.S. acquiescence, if not active support. On the Palestinian side suicide attacks deep into Israel, and guerrilla raids on Jewish settlements and military outposts became (by March 2002) a daily feature. Eventually Israeli retaliation took the form of attacks on Arafat's headquarters and he was officially categorized as an 'enemy'. In a major military operation in April 2002 the Israeli army reoccupied the main PA controlled population centers on the West Bank, with Jenin's refugee camp being savagely assaulted in an Israeli search and destroy operation with scores killed and hundreds wounded, with the loss of 23 Israeli soldiers. Civilian casualties on both sides mounted steadily, and the situation in many Palestinian towns amounted to a state of war.[13]

This conflagration, covered on prime time television forced a reluctant U.S. diplomatic intervention in the form of Colin Powell, the U.S. Secretary of State. This high profile regional swing was a watershed for the Bush administration with regard to the Palestinian/Israeli conflict. President Clinton was personally heavily involved in attempted peace making right up to the end of his term of office. The Bush administration's approach was markedly different. Seeing no advantage in U.S. entanglement Bush adopted a hands-off approach – conflict management rather than conflict resolution.[14] This continued until the U.S. was forced to adopt a pro-active approach when many Arab capitals erupted in anti-Israeli and anti-U.S. demonstrations, on a scale not seen since 1967, in support of the Palestinians. And these unprecedented manifestations of popular anger crossed regime-imposed red lines – spontaneous eruptions in Syria and Saudi Arabia, beyond university campuses in Egypt, almost out of control in Jordan, with criticism aimed at the regimes themselves, and not just against Israel and the U.S.

As far as many in the American administration were concerned, the MEPP, despite its complete collapse, was less a U.S. priority than dealing with Iraq. But even the hard liners realized there would be little hope of any Arab support, even from traditional friends in the region, for a new confrontation with Baghdad unless Washington could be seen to be actively involved in reviving the peace process, and in an even-handed manner. To do this President Bush needed to rein in the Israelis, even though he shared Ariel Sharon's views on the Palestinians as terrorists, as well as his dislike for and distrust of Chairman Arafat. Dramatic progress seemed unlikely. Soon after 9/11 there were attempts to create two possible building blocks. Saudi Arabia's Crown Prince Abdullah's proposal was endorsed at an Arab summit in Beirut on 27 March 2002 (but rejected by Tel Aviv), for Israeli withdrawal from the Occupied Territories as a basis for a peace settlement in exchange for Arab recognition of Israel and its right to live within secure boundaries. Second, Security Council Resolution 1397,[15] for the first time specifically endorsed a 'vision' of a Palestinian State alongside an Israeli one. This was a U.S. proposal and had the grudging acquiescence of Israel, although the main Israeli coalition partner Likud formally rejected the concept of a Palestinian state on the West Bank of the Jordan.

Given the constant prospect of violence the auguries have been unpromising. Colin Powell's earlier inability to broker a cease-fire against the background of Israel's search and destroy operations in Jenin and other Palestinian cities demonstrated the limits of U.S. influence when Israel feels its basic national interests (perhaps its survival) are at stake. Powell's failure led to Arab accusations that Washington was not serious about disciplining Israel and was, in effect, continuing to allow Ariel Sharon a free hand to deal with his opponents. More suicide bombings in the aftermath of Jenin throughout the summer of 2002 did not make for productive negotiations. With so much blood spilt, and after such widespread destruction, Chairman Arafat proved unable (or unwilling to try) to control the extremist groups and enforce a viable Palestinian cease-fire. Sadly, suicide bombings and tough measures by Sharon's administration were highly popular amongst their respective peoples. The Palestinian response is born of despair and the Israelis' of fear. Some kind of enforced solution by the international community may be the only viable option. Following the war on Iraq, however, U.S. pressure on both parties led to Israel and the Palestinians agreeing to the newly formulated 'Road Map' for peace. This was drawn up by the U.S., in consultation with the EU, Russia, and the UN. The appointment of Mahmoud Abbas as the Palestinians' new prime minister allowed the Israeli government an opening to direct talks with the PA, without having to deal directly with Arafat.

British interests in the Middle East

Britain's historic links, especially with the more conservative and monarchical regimes in the Middle East, are an important if somewhat intangible asset.[16] These links lend a degree of perceived prominence and influence to the British presence in a number of countries that were once dependencies or protectorates, not strictly justified by the U.K.'s real (military) power. By the same token Britain's imperial past plays against it in other countries like Iraq, Iran, Yemen and Egypt where British sponsored regimes were swept away as a result of popular revolutions. The familiarity of the ruling elites with Britain, especially London, as a second home, higher educational links and appreciation of British goods and services have strengthened U.K./Arab ties, especially with monarchical regimes. The ties include the provision of defense equipment, military training, joint exercises and close personal contacts between the defense establishments.[17] The fact that English is the second language of many Gulf Arabs is also a decided advantage for British businessmen, although 'English English' is fighting a losing battle against the transatlantic variety – something likely to be exacerbated following the American-led occupation of Iraq in March 2003.

The stability and prosperity of the region, with its rapidly growing population is a priority for a trading nation like the U.K. The Middle East and, particularly, the Gulf Cooperation Council (GCC) monarchies are important markets for British goods and services and as a source of inward investment. From 1997 to 2000 U.K. exports in trade and services to the Arab world and Iran (hence not including Israel and Turkey) averaged over £10 billion. Of U.K. trade (visible) exports in 2001 of £7.8 billion, £4.1 billion went to the seven GCC countries (a figure twice as large as British exports to China). Egypt and Morocco are also significant markets. In addition Israel imported £1.4 billion worth of British goods in 2001, making it Britain's third biggest market in the region.[18] Ironically, lack of stability, especially the threat posed by Iraq, was also beneficial to British trade in the same period. In this period (1997-2000) the U.K. supplied 26 per cent of arms delivered to the region worth about £1billion in 2000 alone.[19] The overall trade balance of £4.7 billion in 2000 was greatly in the U.K.'s favor. The gradual liberalization of many Arab economies and economic reform in the area could open up areas where U.K. expertise is strong, for example with privatization and private capital investment in infrastructure. This market has enormous potential with a population growth predicted to rise from 164 million in 2000 to 240 million in 2015 and with important infrastructure projects coming on stream. The requirement for reconstruction in Iraq complicated matters, although in terms of oil, the overthrow of Saddam's regime should be a long-term bonus for the U.K. And of course, having supported the U.S. both politically and militarily in the war against Iraq, Britain stands to gain economically in its reconstruction.

Continued access to the region's oil (and gas) resources and especially the stability of the oil market is a key British interest. Not so much as a direct source of supply – the U.K. is a net oil exporter thanks to the North Sea oilfields – but for the sake of maintaining an adequate global supply to meet the needs of the industrialized world. Global dependency on the OPEC 'core': Saudi Arabia, Iraq. Iran, UAE, Kuwait and Qatar, which between them control 60 percent of the world's oil reserves, is not likely to change in the medium term. The threat to a stable market comes from interruption of supplies (for example as a result of political decisions by OPEC's Arab producers to put pressure on the West), as Iraq had done to protest U.S. support for Israel before the recent war. Or through physical blockage of the Straits of Hormuz because of war and post-9/11 acts of terrorism. Another threat could arise from political instability in Saudi Arabia. There must be serious concerns about the security of a regime where many of citizens are thought to be active supporters of the al Qaeda network, including twelve of the nineteen hijackers on 11 September. Military action against Iraq also risked a sharp increase in oil prices. Any of these factors sending prices up could cause serious damage to Western economies including that of the U.K.[20] The war on Iraq was short and successful, at least in terms of the initial objective of removing Saddam's regime from power. This has enabled the U.K., as the main ally of the U.S. in undertaking the military operations against the Iraqi regime, to have a say in the post-war running of that country, including control over oil production and sales. The instability of the Saudi regime has been evident for some time, and, given the Western dependency on oil from the region, strategically the war against Iraq has facilitated a more secure future for oil supplies. The British government was fairly open leading up the war on Iraq that the U.K. had important oil interests in the region. Since the war and following the terrorist attacks on U.S. personnel (and other foreigners) in Riyadh, American troops are likely to be redeployed elsewhere in the region.

Global demand for gas is growing faster than for oil. This trend will be encouraged by Kyoto-compliant measures, which favor gas as a relatively clean fuel. Egypt and Libya are poised to compete with existing Algerian exports across the Mediterranean. Qatar and Oman are major exporters of gas (in the form of LNG). Iran has the world's second biggest reserves and is engaged on a major development programme in preparation for exports, possibly westwards to Europe. It could also be a major transit route for gas from Central Asia. All this will contribute to Western energy security, not least by reducing dependency on Russian supplies. However, trans-Mediterranean pipelines and pumping stations could present tempting targets for terrorists.

The proximity of the Arab world to Europe is another reason why the stability of the region is a vital interest. Refugees fleeing oppression or extreme economic hardship (especially Kurds and Iraqis) are a growing problem, since the U.K. is a very popular destination.[21] But migration has a positive aspect as well as being a social threat. The EU has an ageing population and a contracting work force, whilst the Arab countries have a rapidly growing one of working age so an influx into Europe of skilled migrants in the search for employment could be of considerable benefit to European economies.

British policies in the Middle East before and after 11 September

At this point I should note that my own personal experience has greatly influenced my perspectives on regional policy-making. Between 1981 and 1997 I headed three British missions in the Arab world: Dubai (1981-85), Kuwait (1987-90) and Jordan (1993-97). It seemed to me then that there was no such thing as a British policy in the sense of an overarching game plan dealing with regional issues as a whole. Rather the 'policy' was the unwieldy sum of a number of separate, individual strategies within a series of bilateral frameworks. Each Embassy had a set of objectives reflecting a perception of British interests and opportunities in the host country. In Dubai the focus was trade almost to the exclusion of all else. In Kuwait the priorities were trade and the encouragement of Kuwaiti investment into the U.K. With Kuwait's strategic location, next to Iraq and close to Iran, we had a close relationship on military matters – the sale of defense equipment and training the Kuwaiti armed forces on its use. In Jordan, there was a close political, military and intelligence relationship given Jordan's position as a pivotal state in the context of the MEPP and its proximity to Iraq. In all three countries the Embassy had a major objective of maintaining and exploiting the very close, often primarily sentimental ties, which for historical reasons linked the elites in those countries with the U.K. Apart from the bonds of history, the U.K. had much, in practical terms to offer in a partnership of equals. Monitoring the stability of these instinctively conservative regimes was also a major preoccupation. My colleagues elsewhere in the Arab world had similar objectives fine-tuned to reflect local (and regional) circumstances, and this remains the case today.

The Middle East Directorate in the FCO has a set of wider, trans-national objectives reflecting a perception of U.K. foreign policy in changing regional circumstances. It would be accurate to describe these as reactive rather than proactive. During my time (and well before it) the constant major preoccupation was the Arab/Israeli conflict. The MEPP as initiated at Oslo in 1993 remained the only viable template or 'Road Map', for a just and lasting peace. The U.K. as part of a cumbersomely coordinated EU approach had an informal division of labor with Washington at U.S. insistence. The Americans, generally speaking, handled the politics facilitating the negotiation process. The received wisdom being that only the Americans had sufficient clout with the Israelis to influence their policies. The Europeans, whilst trying to use their collective voice in support of the MEPP, provided the bulk of the finance for peace building.[22] The EU has financed much of the infrastructure of the Palestinian Authority and a significant proportion of its running expenses. The EU was also a major player in a series of multilateral post-Oslo financial institutions. These were partly developmental, but were also intended as confidence building measures encouraging positive contacts between Israel and the Arab states in the region. They have now lapsed, as attitudes hardened on the Arab side following the advent of a conservative Israeli Government under Benyamin Netanyahu, and the subsequent steady erosion of the MEPP. But any lasting peace benefiting the region should have as an objective an economically linked Levant in which Israel could play a dynamic role as a driving economy of the region.

The other major foreign policy issue high on the agenda since 1990 was Iraq. London remained a junior partner with Washington in a policy of isolating and containing Iraq, identifying Saddam as a continuing threat to his neighbors and to the stability of the region. U.S.-British co-operation within the UN Security Council ensured the maintenance of a comprehensive sanctions regime. Joint military activity included air strikes on Baghdad to try and ensure Iraqi compliance with the activities of UN arms inspectors seeking to identify and neutralize Iraq's WMD capability. Following the expulsion of the weapons inspectors in 1998 U.S./U.K. air activity enforced a no fly zone in southern Iraq with occasional air attacks on Iraqi radar and anti aircraft installations. The Kurds in northern Iraq were also protected and enjoyed *de facto* autonomy.

Despite attempts by the UN to soften sanctions for humanitarian purposes[23] Iraq cleverly convinced most of the international community that sanctions were having disastrous effects on the civilian population without being able to influence the behavior of the ruling elite. Nor was there agreement as to the extent of the threat that Iraq posed via its possession of WMD, although countries in the region such as Saudi Arabia and the UAE, whatever they may say publicly, remained frightened of the 'Butcher of Baghdad'. The same was true of most of Saddam's subjugated people. However, many of the U.K.'s EU partners, plus Russia and China favored a less confrontational approach towards Baghdad. And most of the Arab world (certainly at a popular level) was united in condemning and contrasting U.S. (and the U.K. as Washington's poodle) 'punishment' of Iraq and its people with a stridently voiced refusal to restrain Israel in its bloody confrontation with the Palestinians.

New lines in the sand?

So to what extent after September 11 were there new 'lines in the sand' for U.K. policy-makers? To what extent has Britain dramatically reordered its priorities in the light of the 'war against terrorism'? Lights still burn late in Whitehall looking at this question and have done so since September 2001. My judgment is that as far as our various bilateral country objectives are concerned little more than fine-tuning will be needed. There is now more emphasis on security issues such as military training, sale of sophisticated defense equipment and the exchange of counter terrorist intelligence with friendly countries. Our bilateral and involvement in multilateral aid programmes aimed at alleviating poverty in the poorer Arab countries will be substantially increased. So will our engagement as a member of the EU in the formalized consultation forums with North African (Maghreb) and GCC countries.

A major priority will be monitoring potential internal threats in those countries with close ties to the West where there is known to be sympathy for al Qaeda, and some of whose nationals have been involved in the terrorist network. Saudi Arabia is probably the most worrying case. Despite the oppressively tight control that the House of Saud maintains over its citizens there is a threat from dissident elements with radical Islamic connections, some of whom will be members of bin Laden's network: he himself is of Saudi origin. Young Saudi radicals are turning to Islam out of disgust with their regime's close ties with the West (especially the U.S., with its support for the Jewish State), and out of despair at the inability of their regimes effectively to help the Palestinians. Stories of corruption on a vast scale amongst the princely elite fuel similar emotions in a country where the economy is struggling and unemployment is rising amongst a young and rapidly expanding workforce. There was some evidence that recent bomb outrages blamed on expatriates are the work of home grown terrorists seeking to destabilize the regime and the bland assurances of senior Saudis that all is well concealed real worries. Following the war on Iraq the terrorist bombings on Western residential compounds in Riyadh, with al Qaeda as the prime suspect, show clearly that the threat is still potent. Despite New Labor's much-vaunted 'ethical' foreign policy, there has been reluctance to talk toughly to the Saudis about their appalling human rights record. Given the link between oppressive regimes and the creation of a climate in which terrorists readily attract support for their anti-regime activities I would expect that the U.K., following the victory over Saddam's regime, will now take a more robust line. This will apply not only to Saudi Arabia, but to other regional countries linked to the west where the treatment of minorities like the Kurds in Turkey[24] or the absence of political rights for women as in Kuwait are becoming increasingly unacceptable to rising generations. The absence of adequate political and social rights generally, especially in the context of close official ties with the West, encourage support for radical dissident elements in a number of 'moderate' Arab countries. It is hoped by Bush and Blair that the outcome of their war on Iraq will be the development of democracy, which will have a spill-over effect in the wider region.

The problem is that there is considerable ambivalence within the Gulf Monarchies (and indeed throughout the Arab world) over the question of political liberalization. Many senior people (including a number of Saudi Princes) recognize the need to allow more popular participation if only as a political safety valve. But others who appear to be calling the shots, perhaps mindful of what happened to the Soviet Union after Gorbachev's reformism, are worried about too much liberalization too quickly for fear of not being able to return the genie to the bottle. Indeed, evidence of opposition from Islamic groups influenced by bin Laden's philosophy may be used by some of these regimes as a pretext for resisting loosening up the system. Or they may be genuinely worried about the extent of radical opposition to their rule and prefer suppression to engagement. And this pertains not just to the Gulf. Indeed, crackdowns on the pretext of confronting terrorism have happened in Egypt, Syria, Jordan, Yemen and North African countries. The late King Hussein of Jordan handled these pressures skillfully and this is a challenge, which the other monarchies must meet to ensure their long-term survival. British and other Western diplomats will doubtless continue to press for more political reforms, including improvements in human rights practices on the more autocratic regimes, but it will be hard going in the present climate. However, the terrorist bombs in Riyadh could have a different impact, making the regime there recognize the need not only to clamp down on terrorism and Islamic fundamentalism, but also to free up societal controls to better facilitate a civil society that allows for dissent to be articulated through more moderate means. Critical also will be the extent to which democracy can be developed in post-Saddam Iraq, to serve as a model to others in the region (the stated hope and objective of American and British political leaders).

Admittedly in the Gulf some cautious steps permitting more popular participation in state legislatures had already been taken, before 9/11, the war in Iraq, and the terrorist attacks in Saudi Arabia. There is also growing awareness of the importance of economic reform to meet the rising expectations of expanding populations. Hence, there has been growth in the support for liberalization and diversification away from total reliance on oil/gas and their derivatives.[25] Here and elsewhere in major markets in the region, the U.K. and other Western trading nations will be urging a more attractive inward investment climate. It has been bureaucratic obstacles and hostility to foreign financial hegemony (threatening the interests of local business leaders) that have discouraged potential overseas investors from entering Middle Eastern markets, rather than the threat of terrorism. U.K. private investment in the Arab world of about £1.5 billion represents only about 1 per cent of Britain's global total. The same paucity applies to investments from other major trading countries that are able to find more attractive opportunities elsewhere (the U.K.'s minimal investment still represents about 15 per cent of total external private inward investment in Arab countries).

Protectionism is short sighted, given the growing need for private finance to expand economies that are unable to cater for the rising expectations of their people. Therefore, ultimately, need may force a change in the investment culture, reinforcing the urging of Western diplomats.

In the current highly charged atmosphere it will require a major effort by the international community to keep the peace process on track. The grievances of the Palestinians and how they are redressed will remain the touchstone of how Arabs view the policies of the West. A comprehensive peace will do more than anything else to dissipate support for bin Laden and other extremist groups. After 9/11 and the war on Iraq there ought to be more of a political role for the EU than hitherto, especially if Washington eventually disengages itself from detailed involvement in future Palestinian/Israeli negotiations should the road map stall. The fact is, as mentioned above, the EU has a poor track record on concerting policy on Arab/Israel. This has been especially the case in finding a political role.[26] Despite an instinctive sympathy with the Palestinians, Europe has a problem with putting effective pressure on Israel, despite the leverage, especially in the form of trade sanctions, at its disposal. The shadow of the Holocaust hangs over German policymakers who are most reluctant to take a strong stance with Israel, or any policy that could be construed as having an anti-Israeli (anti-Semitic) bias. The U.K. will play a major part in any joint EU initiative whilst maintaining the closest of links with Washington. Two joint U.K./U.S. initiatives had already partially resolved crises in Ramallah (the 'release' of Arafat and Bethlehem) contributing to a lowering of the political temperature. Britain will certainly continue to be a significant financial contributor to future Palestinian 'nation building'. Following the recent violence, reconstruction rather than development will be the first priority. The map laid out after the Iraq war provides some hope for a settlement, but the sticking points of Israeli settlements and the right of return for Palestinians will be very difficult to resolve.

Iraq was a major dilemma for the U.K. The instincts of the Prime Minister and the Foreign Secretary favored Washington's policy of aggressive confrontation as the next stage of the war against terrorism. It was widely assumed soon after 9/11 that sooner or later the U.S. would be engaged in some kind of attempt to overthrow Saddam. Whether by a variation on the Afghan template of using internal opposition groups (drawn from the Shia community and/or the Kurds) or through supporting the multifarious (and so far ineffectual) exile opposition parties was not clear. Washington did however make it clear, no matter what the UN might or might not say, or even what the weapons inspectors might or might not find, that it was not going to let Saddam remain in power. 'Regime change' became the catch-cry in this instance.

Opinion polls suggested that popular support in the U.K. for 'dealing' with Saddam Hussein, although significant (42 per cent according to *The Independent* following the Bali bombing), was falling, in the absence of any proof linking him with al Qaeda. The prospect of U.K. military action in support of the U.S. split the ruling

Labor party. By 6 April 2002 over 120 Labor MPs had signed a parliamentary motion expressing disquiet at this possibility. There was thought to be widespread misgivings amongst senior military officers, especially about British forces being overstretched.[27] Labor and opposition MPs were concerned that an attack on Iraq at a time of continued stalemate in the MEPP would destroy any prospect of attracting support from other Arab countries, and could become the cause of serious instability as popular passions erupted.[28] Moreover, despite determination to deal with international terrorists the EU as a body did not support a military campaign. Tony Blair has attached importance to the 'special relationship' with the U.S., presumably as a means of enhancing British power and international standing. He may also see Britain as a moderating influence countering the excesses of the U.S. extreme right. One therefore has to understand Blair's support for the U.S.-led war against Iraq with these issues in mind.

Certainly there are important differences of emphasis between the British and U.S. approaches to terrorism and rogue states. Britain has been more ready to be engaged with such countries as Iran, Syria and Libya than have the Americans. And the U.K. will talk to extremist organizations like Hezbullah, while the U.S. remains most reluctant to do so. The U.K., rather than the U.S., is playing a major part in bringing peace to Sudan. Moreover Britain, in contrast to the U.S., is making a serious effort to understand why foreign policy 'messages' are not getting through to the Arab/Islamic world and to the domestic Islamic constituency. A special Islamic media unit has been set up in the FCO to tackle this serious deficiency. As for Iraq, I do not doubt that Blair genuinely perceived Saddam's WMD potential as a major international threat and was most reluctant to break ranks with President Bush whatever the consequences in term of international reaction.

British diplomats had their work cut out in attracting the support of any of our traditional allies for increasing the spiral of confrontation. The U.K. very much hoped that any action against Baghdad would have the endorsement of the UN Security Council, and tried to carry Washington with it. This was hard going against the Bush administration's instinctive distrust of the UN as a talking shop predisposed to favor Third World U.S. bashing. However, the U.K. and other allies at least persuaded Washington to go down the UN route in the first instance. President Bush's address to the UN General Assembly on 12 September 2002 strongly emphasized his wish for the UN to be proactive in taking action against Iraq.

In the final analysis the U.K. and the U.S. went to war against Iraq without UN approval. This has clearly complicated matters in the war on terror. The war on Iraq came directly out of the terrorist attacks of 9/11. The U.S. in particular has made it clear that even without the 'smoking gun' evidence of Iraq's WMD programme, or its links with al Qaeda, that the war against Iraq was necessary as part of its wider war on terrorism. The U.K., having supported military action against Iraq has complicated its relationship with its European neighbors, and left it committed to a much greater degree than hitherto to dealing with the myriad problems of the Middle East region, especially relating to the reconstruction of post-war Iraq and the resolution of the Israeli-Palestinian issue. For better or worse now the U.K. cannot simply walk away from this commitment. Clearly a new line in the sand has been drawn in relation to British policy in the Middle East, and this stems directly from 9/11.

Notes

1.   'The day the world changed'. Cover headline in *The Economist* of 15 September 2001 which typified the Western media reaction to 9/11.

2.   1997 figures put the Muslim community in the U.K. at between 1.5 and 2 million. Over 60 per cent from Pakistan and Bangladesh, with about 25 per cent from the Middle East and North Africa. Over 1400 different organizations represent the various Muslim communities with no single body competent to speak for the British Islamic community as a whole.

3.   As an indication of American insularity a commentator speaking on BBC Radio 4 Breakfast programme on 12 September 2001 stated that only 6 per cent of U.S. citizens possessed passports.

4.   Despite this apparent widespread interest in international affairs a poll commissioned by the *Council for the Advancement of Arab-British Understanding* (CAABU) revealed that '83 per cent of the British population knows little or nothing about Islam': *CAABU News*, vol. 4, no. 1, February 2002.

5.   The November 1917 'Balfour Declaration' in the form of a letter from the U.K.'s Foreign Secretary to a prominent British Zionist envisaged a homeland rather than a state for the Jews. But the Mandatory authorities failed to reconcile Jewish national aspirations with the anger of the Palestinians who rejected Jewish immigration and any attempt to construct a Zionist entity on their ancestral lands.

6.   Geoff Hoon, U.K. Minister of Defense, made the announcement for on 18 March. It took most observers by surprise although these Marine Commandos had been on standby for possible action in Afghanistan since September 2001.

7.   See for example, '9/11 Six Months On', *The Observer*, Special Report, 10 March 2002, p. 3.

8.   *'Six Months on. A balance-sheet'*, *The Economist*, 9 March, 2002, pp. 11-12. A thoughtful analysis of what has changed internationally over a six month period.

9.   The target countries nominated by the Pentagon in the leaked classified document were the Axis of Evil gang of three plus China, Russia, Libya and Syria. The Nuclear Posture Review widened the circumstances thought to justify a possible nuclear response and expands the list of targets. (See the numerous press reports summarized in *The Week*, 16 March, 2002, p. 4.)

10.   First coined by a State Department spokesman on 11 September 2002.

11.   In contrast to the cool reception U.S. Vice President Cheney received from a number of Arab countries on his tour in March and criticism of a possible U.S. attack on Iraq from some other EU leaders the U.K. was markedly supportive. At a joint press conference with Vice President Cheney on 11 March British Prime Minister Tony Blair stated 'There is a threat from Saddam Hussein and the weapons of mass destruction that he has acquired. It is not in doubt at all'. A Downing Street source later said that 'no decisions' had been taken about military action against Iraq. See *Independent*, 12 March 2002.

12 From Camille Mansour's excellent article on the Palestinian/Israeli conflict pre and post 11 September. See Mansour, C., 'The impact of 11 September on the Israeli-Palestinian Conflict', *Journal of Palestinian Studies*, vol. 31, no. 2, 2002, pp. 5-18 (p. 13).

13 Excluding the still unknown number of casualties in Jenin at least 1,264 Palestinians and 452 Israelis had died since September 2000. According to Medical Aid for Palestinians (MAP) 35,000 Palestinians have been wounded in the same period. (*MAP Appeal April 2002.*)

14 Aluf Benn brilliantly analyses George W. Bush's attitude towards the MEPP in his online article: 'George Bush: Ariel Sharon's Most Powerful Weapon', at http://www.salon.com/news/features/2002/03/08/weapon.

15 SCR 1397, adopted on 12 March, 2002, affirms 'a vision of a region where two states, Israel and Palestine, live side by side within secure and recognized borders'.

16 Perhaps as illustrated during my time as British Ambassador in Jordan when I was frequently told: 'King Hussein receives the U.S. Ambassador because he had to and the British Ambassador because he wanted to!' Sentimental ties have considerable practical value in countries like Jordan and the GCC monarchies (Saudi Arabia excepted).

17 Both the late King Hussein of Jordan and the present King Abdullah went to U.K. schools and graduated from the Royal Military Academy, Sandhurst. Many other senior Hashemites had similar exposure to the British system at King Hussein's insistence. The same applies to a number of members of the ruling families and senior military officers in the GCC monarchies. For example Sheikh Mohamed bin Rashid of Dubai, the UAE Minister for Defense is a graduate of Mons Officer Cadet School.

18 I am indebted to the *Foreign and Commonwealth Office*'s (FCO) Economic Policy Department for the bulk of these statistics, and also the *Middle East Association*, the *Arab-British Chamber of Commerce* and the *ABC International Bank plc*.

19 Arms Trade Oversight Project: Council for a Liveable World, available at www.clw.org.

20 For more detail see U.S. Dept of Energy's analysis of dependence on the 'Persian Gulf' at www.eia.doe.gov/emeu/cabs/pgulf.html.

21 Refugees seeking political asylum in the U.K. based at a camp near the French entrance to the Channel Tunnel have severely disrupted freight train services from France to Britain with their persistent and increasingly desperate attempts to get through the tunnel.

22 See Dhonte, Bhattacharya and Yousef, 'Demographic Transition in the Middle East', *IMF Working Paper*, 00/41 for an interesting analysis of the implications of the rapid population growth in the Arab region.

23 Attempts to coordinate an EU 'foreign policy' have so far not been particularly successful and the procedures remain cumbersome. The Middle East is a case in point. See Ginsburg, R.H., *The European Union in International Politics*, Rowman and Littlefield. Lanham, Maryland, 2001. Chapter 5 focuses on the EU's impact on the MEPP.

24 These included a number of SCR resolutions allowing Iraq to sell oil to fund imports of food whilst keeping the rest of the sanctions regime in place. The emphasis is now on 'smart' sanctions targeting the supply of arms (or the means to make them) to Iraq whilst suspending the ban on the import of a range of normal goods. The latest example is SCR 1382 of 29 November 2001.

25   *The Economist* of 23 March has an excellent survey of the social and economic
      problems faced by the Gulf Monarchies.

26   Ginsburg, R.H., *The European Union in International Politics*, chapter 5.

27   *The Independent* of 25 March reported that 'senior military officers' denied any
      evidence of an intention by Saddam's regime to pass WMD to al Qaeda. They also
      were worried about fulfilling too many simultaneous military commitments.

28   Widespread popular demonstrations in April throughout the Arab world in support
      of the Palestinians and expressing outrage at Israeli and U.S. policies were the
      biggest since 1967.

References

'9/11, Six Months On', *The Observer*, Special Report, 10 March 2002, p. 3.

'After September 11: A conversation', *National Interest*, vol. 65, no. 4, 2001, pp. 66-116.

Ajami, F., 'The Summoning', *Foreign Affairs*, vol. 72, no. 4, 1993, pp. 26-35.

'Amerikanstsy v Gruzii', *Nezavisimoe Voennoe Obozrenie*, no. 7, 2002, p. 1.

'An Attack on Us All: NATO's Response to Terrorism', *Military Technology*, vol. 25, no. 11, 2001, pp. 15-16.

Andréani, G., 'Gouvernance globale: origines d'une idée', *Politique étrangère*, vol. 66, no. 3, 2001, pp. 549-68.

Antonenko, O., 'Russia, NATO and European Security After Kosovo', *Survival*, vol. 41, no. 4, 1999-2000, pp. 124-144.

Arms Trade Oversight Project: Council for a Liveable World, available at http://www.clw.org.

'A Shield in Space', *Economist*, 3 June, 2000.

Baker, J., 'Russia in NATO?', *The Washington Quarterly*, vol. 25, no. 1, 2002, pp. 95-103.

Barber, B., *Jihad vs McWorld – Terrorism's Challenge to Democracy*, New York, Ballantyne Books, 2001.

Bartley, R., 'The Case for Optimism', *Foreign Affairs*, vol. 72, no. 4, 1993, pp. 15-18.

Barynkin, Victor, 'Russia's Stand on Plans for Enlargement of NATO', *Military News Bulletin*, vol. 5, May 1996.

Baxter, J. and Downing, M., *The Day That Shook The World: Understanding September 11*, London, BBC Worldwide, 2001.

Baylis, J. 'International and Global Security in The Post-Cold War Era', in Baylis, J. and Smith, S. (eds), *The Globalization of World Politics: An Introduction to International Relations*, Oxford, Oxford University Press, 2nd edition, 2001, pp. 253-276.

Baylis, J. and Smith, S. (eds), *The Globalization of World Politics: An Introduction to International Relations*, Oxford, Oxford University Press, 2nd edition, 2001.

Benn, A., 'George Bush: Ariel Sharon's Most Powerful Weapon', available at http:www.salon.com/news/features/2002/03/08/weapon.

Bennet, C., 'Aiding America', *NATO Review*, Winter 2001-2002, p. 6.

Bergen, P.L., *Holy War: Inside the Secret World of Osama bin Laden Inc*, London, Weidenfeld & Nicolson, 2001.

Bhatty, R. and Bronson, R., 'NATO's Mixed Signals in the Caucasus and Central Asia', *Survival*, vol. 42, no. 3, 2000, pp. 129-145.

Blair, T., 'Doctrine of the International Community', 23 April, 1999, at www.primeminister.gov.uk.

Blinken, A., 'The United States, France, and Europe at the Outset of the New Administration', Washington D.C., Brookings Institution, Center on the United States and France, March, 2001.

Bodansky, Y., *Bin Laden: The Man Who Declared War on America*, Roseville, California, Prima Publishing, 2001.

Bollaert, B., 'French Nuclear Power and Its Alternatives', Washington D.C., Brookings Institution, Center on the United States and France, January, 2001.

Booth, K. and Dunne, T. (eds), *Worlds in Collision: Terror and the Future of Global Order*, Houndsmills, Palgrave, 2002.

Brooks, S. and Wohlforth, W., 'Power, Globalization, and the End of the Cold War: Reevaluating a Landmark Case for Ideas', *International Security*, vol. 25, no. 3, 2000-2001, pp. 5-53.

Bull, H., *The Anarchical Society: A Study of Order in World Politics*, London, Macmillan, 1977.

Bush, G.W., 'Freedom at war with Fear', speech to joint session of Congress, September 20, 2001. Available on the World Wide Web at www.whitehouse.gov/news/releases/2002/01/20020129-11.html.

Buzan, B. and Little, R., 'Why International Relations has Failed as an Intellectual Project and What to do About it', *Millennium*, vol. 30, no. 1, 2001, pp. 19-39.

Buzan, B., *People States and Fear: An Agenda for International Security Studies in the Post-Cold War Era*, Hemel Hempstead, Harvester Wheatsheaf, 2nd edition, 1991.

Carlsnaes, W., Risse, T. and Simmons, B.A. (eds), *Handbook of International Relations*, London, Sage, 2001.

Checkel, J., 'The Constructivist Turn in International Relations Theory' (Review Article), *World Politics*, vol. 50, no. 1, 1998, pp. 324-348.

Chirac, J., '2010: The Challenges to Global Security', *Jane's Defense Weekly*, 22 December, 1999.

Chomsky, N., *Power and Terror*, New York, Seven Stories Press, 2003.

Chomsky, N., *September 11*, Crows Nest, New South Wales, Allen & Unwin, 2001.

Clarke, W.K., *Waging Modern War*, New York, Perseus, 2001.

Cohen, E., 'A Tale of Two Secretaries', *Foreign Affairs*, vol. 81, no. 3, May/June 2002, pp. 33-46.

'Combating Terrorism: How Five Countries Are Organized to Combat Terrorism' Report to Congressional Requesters, GAO, Washington D.C., April, 2000.

'Contrary to Common Sense', *Military News Bulletin*, vol. 1, January, 1997.

Cox, M., 'September 11 and U.S. Hegemony – or Will the 21st Century be American Too?', *International Studies Perspectives*, vol. 3, no. 1, 2002, pp. 53-70.

Cox, M., 'American Power Before and After September 11: Dizzy with Success?', *International Affairs*, vol. 78, no. 2, 2001, pp. 261-276.

Creveld, M. Van, *The Rise and Decline of the State*, Cambridge, Cambridge University Press, 1999.

Daalder, I. and Lindsay, J.M., 'Nasty, Brutish, and Long: America's War on Terrorism', *Current History*, December, 2001, pp. 403-406.

Daalder, I., 'A U.S. View of European Security and Defense Policy', Washington D.C., Brookings Institution, Center on the United States and France, March, 2001.

Daley, S., 'Europe's Dim View of U.S. is Evolving into Frank Hostility', *New York Times*, 9 April, 2000, pp. A1, A8.

David, D., '11 septembre: premières leçons stratégiques', *Politique étrangère*, vol. 66, no. 4, 2001, pp. 765-775.

Davis, A., 'Afghanistan Top of Central Asia Security Agenda', *Jane's Defense Weekly*, 17 January, 2001, p. 16.

Davis, A., 'Putting Pressure on Kabul', *Jane's Defense Weekly*, 20 December, 2000, p. 17.

Davis, A., 'Shanghai Five Step Up War on Terrorists', *Jane's Defense Weekly*, 2 May, 2001, p. 17.

Davis, A., 'Uzbekistan Emerges as Key to Allied Effort', *Jane's Defense Weekly*, 10 October, 2001, p. 3.

De Witte, P., 'Fostering Stability and Security in the Southern Caucasus', *NATO Review*, no. 1, 1999, pp. 14-16.

Deudney, D. and Ikenberry, J., 'The Nature and Sources of Liberal International Order', *Review of International Studies*, vol. 25, no. 4, 1999, pp. 179-196.

Deutscher Bundestag, 'Beschluß des Deutschen Bundestages vom 21 Dezember über die Beteiligung bewaffneter deutscher Streitkräfte an dem Einsatz einer Internationalen Sicherheitsunterstützungstruppe', *Blätter für deutsche und internationale Politik*, vol. 47, no. 3, 2002.

Dibb, P., 'The Future of International Coalitions: How Useful? How Manageable?', *Washington Quarterly*, vol. 25, no. 2, 2002, pp. 131-144.

Dinan, D., *Ever Closer Union? An Introduction to the European Community*, 2nd ed, New York, Lynne Reiner, 1999.

Dorient, R., 'Un septennat de politique asiatique: quel bilan pour la France?, *Politique étrangère*, vol. 67, no.1, 2002, pp. 173-188.

Duffield, John S., 'NATO's Functions After the Cold War', *Political Science Quarterly*, vol. 109, no. 5, 1994-95, pp. 763-787.

'Ekho Tragedii', *Krasnaya Zvezda*, 15 September, 2001, p. 3.

Elshtain, J.B., *Just War Against Terror: The Burden of American Power in a Violent World*, New York, Basic Books, 2003.

European Parliament, *Conference Intergouvernmentale: la politique étrangère et de sécurité commune*, Brussels, Office for Official Publications, 21 March, 1997.

Falk, R., 'Appraising the War Against Afghanistan', *Social Science Research Council (SSRC) Papers*, available at www.ssrc.org.

Fallows, J., 'The Unilateralist: A Conversation With Paul Wolfowitz', *The Atlantic Monthly*, March, 2002, at www.theatlantic.com/issues.2002/03/fallows.

Field, H., 'Problems of Enlargement, Security and Foreign Policy in Europe', paper presented to the National Europe Centre Workshop, Australian National University, Canberra, 8 December, 2000.

Finn, P., 'In Germany, harsh words for Israel', *International Herald Tribune: The IHT Online*, 10 April, 2002, pp. 1-2.

Fouda, Y. and Fielding, N., *Masterminds of Terror*, Penguin, Camberwell, Victoria, Australia, 2003.

Fougier, E., 'Perceptions de la mondialisation en France et aux Etas-Unis', *Politique étrangère*, vol. 66, no. 3, 2001, pp. 569-585.

Fukuyama, F., *The End of History and the Last Man*, New York, Free Press, 1992.

Gaddis, J.L., 'International Relations Theory and the End of the Cold War', *International Security*, vol. 17, no. 4, 1992-1993, pp. 5-58.

Galeotti, M., 'Kaliningrad at the Crossroads', *Jane's Intelligence Review*, vol. 14, no. 9, 2002, pp. 50-51.

Galeotti, M., 'The View From the Kremlin', *Jane's Intelligence Review*, vol. 14, no. 7, July 2002, p. 16.

Garrity, P. and Maaranen, S., (eds), *Nuclear Weapons in a Changing World: Perceptions from Europe, Asia and North America*, New York, Plenum Press, 1992.

Gill, B., 'China: Can Engagement Work?', *Foreign Affairs*, vol. 78, no. 4, July/August 1999, pp. 65-76.

Ginsburg, R.H., *The European Union in International Politics*, Rowman and Littlefield, Lanham, Maryland, 2001.

Glinski-Vassiliev, D., 'Suffocation by Embrace: The Putin-Bush Alliance and the Cultural Threat to Western Democracy', *Program on New Approaches to Russian Security (PONARS)*, Harvard University, memo no. 226, 25 January, 2002.

Goldstone, J., 'Responses to Tilly's "Predictions"', *SSRC Papers*, www.ssrc.org.

Golts, A. and Novichkov, N., 'Putin Outlines Cooperation', *Jane's Defense Weekly*, 10 October, 2001, p. 3.

Gompert, D. and Larrabee, F.S. (eds), *America and Europe: A Partnership for a New Era*, New York, Cambridge University Press, 1997.

Gordon, P.H., 'Reforging the Atlantic Alliance', *The National Interest*, no. 69, 2002, pp. 91-97.

Gordon, P.H., 'NATO after 11 September', *Survival*, vol. 43, no. 4, 2001-02, pp. 1-18.

Gordon, P.H., 'All Treaties Are Not Equal', *Le Monde*, 8 September, 2001.

Gordon, P.H., 'The French Position', *The National Interest,* no. 61, Fall 2001, pp. 85-96.

Gordon, P.H., 'Bush, Missile Defense and the Atlantic Alliance', *Survival*, vol. 43, no. 1, 2001, pp. 17-36.

Gordon, P.H., 'Bush's Unilateralism Risks Alienating America's Allies', *Handelsblaat*, 2 April, 2001.

Gordon, P.H., 'Bush, the Europeans, and Missile Defense', *Libération*, 18 May, 2001.

Gordon, P.H., 'How Bush Could Help Europe to Change its Mind', *International Herald Tribune*, 12 June, 2001.

Gordon, P.H., *France in an Age of Globalization*, Washington, D.C., Brookings Institution, 2001.

Gordon, P.H., *A Certain Idea of France: French Security Policy and the Gaullist Legacy*, Princeton, Princeton University Press, 1993.

Gordon, P.H. and Blinken, A.J., 'September 11 and American Foreign Policy', *Aspenia*, November, 2001.

Gordon, P.H. and Blinken, A.J., 'France, the United States and the "War on Terrorism"', Washington D.C., Brookings Institution, Center on the United States and France, October, 2001.

Gordon, P.H. and Blinken, A.J., 'NATO Is Ready to Play a Central Role', *International Herald Tribune*, 18 September, 2001.

Gordon, P.H. and Gnesotto, N., 'It's Time for a Trans-Atlantic Summit', *International Herald Tribune*, 13 March, 2002.

Griffiths, M. and O'Collaghan, T., *International Relations: The Key Concepts*, London, Routledge, 2002.

Guerot, U., 'France, Germany and the Constitution of Europe', Washington D.C., Brookings Institution, Center on the United States and France, 1 March, 2002.

Gunaratna, R., *Inside Al Qaeda: Global Network of Terror*, Carlton, Victoria, Australia, Scribe Publications, 2002.

Habermas, J., 'Fundamentalismus und Terror', *Blätter für deutsche und internationale Politik*, vol. 47, no. 2, 2001, p. 172.

Halliday, F., *Two Days That Shook the World: September 11, 2001: Causes and Consequences*, London, Al Saqi Books, 2002.

Halliday, F., 'Aftershocks that will eventually shake us all', *Observer*, 25 November, 2001.

Halliday, F., 'Beyond Bin Laden', *Observer*, 23 September, 2001.

Halliday, F., 'New World, But the Same Old Disorder', *Observer*, 10 March, 2002.

Harnisch, S. and Brauner, W., 'The German Response to the September 11th Terrorist Attacks: A Shift in the Domestic Political Debate and Party Politics?' *German Foreign Policy in Dialogue*, Newsletter, Issue 5, 23 November, 2001.

Harries, O., 'An End to Nonsense', *The National Interest*, vol. 65, no. 4, 2001, pp. 117-120.

Harris, S. et al., *The Day The World Changed? Terrorism and World Order*, Keynotes, RSPAS, The Australian National University, Canberra, October, 2001.

Harkavy, R.E. and Neuman, S.G., *Warfare and the Third World*, New York, Palgrave, 2001.

Hefner, R.W., 'Muslim Politics in Indonesia After September 11', paper prepared for the U.S. House Committee on International Relations. Available at www.house.gov/international_relations/hefn1212.htm.

Heibourg, F., 'Défenses antimissiles: l'analyse stratégique et l'intérêt européens', *Politique étrangère*, vol. 66, no. 3, 2001, pp. 619-630.

Heibourg, F., 'Europe and the Transformation of World Order', *Survival*, vol. 43, no. 4, 2001, pp. 143-148.

Held, D., *Democracy and the Global Order: From the Modern State to Cosmopolitan Governance*, Cambridge, Cambridge University Press, 1995.

Heymann, P.B., 'Dealing with Terrorism: An Overview', *International Security*, vol. 26, no. 3, 2001, pp. 24-38.

Hill, L. and Golts, A., 'NATO Fails to Warm Putin', 7 November, 2001, p. 21.

Hill, L., 'NATO Responds, Rivalries Remain', *Jane's Defense Weekly*, 17 October, 2001, p. 4.

Hill, L., 'NATO Set for "Big Bang"', *Jane's Defense Weekly*, 17 April, 2002, p. 21.

Hill, L., 'War on Terrorism Spur Closer NATO-Russia Ties', *Jane's Defense Weekly*, 12 December, 2001, p. 2.

Hirsh, M., 'Bush and The World', *Foreign Affairs*, vol. 81, vol. 5, September-October, 2002, pp. 18-43.

Hoffman, S., 'On the War', *New York Review of Books*, 10 November, 2001, pp. 4-5.

Hoge Jnr., J.F. and Rose, G. (eds), *How Did This Happen? Terrorism and the New War*, New York, Council on Foreign Relations, 2001.

Holbrooke, R., *To End a War*, London, Random House, 1999.

Holliday, L., *Children of the Troubles*, New York, Washington Square Press, 1997.

Huntington, S., 'Cultures in the 21st Century: Conflicts and Convergences', at www.coloradocollege.edu/anniversary/Transcripts/HuntingtonTXT.

Huntington, S., 'Global Perspectives on War and Peace (Or Transiting A Uni-Multipolar World)', at: www.aei.org/bradley/b1051198.htm.

Huntington, S., 'The Erosion of American National Interests', *Foreign Affairs*, vol. 76, no. 5, 1997, pp. 26-49.

Huntington, S., *The Clash of Civilizations and the Remaking of World Order*, New York, Touchstone, 1996.

Huntington, S., 'The West: Unique, Not Universal', *Foreign Affairs*, vol. 75, no. 6, 1996, pp. 28-46.

Huntington, S., 'The Clash of Civilizations?', *Foreign Affairs*, vol. 72, no. 3, 1993, pp. 23-49.

Huntington, S., *The Third Wave: Democratization in the Late 20th Century*, Norman, University of Oklahoma Press, 1991.

Huntington, S., *The Soldier and the State: The Theory and Politics of Civil-Military Relations*, New York, Belknap, 4th edition, 1981.

Huntington, S., *Political Order in Changing Societies*, New Haven, Yale University Press, 1968.

Hutton, W., *The World We're In*, New York, Little Brown, 2002.

Hyde-Price, A., 'Of Dragons and Snakes: Contemporary German Security Policy', in Smith, G., Paterson, W.E. and Padgett, S. (eds), *Developments in German Politics*, 2nd ed, Houndsmills, Basingstoke, Macmillan, 1996, p. 178.

Ikenberry, J., *After Victory: Institutions, Strategic Restraint, and The Rebuilding of Order after Major Wars*, Princeton, Princeton University Press, 2001.

Ikenberry, J. et al, 'The West: Precious not Unique', *Foreign Affairs*, vol. 76, no. 2, March/April, 1997, pp. 162-165.

Indyk, M., 'Back to the Bazaar', *Foreign Affairs*, vol. 81, no. 1, 2002, pp. 75-88.

'Iraq: the myth and the reality', *The Guardian*, 15 March, 2002, p.16.

Israelyan, Victor, 'Russia at the Crossroads: Don't Tease a Wounded Bear', *Washington Quarterly*, vol. 21, no. 1, Winter 1998, pp. 53-54.

'Itum-Kalinskiy Proryv', *Nezavisimoe Voennoe Obozrenie*, no. 26, 2002, p. 2.

Ivashov, L., 'Europe Needs a New Security System', *Military News Bulletin*, vol. 2, February 1997.

Janes, J., 'Transatlantic Relations', *German Foreign Policy in Dialogue*, Newsletter, Issue 5, 23 November, 2001.

Jentleson, B.W., 'The Need for Praxis: Bringing Policy Relevance Back In', *International Security*, vol. 26, no. 4, 2002, pp. 169-183.

Joffe, J., 'Of Hubs, Spokes, and Public Goods', *The National Interest*, vol. 69, Fall 2002, pp. 17-20.

Johnson, C., *Blowback: The Costs and Consequences of American Empire*, London, Time Warner Paperbacks, 2002.

Kagan, R., 'Power and Weakness', *Policy Review*, no. 113, June-July 2002, pp. 3-28.

Kagan, R., *Paradise and Power: America and Europe in the New World Order*, London, Atlantic Books, 2003.

Kaldor, M., 'American Power: from "compellance" to "cosmopolitanism?"', *International Affairs*, vol. 79, no. 1, 2003, pp. 1-22.

Kaldor, M., 'Beyond Militarism, Arms Races, and Arms Control', SSRC, available at http://www.ssrc.org/sept11/essays/kaldor_text_only.htm.

Kaldor, M., *New and Old Wars: Organized Violence in a Global Era*, Cambridge, Polity, 1999.

Kaplan, R.D., 'Looking the World in the Eye', *Atlantic Monthly*, vol. 288, no. 5, 2001, pp. 68-82.

Kaplan, R.D., 'The Coming Anarchy', *Atlantic Monthly*, vol. 273, no. 2, 1994, pp. 44-76.

Katzenstein, P (ed.), *The Culture of National Security: Norms and Identity in World Politics*, New York, Columbia University Press, 1996.

Keller, B., 'Nuclear Nightmares', *New York Times Magazine*, 26 May, 2002, pp. 1-7.

Khodarenok, M., 'Amerikanskiy Desant v Kazakhstane', *Nezavisimoe Voennoe Obozrenie*, no. 11, 2002, p. 3.

Khodarenok, M., 'Ozherelie iz Amerikanskikh Baz', *Nezavisimoe Voennoe Obozrenie*, no. 10, 2002, p. 4.

King, A., *Britain Says Yes: The 1975 Referendum on the Common Market*, Washington D.C., The American Enterprise Institute, 1977.

Kirkpatrick, J., 'The Modernizing Imperative', *Foreign Affairs*, vol. 72, no. 4, 1993, pp. 22-26.

Kissinger, H., 'America and the Apex: Empire or Leader?', *The National Interest*, no. 64, Summer, 2001, pp. 1-17.

Kissinger, H., *Years of Upheaval*, Boston, Little Brown, 1982.

Klein, J., *The Natural: The Misunderstood Presidency of Bill Clinton*, London, Hodder and Stoughton, 2002.

Korotchenko, I., 'Putin Dazhe ne Vspomnil o Rasshirenii NATO', *Nezavisimoe Voennoe Obozrenie*, no. 17, 2002, p. 1.

Krasner, S., *Sovereignty: Organized Hypocrisy*, Princeton, Princeton University Press, 1999.

Krause, J., 'The Consequences of September 11 2001 for transatlantic relations', *German Foreign Policy in Dialogue*, Newsletter, Issue 5, 23 November, 2001.

Krauthammer, C., 'The Unipolar Moment Revisited', *The National Interest*, Winter 2002/03, pp. 5-17.

Kutscha, M., 'Anti-Terror-Paket, Fortsetzungslieferung', *Blätter für deutsche und internationale Politik*, no. 46, 11 November, 2001.

Kuzio, T., 'NATO and the Baltic States', *Jane's Intelligence Review*, vol. 12, no. 11, November, 2000, p. 1.

Lapid, Y. and Kratochwil, F. (eds), *The Return of Culture and Identity in IR Theory*, Boulder, Colorado, Lynne Reinner, 1996.

Laqueur, W., *The New Terrorism: Fanaticism and the Arms of Mass Destruction*, Oxford, Oxford University Press, 1999.

Laurence, J., 'Islam in France', Washington D.C., Brookings Institution, Center on the United States and France, December, 2001.

'Le monde entier reconnaîtra que les Etats-Unis sont en situation de légitime défense', *Le Monde*, 18 September, 2001.

'Jacques Chirac annonce la participation des forces françaises', *Le Monde*, 7 October, 2001.

Lebow, R.N., 'The Long Peace, the End of the Cold War, and the Failure of Realism', in Richard Ned Lebow and Thomas Risse-Kappen (eds), *International Relations Theory and the End of the Cold War*, New York, Columbia University Press, 1995, pp. 23-56.

Lewis, B., 'License to Kill: Usama Bin Laden's Declaration of Jihad', *Foreign Affairs*, vol. 77, no. 4, 1998, pp. 14-19.

Lewis, B., 'The Roots of Muslim Rage', *Atlantic Monthly*, Issue 266, 1990, pp. 60-71.

Lieven, A., 'The Secret Policemen's Ball: The United States, Russia and the International Order after 11 September', *International Affairs*, vol. 78, no. 2, 2001, pp. 245-259.

Lindsay, J., 'La politique américaine de defense antimissile: la troisième fois sera-t-elle la bonne?', *Politique étrangère*, vol. 66, no. 3, 2001, pp. 631-45.

Lukacs, J., *Churchill: Visionary, Statesman, Historian*, Melbourne, Scribe Publications, 2002.

Lundestad, G., 'Empire by Invitation', *Journal of Peace Research*, vol. 23, no. 3, 1999, pp. 263-276.

Mahbubani, K., 'The Dangers of Decadence', *Foreign Affairs*, vol. 72, no. 4, 1993, pp. 14-18.

Makarenko, Boris, 'Where Does the Potential Threat to Russia Come From: The West or the South?', *Moskovskiy Komsomolets*, 15 October, 1996.

Mandelbaum, M., 'How the West is torn on dealing with Iraq', *The Age*, 12 February, 2003.

Mandelbaum, M., *The Ideas that Conquered the World*, New York, Public Affairs, 2002.

Mansfield, E. and Snyder, J., 'Democratization and the Danger of War', *International Security*, vol. 20, no. 1, 1995, pp. 5-38.

Mansour, C., 'The impact of 11 September on the Israeli-Palestinian Conflict', *Journal of Palestinian Studies*, vol. 31, no. 2, 2002, pp. 5-18.

Maull, H.W., 'The Guns of November? Germany and the Use of Force in the Aftermath of 9/11', *German Foreign Policy in Dialogue*, Newsletter, Issue 5, 23 November, 2001.

Mazaar, M., 'Saved From Ourselves?' *Washington Quarterly*, vol. 25, no. 2, 2002, pp. 221-232.

Mearsheimer, J., *The Tragedy of Great Power Politics*, New York, W.W. Norton, 2001.

Mearsheimer, J., 'A Realist Reply', *International Security*, vol. 20, no. 1, 1995, pp. 82-93.

Miller, J., 'The Challenge of Radical Islam', *Foreign Affairs*, vol. 72, no. 2, 1993, pp. 43-56.

Ministry of Foreign Affairs of the French Republic, 'Entretien du Ministre des Affaires Etrangères M. Hubert Védrine avec la Revue Trimestrielle Politique Internationale', press release, November, 2000.

'Missiles Over the Moors', *Economist*, 20 January, 2001.

Moravcsik, A., 'De Gaulle Between Grain and Grandeur: The Political Economy of French EC Policy, 1958–1970 (Part 2)', *Journal of Cold War Studies*, vol. 2, no. 3, 2000, pp. 4–68.

Morgenthau, H.J., *Politics Among Nations: The Struggle for Power and Peace*, 2nd ed, New York, Alfred A. Knopf, 1948.

'Moskva Gotova Delitsya Informatiei s Vashingtonom', *Krasnaya Zvezda*, 19 September, 2001, p. 1.

Muller, H., 'Security Cooperation', in Walter Carlsnaes, Thomas Risse and Beth A. Simmons (eds), *Handbook of International Relations*, London, Sage, 2002, pp. 350-368.

Muravchik, J., 'The European Disease', *The American Enterprise*, vol. 13, no. 8, December, 2002, pp. 24-27.

Nardon, L., 'France Cedes Leading Role in Space to Europe', Washington D.C., Brookings Institution, Center on the United States and France, April, 2001.

Nardon, L., 'Espace militaire: les débuts aux Etas-Unit, les avancées de l'Europe', *Politique étrangère*, vol. 67, no. 1, 2001, pp.189-198.

NATO, 'The Alliance's Strategic Concept', Rome, 8 November, 1991. Available online at: http://www.nato.int/docu/basictxt/b911108a.htm.

Nelan, Bruce W. 'Present Danger', *Time*, 7 April, 1997, p. 49.

'New Russia-NATO Relationship off to Rocky Start', *Jane's Defense Weekly*, 2 January, 2002, p. 2.

Novichkov, N., 'Putin Pledges to Supply Equipment to UF', *Jane's Defense Weekly*, 24 October, 2001, p. 5.

Nye, J., *The Paradox of American Power*, New York, Longman, 2002.

Nye, J., *Bound to Lead: The Changing Nature of American Power*, New York, Basic Books, 1990.

Parmentier, G., *After Nice: The Discreet Emergence of a Military Partner for the United States*, Washington D.C., Brookings Institution, Center on the United States and France, April, 2001.

Pishchev, N., 'NATO: Myths and Reality', *Krasnaya Zvezda*, 4 January, 1997.

'Pomoshch SSHA', *Nezavisimoe Voennoe Obozrenie*, no. 11, 2002, p. 3.

Posen, Barry, R., 'The Struggle against Terrorism: Grand Strategy, Strategy, and Tactics', *International Security*, vol. 26, no. 3, 2001/2002, pp. 39-55.

Prentice Hall Authors Speak Out: September 11 and Beyond, Prentice Hall, Upper Saddle River, NJ, 2002.

Price, R., 'Is It Right To Respond With Military Attacks?', in Christian Reus-Smit, Amin Saikal, William Maley, Richard Price and Stuart Harris, *The Day the World Changed? Terrorism and World Order*, Canberra, Department of International Politics (RSPAS), Australian National University, 2001, pp. 25-31.

Proceedings of the US-Russia Binational Commission (GCC-6), Washington, D.C, 29-30 January, 1996.

'Protivniki ili Partnery', *Nezavisimoe Voennoe Obozrenie*, no. 22, 2001, p. 1.

Prudnikov, V., 'Main Lines of Air Defense Development in Russia', *Military Parade*, July-August, 1996.

Ray, J.L., *Democracy and International Conflict*, Columbia, S.C., University of South Carolina Press, 1995.

Recknagel, C., 'Iraq: Bush and Blair Opt for Diplomatic Offensive for Now', *RFE/RL Newsline*, 8 April, 2002.

Reeve, S., *The New Jackals*, London, Andre Deutsch, 1999.

Reus-Smit, C., 'The Return of History', in Christian Reus-Smit, Amin Saikal, William Maley, Richard Price and Stuart Harris, *The Day the World Changed? Terrorism and World Order*, Canberra, Department of International Politics (RSPAS), Australian National University, 2001, pp. 1-8.

Rice, C., 'Promoting the National Interest', *Foreign Affairs*, vol. 79, no. 1, 2000, pp. 45-62.

Ritter, S., *Endgame: Solving The Iraq Problem – Once and For All*, New York, Simon & Schuster, 1999.

Ritter, S. and Pitt, W.R., *War on Iraq: What Team Bush Doesn't Want You To Know*, Crows Nest, New South Wales, Allen and Unwin, 2002.

Roberts, A., 'Counter-terrorism, Armed Force and the Laws of War', *Survival*, vol. 44, no. 1, Spring 2002, pp. 7-32.

'Rossiya Pomozhet Naseleniu Afganistana', *Krasnaya Zvezda*, 5 October, 2001, p. 1.

'Rossiya-NATO: Novy Format', *Krasnaya Zvezda*, 15 May, 2002, p. 1.

Rühe, V., 'Zukunft der Bundeswehr--Zehn Thesen', available on the Web at http://www.cdu.de/ueber-uns/buvo/ruehe/040802bw.pdf.

Rumsfeld, D., 'A War Like No Other', reprinted in the *Guardian Weekly*, 4-10 October, 2001, p. 11.

Rumsfeld, D., 'Transforming the Military', *Foreign Affairs*, vol. 81, no. 3, 2002, pp. 20-32, p. 23.

Schmid, John. 'A new vision for Germany', *International Herald Tribune. The IHT Online*, 8 April, 2002, pp. 1-2.

Segal, G., 'East Asia and the 'constrainment' of China', *International Security*, vol. 20, no. 2, 1996, pp. 107-135.

Serfaty, S, 'The Nice Summit: Deciding Without Choosing', Washington D.C., Brookings Institution, Center on the United States and France, January, 2001.

Shadid, A., 'Iraqi Hurls Abuse at Kuwaiti Delegate', *Washington Post*, 6 March, 2003, p. A5.

Shapiro, J., 'The Role of France in the War on Terrorism', Washington D.C., Brookings Institution, Center on the United States and France, May, 2002.

Shearman, P., 'New Wars and Russia's War in Chechnya', 4th Pan-European International Relations Conference, University of Canterbury, Kent, 6-10 September, 2001.

Shearman, P., 'Nationalism, the State, and the Collapse of Communism', in Vandersluis, S.O. (ed.), *The State and Identity Construction in International Relations*, Houndsmills, Basingstoke, Macmillan, 2000, pp. 76-108.

Shearman, P., 'Britain, the European Union and National Identity', in John Milfull (ed.), *Britain in Europe: Prospects for Change*, Aldershot, Ashgate, 1999, pp. 91-102.

Shearman, P. and Sussex, M., 'Foreign Policy-making and Institutions', in Neil Robinson (ed.), *Institutions and Political Change in Russia*, London, Macmillan, 2000, pp. 151-172.

Silvers, R.B. and Epstein, B. (eds), *Striking Terror: America's New War*, New York, New York Review Books, 2002.

Simes, D., 'What War Means', *The National Interest*, no. 65, Fall, 2001, pp. 34-42.

SIPRI Yearbook 1998, London, Brasseys/International Institute for Strategic Studies, 1998.

SIPRI Yearbook 1991, London, Brasseys/International Institute for Strategic Studies, 1991.

'Six Months on. A balance-sheet', *The Economist*, 9 March, 2002, pp 11-12.

Smith, S., 'The End of the Unipolar Moment: September 11 and the Future of World Order', *SSRC Papers*, www.ssrc.org.

Snow, D.M., *September 11, 2001; The New Face of War?*, New York, Longman, 2001.

Snyder, G.H., 'Mearsheimer's World – Offensive Realism and the Struggle for Security: A Review Essay', *International Security*, vol. 27, no. 1, 2002, pp. 149-173.

Snyder, J., *From Voting to Violence: Democratization and Nationalist Conflict*, New York, W.W. Norton, 2000.

Sofka, J., 'American Neutral Rights Reappraised: Identity or Interest in the Foreign Policy of the Early Republic?', *Review of International Studies*, vol. 26, no. 4, 2000, pp. 599-622.

Solana, J., 'The Transatlantic Rift: U.S. Leadership After September 11', *Harvard International Review*, vol. 34, no. 4, Winter 2003, pp. 62-66.

Soloviev, V., 'Po Stsenariu Chechenskikh Boevikov', *Nezavisimoe Voennoe Obozrenie*, no. 26, 2002, p. 1.

Stern, J., 'The Protean Enemy', *Foreign Affairs*, vol. 82, no. 4, 2003, pp. 27-40.

Streshnev, R., 'Shchit Sotruzhestva Derzhit Udar', *Krasnaya Zvezda*, 18 June, 2002, p. 1.

Streshnev, R., 'Sovmestno Protiv Obshchei Ugrogy', *Krasnaya Zvezda*, 19 April, 2002, p. 3.

Suhrke, A. 'Human Security and the Interests of States', *Security Dialogue*, vol. 30 no. 3, 1999, pp. 265-276.

Sussex, M., *Power, Interests and Identity in Russian Foreign Policy*, PhD dissertation, The University of Melbourne, 2001.

Synovicz, R., 'Islamic Conference Fails To Define "Terrorism", Condemns Israel', *Radio Free Europe/Radio Liberty (RFE-RL) Newsline*, 3 April, 2002, available at www.rferl.org/nca/features/2002/04/03042002083906.asp.

Takeyh, R., 'Two Cheers From the Islamic World', *Foreign Policy*, vol. 21, no. 3, 2001, pp. 70-71.

Talbott, S. and Chanda, N. (eds), *The Age of Terror: America and The World After September 11*, New York, Basic Books, 2001.

The Military Balance 1998–1999, London, International Institute for Strategic Studies, 1999.

Tiersky, R., 'The Mitterrand Legacy and the future of French Security Policy', *McNair Papers*, no. 5, National Defense University, 2001.

Townsend, C., *Terrorism: A Very Short Introduction*, Oxford, Oxford University Press, 2002.

Tuman, M. (ed.), *September 11, 2001: Readings for Writers*, New York, Longman, 2002.

'Ukreplaya Bezopasnost v Azii', *Krasnaya Zvezda*, 16 May, 2002, p. 1.

'US Plans Military Base in Hungary', *The Times*, 3 July, 1996.

'US Security Policy in Asia and the Pacific: The View From Pacific Command', House Committee on International Relations, 27 February, 2002, at www.house.gov/international_relations/77895.pdf.

Vaïsse, J. 'Un traumatisme d'une magnitude historique', Washington D.C., Brookings Institution, Center on the United States and France, 1 October, 2001.

Vaïsse, J., 'Two Scenarios for the Future', *Libération*, 21 September, 2001.

Vaïsse, J., 'America and Multilateralism: Why George W. Bush is No Different', *Handelsblatt*, 26 July, 2001.

Vaïsse, J., 'Senate Shift Might Soften the U.S. Stance Abroad', *Handelsblatt*, 29 May, 2001.

Vaïsse, J., 'French Views on Missile Defense', Washington D.C., Brookings Institution, Center on the United States and France, April, 2001.

Vaïsse, J., 'French Reactions to the 2000 US Presidential Election', Washington D.C., Brookings Institution, Center on the United States and France, January, 2001.

Vedrine, H. *Les Cartes de la France à l'heure de la mondialisation*, Paris, Fayard, 2000.

Verluise, P., 'Quelle France dans le monde au XXIe siècle?', *Diploweb*, January, 2001.

Waever, O., Buzan, B., Kestrup, M. and Lemaitre, P., *Identity, Migration and the New Security Agenda in Europe*, London, Pinter, 1993.

Walker, M., 'Post 9/11: The European Dimension', *World Policy Journal*, vol. 18, no. 4, 2001-2002, pp.1-10.

Wallace, W., 'Living With The Hegemon: European Dilemmas', 2002, available at www.ssrc.org/sep11/essays/wallace.

Wallace, W., 'Europe, the Necessary Partner, *Foreign Affairs*, vol. 80, no. 3, 2001, pp. 16-34.

Wallerstein, I., 'America and the World: The Twin Towers as Metaphor', available at www.ssrc.org/sept11/essays/wallerstein.

Walt, S.M., 'Beyond bin Laden: Reshaping U.S. Foreign Policy', *International Security*, vol. 26, no. 3, Winter 2001/02, pp. 56-78.

Waltz, K.N., 'The Continuity of International Politics', in Ken Booth and Tim Dunne (eds), *Worlds in Collision: Terror and the Future of the Global Order*, Houndsmills, Basingstoke, Palgrave, 2002, pp. 348-354.

Waltz, K.N., *Theory of International Politics*, Reading, MA, Addison-Wesley, 1979.

Wedemeyer, G., 'Anfällig für Sündenfäll', *Stern*, no. 4, 2002, p. 34.

Weeks, A., 'Do Civilizations Hold?', *Foreign Affairs*, vol. 72, no. 4, 1993, pp. 53-54.

Wijk, R. de, 'The Limits of Military Power', *The Washington Quarterly*, vol. 25, no. 1, pp. 75-92.

Wright, R., 'Islam, Democracy, and the West', *Foreign Affairs*, vol. 71, no. 3, 1992, pp. 131-145.

Yost, D., 'Transatlantic relations and peace in Europe', *International Affairs*, vol. 78, 2002, pp. 277-300.

Zinn, H., *Terrorism and War*, Crows Nest, New South Wales, Allen & Unwin, 2002.

Zinsmeister, K., 'Old And In the Way', *The American Enterprise*, symposium on 'Continental Drift: Europe and the U.S. Part Company', vol. 13, no. 8, December 2002, pp. 4-9.

Index

acquis communitaire 72
Africa 42, 138-9
Airborne Warning and Control Systems
   (AWACS) 101
aircraft (as weapons) 14
airpower 91, 109, 120
Albright, M. 69
anarchy, international 10*n*, 12, 42
Anti Ballistic Missile Treaty (ABM) 16,
   35, 39, 77-8,
Antonenko, O. 111
Afghanistan
  al Qaeda 5, 14-15, 21, 34, 77, 80, 92,
    113-14, 119
  and Taliban 2, 4-5, 13-14, 21, 34, 55-6,
    69, 76-80, 90, 92, 102, 104,
    113-15, 119, 129
  NATO's role 19, 51, 71, 75, 100, 113
  Northern Alliance 77, 113-15
  Soviet invasion of 5, 21, 34, 65
  U.S. intervention in 13, 14, 19, 34, 39,
    75, 80, 100, 119, 131
alliances 12, 17-19, 39, 41, 52-3, 57, 64
al Qaeda
  and Afghanistan 14, 21, 34
  and clash of civilizations 31, 38
  alleged links to Iraq 15
  destruction of WTC 3
  operatives in Europe 2, 75
  recruitment and training 77, 114
ANZUS 17, 19
Armenia 119, 125n
Arab people 4, 58, 132, 134, 140
arms control 17, 54, 72, 78
Asia 5, 16, 18, 38, 42, 57, 74, 76, 85,
   118-20, 130
Australia 17, 19, 33
Austria 81
Azerbaijan 118-19

Baader-Meinhoff Gang 14, 98
balance of power 4, 9*n*, 12, 18, 30, 35,
   52-3

balancing and bandwagoning 3-4, 24, 30,
   35-6, 40
Baltic states (Latvia, Lithuania, Estonia)
   81, 108, 118, 120-122
Barber, B. 29
Basques 14, 62
Belgium 75, 92
Berlusconi, S. 37, 81
bin Laden, Osama
  and clash of civilizations 29, 33-4, 74,
    103
  and international terrorism 3, 21
  and U.S. foreign policy 21
  and world media 128, 141
  as reflection of radical Islam 37-8, 79,
    114, 131, 138-40
  perception of in Islamic world 34
  in Afghanistan 5, 114
  rejection of Israel 14, 34
  role as leader of al Qaeda 128
  root causes of terrorism 20-22
  speeches, videos and threats 44, 45
bipolarity 6, 11, 20, 51-2, 59, 80, 100
Blair, A.
  ambivalent on institutions 4, 61, 71
  and UN 60, 82
  as UK Prime Minister 21
  as leading partner of U.S. 4, 129
  criticism of 37, 63
  diplomacy in Middle East 129-30, 139
  doctrine of the international
    community 23
  dissent from Labor Party over war in
    Iraq 37
  proponent of war in Iraq 23, 58, 141
  strategic vision 4, 23
  relationship with George W. Bush 23,
    37, 60, 141
bombings
  Moscow apartment blocks 113
  Bali 14, 38, 129
  Casablanca 14, 131
  in Israel 79, 132-3
  Karachi 84

Bulgaria 81, 118
Bull, H. 42
Bundestag 95-6, 99-101
Bundeswehr 71, 102-104
Bush, G.H.W. Snr 14, 17, 51
Bush, G.W. Jnr
  as president of U.S. 79
  'axis of evil' reference 2-3, 32, 36, 39,
        63, 103, 131
  comparison to Hitler 4, 68, 83
  critics 21, 63, 83, 87, 103
  diplomacy of 21, 39, 41, 83, 133
  domestic support 36
  foreign policy before 9/11 35, 57, 66,
        133
  leadership 85
  relationship with Blair 23, 37, 60, 141
  response to 9/11 24
  speeches 2, 19-20, 37, 60,
        73-4, 84, 131
  stance on NATO's utility
        56-57, 86
  strategic vision 4, 17, 18-20
  unilateralism 4, 16, 19, 35, 38, 59-65,
        76, 81, 84, 141

capitalism 6, 65
CFSP 55, 60, 62, 69, 71-2, 76, 84-6
Chechnya 5, 13, 31, 114, 117, 122
Chirac, J. 4, 36, 71-84, 86
Christian Democratic Union (CDU)
        93-4, 98-9, 102-3
Christian Socialist Union (CSU) 93-5, 99
Clarke, General Wesley 56
clash of civilizations 6, 8, 16, 28, 30, 32,
        36-8, 42, 74, 92
Clinton, Bill 22, 33, 66, 71-2, 77, 86,
        108, 132-3
coalition of the willing 41
Cohen, W. 72
Cold War
  and international security 3, 5, 20, 23,
        53
  as contest of ideologies 52, 54, 64, 65
  as contest of power 39, 54
  nature of international system 5, 12,
        16, 56-9, 64
  role of interests 22, 52-4, 55, 61, 65
  superpower policies 12, 18, 53, 79, 108
collective security 18, 54, 113

Commonwealth of Independent States
        113, 116-19
communism 3, 54, 62, 65
Comprehensive Test Ban Treaty (CTBT)
        35, 77, 78
CSCE 110 (*see also* OSCE)
containment 53, 59, 70
critical theory 28
Cuba 39, 129
culture
  and IR theory 29, 30-33
  clash of civilizations thesis 29-30,
        40-43
  ideas and identity 33, 40
  Islamic 37, 38, 138-39
  Western 34-5, 36-8
Czech Republic 108-110

decolonization 129
defense spending 15, 72, 77-9, 102, 104
democratic peace thesis 54
demographics 11
Denmark 81
deterrence 20, 59, 71, 78
'divide and rule' 43

Egypt 31, 33, 37, 74, 133-6, 139
Einstein, A. 18
Euro 86
European Coal and Steel Community
        (ECSC) 53
European Defense Community (EDC) 70
European Security and Defense Policy
        (ESDP) 72
European Union (EU)
  and CFSP 55, 60, 62, 69, 71-2, 76
  as power bloc 62-3, 66, 80
  divisions over Iraq 2, 4-5, 8, 35, 60-63,
        66, 81-84, 137, 141
  Justice and Home Affairs 60, 74, 91
  Treaty on European Union 71, 72, 91

failed states 41, 66
Field, H. 72
Financial Action Taskforce on Money
        Laundering (FATF) 73-4
Fischer, J.
  and German Green Party 94-5
  as German foreign minister 92, 103
  domestic politics 94-5
  flexible response 79

Foreign and Commonwealth Office
(UK) 137, 141
France
  and CFSP 84-6, 72
  and NATO 56, 79-82
  and UN 64, 70, 86
  diplomacy in Asia 74-6
  domestic politics 79-80, 104
  'exceptionalism' 71, 76-77
  foreign and security policy
    61-62, 70-2
  Jacques Chirac 4, 36, 71-84, 86
  legacy of de Gaulle 56, 70, 76
  multipolarism 80, 84
  relations with Germany and U.K.
    70-71, 83-84, 86
  relations with U.S. 62, 76-80, 104
  responses to 9/11 72-76
  role in 'war on terror' 19, 70-72, 73-5
  transatlantic split over Iraq 7, 34-7,
    61-3
Free Democratic Party (FDP) 93-4, 98,
  103
fundamentalism, Islamic 29, 30, 34, 37,
  42, 65, 93, 99, 139

geopolitics 6, 51, 65, 107-8, 110
Georgia 39, 118-20
Germany
  and CFSP 71, 72, 83
  and transatlantic split over Iraq 7, 34-7,
    61-3
  armed forces 71, 102-104
  as key state during Cold War 61
  as NATO member 90, 91-3, 95
  domestic politics 61, 93-5, 102
  emerging as 'normal' state 78, 91,
    100-101, 104
  preference for UN 63-4, 95
  public opinion 93, 95, 96-7, 105
  relations with France 83-4, 86
  relations with U.S. 101, 104-05
  responses to 9/11 95, 97-99
  reunification 61, 99, 102, 104
  role in 'war on terror' 100-101
Ghent European Council 75
global cosmopolitanism 11, 24, 58
globalization
  and U.S. power 5, 42, 84
  and inequality 5, 42, 74
  and interdependence 29, 65, 66

failed states 41, 66
state sovereignty 43
terrorism 23
Gordon, P.H. 84, 90, 100
great powers 4, 6, 12-13, 16 18, 30, 37,
  42, 84, 85, 122
Greens (Germany) 90, 94-6, 97, 98-9,
  102
Gulf Cooperation Council (GCC) 134,
  138
GUUAM 119

Halliday, F. 6, 30, 35, 42
Hoffman, S. 35, 36
homeland security (U.S.) 20, 21, 97, 104
Holbrooke, R. 55
humanitarian intervention 24, 55, 95
Hungary 81, 108-10
Huntington, S.
  after 9/11 6, 8, 39
  clash of civilizations thesis 28-9, 30,
    31-3
  conception of culture 29-33
  critics 34, 38, 42
Hussein, Saddam 15, 21, 22, 29, 31, 37,
  41, 58-60, 62, 81-2, 122, 132, 135,
  137, 140

ideas and identity 33, 40
ideology 3, 54, 62, 65
IFOR 91, 111
India 3, 14, 17, 40, 76, 78, 128
intelligence
  European efforts 72, 75-6, 97-8, 101,
    104
  flawed on Iraq 24
  gathering of after 9/11 21, 113, 114,
    115, 138
Intermediate Nuclear Forces Treaty
  (INF) 77, 88*n*
International Criminal Court (ICC) 66
international law 81
International Monetary Fund (IMF) 64,
  83
institutions
  in IR 4, 18-19, 24, 42, 53, 59, 63-5, 69
  role of during Cold War 23, 53, 59, 64
Iran 39, 58, 63, 77, 103, 131, 134-6
Iraq
  alleged WMD program 15, 24, 34, 60,
    62, 137, 141

and Saddam Hussein 15, 21, 22, 29,
    31, 37, 41, 58-60, 62, 81-2,
    122, 132, 135, 137, 140
and U.S.-led war 3, 22, 34, 55, 63, 66,
    76, 80-82, 93, 95, 117, 121,
    138, 141
links with terrorists 15
European objections to war 7, 34-7,
    61-3, 80, 82, 93, 96, 100, 103,
    117, 121
postwar 69, 142
UNSC debates over 60, 81-3, 137
weapons inspectors 82, 137, 140
IR theory 4, 18-19, 24, 28-31, 35, 39-41,
    42, 53, 59, 63-5, 69, 72
Irish Republican Army (IRA) 14, 62
Iron Curtain 60
Islam 6, 21, 33, 36, 39, 40, 42, 79, 103,
    130, 138
Israel
    and Palestinian problem 32, 36-7, 43,
        103, 132, 133, 137
    and wars in Middle East 129
    policy after 9/11 132, 137
    relationship with U.S. 14, 21, 22, 24,
        36, 37, 43, 76, 79, 132, 133-4
Italy 36, 81

Jackson-Vanik 39
Janes, J. 91, 102
Japan 32, 39, 52, 61, 74, 76, 78, 80
Jihad 29, 131-2
Joffe, J. 56
Jospin, L. 73-4

Kagan, R. 57
Kant, I. 51
Kaplan, R. 28
Kaldor, M. 24, 33
Kashmir 14, 40
Kazakhstan 116, 119
Kirkpatrick, J. 38
Kissinger, H. 53, 78, 85
Kohl, H. 71-2, 74, 102
Kosovo 16, 40, 54-6, 75, 76, 85, 91, 107,
    111-12
Krasner, S. 58
Krause, J. 92, 93
Krauthammer, C. 80
Kurds 136-8, 140
Kursk 109

Kuwait 14, 59, 80 135-6, 138
Kyoto Protocol 16, 35, 66, 83, 136
Kyrgyzstan 116, 119

Latin America 42
law enforcement 97-9, 104
League of Nations 59, 129
Liberalism 18, 29, 64, 95
Libya 29, 141
Likud Party 133

Maastricht, Treaty of 71, 72, 91
Macedonia 107, 118
Mandelbaum, M. 51
Mearsheimer, J. 7, 52
Miller, J. 38
mission-creep 36
Mitterand, F. 71, 72, 79, 80, 84
modernity 6, 31
Moldova 118
Morgenthau, H.J. 7, 30
multilateral cooperation 4, 39, 55-7, 60,
    63, 64-5, 86, 98, 116, 119, 137,
    138
multipolarity 7, 8, 16, 40, 43, 80, 84,
    104, 112, 116
Muslims 6, 21, 33, 36, 39, 40, 42, 79,
    103, 130, 138

National Missile Defense (NMD) 35-6,
    39, 77-9
Nationalism 1, 14, 42
naval forces 101, 109, 120
neo-conservatives – U.S. 17, 22, 57
Netherlands 81, 92
Newspapers 11
Nixon, R.M. 53
North Atlantic Treaty Organization
    (NATO)
    no threat after Cold War 55, 59
    and 'war on terror' 19, 51, 71, 75, 100,
        113
    and U.S. foreign policy 56-7, 86
    article five 17, 19, 54, 55, 71-2
    as Cold War alliance 12, 18, 53, 79,
        108
    dwindling relevance 56-7
    expansion 8, 40, 69, 108-10, 117-19
    new post-Cold War role 54, 110
    Prague summit 2002 118

role in Afghanistan 19, 51, 71, 75, 100, 113
Russia-NATO Council 122
Russian perceptions 109-12
split over war in Iraq 7, 34-7, 61-3, 80, 82, 93, 96, 100, 103, 117, 121
strategic concept 112
North Korea 34, 39, 62, 66, 77-8, 103, 131
Nye, J. 30, 53, 55, 83

oil 17, 21, 32, 34, 37, 58, 82, 135-6, 139
Operation Enduring Freedom 114-15
Organization of Islamic Conferences (OIC) 32
Organization for Economic Cooperation and Development (OECD) 74
Organization for Security and Cooperation in Europe (OSCE) 110 (*see also* CSCE)

pacifism 97-8
Pakistan 3, 14, 35, 38-9, 40, 76, 78, 132
Palestine
  and British policy 128-9
  and Israel 32, 36-7, 43, 103, 132, 133, 137
  role of Yasser Arafat 132-4, 140
  self-determination claims 36-7, 43, 103
  support from Islamic states 32 133-4, 137, 148
Partei Rechtsstaatliche Offensive (PRO) 98
Partnerships for Peace 118-19
Party of Democratic Socialism (PDS) 94, 96
patriotism in U.S. 14
Pearl Harbor 11, 16, 17, 52
Pentagon 2, 3, 11, 17, 28, 115, 131
People's Republic of China 3, 16-17, 35, 39, 40-41, 78, 80, 82, 85-6, 116, 132
Perle, R. 4, 17, 41
Poland 36, 81, 108-10
political culture 96-7, 100
postpositivism 29
Powell, C. 82, 83, 133-4
power
  and culture 30-33
  as determinant of interests 32, 38, 64
  changing nature 43

U.S. 59-65
pre-emptive strikes 20, 59
Prodi, R. 75, 81
Putin, V. 5, 37, 39, 58, 81, 83, 112-15, 117, 122

Reagan, R. 17, 37, 77, 131
Reid, Richard. 33, 129
realism
  and anarchy 12, 42
  and clash of civilizations thesis 6, 36-8, 42, 74, 92
  assumptions 6-7
  classical realism 7, 30
  critics 6
  dominant paradigm in IR 28-9
  international system 56-9, 64
  emphasis on power 6, 7
  neorealism 6, 29
  security dilemma 12
  state interests 39-41, 57-9
Red Brigades 14, 98
resource scarcities 11
Rice, Condoleeza 4, 17, 36, 57, 113
Road Map for peace 21, 37, 43, 134, 137, 140
Robertson, George 17, 115, 117-19
rogue states 3, 13, 34-5, 59, 62-6, 77, 131, 141
Romania 109, 118
Rome, Treaty of 71
Rumsfeld, D.
  as Pentagon hawk 4, 18-19, 24, 36
  defense spending 15
  desire to enhance role of military 15
  speeches 18-19
  strategic policy of U.S. 4, 17, 18-20, 63, 83, 113
Russia
  and NATO expansion 85, 109-12
  armed forces 108
  in European security 83, 110-11, 118, 121-3
  conflict in Chechnya 5, 13, 31, 114, 117, 122
  criticism of U.S. policy 21, 63, 83, 87, 103
  domestic politics 108, 111, 121
  foreign policy 39-40
  military aid to Tajikistan 114-15, 119
  military doctrine 113

multipolarism 40, 43, 104, 112, 116
participation in Shanghai Group 39, 116
partnership with China 16, 40, 116
relations with 'near abroad' 119-20
response to NMD 35-6, 39, 77-9
role of Vladimir Putin 5, 37, 39, 58, 81, 83, 112-15, 122
U.S. bases around 39, 118-20
see also USSR

St. Petersburg 119
sanctions, economic 17, 20, 37, 40, 59, 76, 80, 86, 137, 140
Saudi Arabia 14, 21, 32-4, 37 40, 74, 133, 135, 137-9
Schengen Convention 91
Schily, O. 98, 99
Schröder, Gerhadt
as German Chancellor 100-01
domestic politics 61, 93-5, 102
foreign policy platform 95, 97-99
rejection of war in Iraq 38, 66, 81-4, 137
security
after 9/11 3, 13, 14, 19, 22, 34, 39, 55, 63, 66, 75-6, 80-82, 93, 95, 100, 117, 121, 131, 138, 141
and alliances 12, 17-19, 39, 41, 52-3, 57, 64
as contested concept 11
conceptualized at different levels 11-12
defined 12
during Cold War 3, 5, 20, 23, 53
referent object 11
security dilemma 12
Security Packages I and II 90, 99, 104
September 11 attacks
and U.S. foreign policy 4, 14, 16-17, 18, 20, 35, 38, 59-65, 76, 81, 84, 144
nationalism in U.S. 14
responses in Europe 2, 4-5, 8, 35, 60-63, 66, 81-4, 137, 141
new partnership with Russia 17, 39-40
Serbia 55, 95, 111
SFOR 91
Shapiro, J. 75, 77
Simes, D. 33
Smith, S. 35

social constructivism 29, 42
Social Democratic Party (SPD) 93-6, 98-9
Spain 2, 62, 81
special forces 114, 119
Stoiber, E. 93, 95, 99
Strategic Defense Initiative (SDI) 77-8
strategic partnership (Russia and U.S.) 17, 39-40
strategic shocks 17-18
Syria 39, 74, 133, 139, 141

Tamil Tigers 14
terrorism
and globalization 5, 42, 74
as age-old problem 3-4
bombings in Bali 14, 38, 129
literature on 1, 4
root causes 20-22
September 11 4, 14, 16-17, 18-20, 35, 38, 59-65, 76, 81, 84, 144
theatre crisis in Moscow 117
Theatre Missile Defense (TMD) 77-9
third world 1, 20, 78, 141
transatlantic partnership 8, 51-2, 57
transnational crime 97-99, 104
Turkey 56, 62, 72, 81, 82
Turkmenistan 119

unilateralism 4, 16, 19, 35, 38, 59-65, 76, 81, 84, 141
United Arab Emirates 135, 137
United Kingdom
and Cold War 60-61
and war in Iraq 23, 58, 141
and 'war on terror' 7, 34-7, 61-3, 80, 82, 93, 96, 100, 103, 117, 121
atlanticism 58-60
domestic politics 37
preference for diplomacy 4, 61, 71, 82
public opinion 37
reactions to 9/11
relations with U.S. 4, 129
role in Middle East 129-30, 139
UN
and humanitarian intervention 24, 55, 95
and institutions 4, 18-19, 24, 42, 53, 59, 63-5, 69, 72
European preference for 4, 61, 63-4, 71, 82

marginalized by U.S. 34, 37, 64
Security Council 60, 81-3, 137
United States
    and anti-U.S. sentiment 61, 82, 133
    and 'coalition of the willing' 41
    and Cold War 12, 18, 53, 79, 108
    and multilateral institutions 4, 34, 37,
        64, 55-7, 60, 63, 64-5, 86
    and NATO expansion 8, 40, 69,
        108-10, 117-19
    as 'hyperpower' 3, 13, 43, 80, 86
    as NATO member 56-7, 86
    defense spending 15, 72, 77-9
    foreign policy under Clinton 22, 33,
        66, 71-2, 77, 86, 108, 132-3
    humanitarian intervention 24, 55, 95
    intervention in Afghanistan 13, 14, 19,
        34, 39, 75, 80, 100, 119, 131
    neo-conservatives 17, 22, 57
    post-9/11 security policy 4, 17, 18-20,
        35, 37-9, 59-63, 81-3. 101-103,
        139-41
    relations with European allies 2, 4-5, 8,
        35, 60-63, 66, 81-84, 137, 141
    role in Iraq 3, 22, 34, 55, 63, 66, 76,
        80-82, 93, 95, 117, 121, 138,
        141
    unilateralism 4, 16, 19, 35, 38, 59-65,
        76, 81, 84, 141
USSR
    and Cold War 5, 21, 34, 65
    bipolarism 6, 11, 20, 51-2, 59, 80, 100
    failure of theory to predict end 32
    foreign policy 51-2
unipolarity 40, 43, 70, 76, 80, 84, 104,
    116
unipolar moment 80
Uzbekistan 39, 119

Van Creveld, M. 33
Védrine, H. 62, 70, 73-4, 76-8, 80

Vietnam War 17, 80
Verhofstadt, G. 75
Visegrad group 108-9

Waltz, K.N. 6-7, 65
Wallace, W. 7, 22, 23, 64
Wallerstein, I. 20
War and warfare
    and states' security policies 12-13
    changing nature of 13-16
    exit strategies 13, 15
    Gulf War 14, 20, 80, 83, 85, 91, 100
    Iran-Iraq 103, 131, 134-6
    rules/norms 13, 15
World Wars I and II 52-3, 59, 129
'War on Terror(ism)'
    and U.S. foreign policy 4, 17, 18-20,
        35, 37-9, 59-63, 81-3. 101-103,
        139-41
    and U.S. power 59-65
    as clash of civilizations 6, 8, 16, 28,
        30, 32, 36-8, 42, 74, 92
    critics 21, 63, 83, 87, 103
    European responses 2, 4-5, 8, 19, 35,
        51, 60-63, 66, 81-4, 137, 141
Warsaw Pact 99, 107-108
Weapons of Mass Destruction (WMDs)
    and NMD 35-6, 39, 77-9
    and terrorists 77, 114
    Iraq's alleged possession of 15, 24, 34,
        60, 62, 137, 141
    nuclear deterrence 20, 59, 71, 78
Westphalia, Treaty of 12
Western European Union (WEU) 71,
    100
Wolfowitz, P. 4, 17, 36, 57
World Trade Centre 3, 11, 28, 113, 115,
World Trade Organization (WTO) 39,
    41, 85, 114, 120

Yugoslavia 16, 31, 55-6, 61, 91, 109